COLORADO

POWDER KEG

Colorado Powder Keg

SKI RESORTS AND THE ENVIRONMENTAL MOVEMENT

Michael W. Childers

 UNIVERSITY PRESS OF KANSAS

Published by the
University Press of
Kansas (Lawrence,
Kansas 66045), which
was organized by the
Kansas Board of Regents
and is operated and
funded by Emporia State
University, Fort Hays
State University, Kansas
State University,
Pittsburg State
University, the University
of Kansas, and Wichita
State University

Library of Congress Cataloging-in-Publication Data

Childers, Michael W.
    Colorado powder keg : ski resorts and the environmental
movement / Michael W. Childers.
        p.   cm.
    Includes bibliographical references and index.
    ISBN 978-0-7006-1869-9 (cloth : alk. paper) 1. Ski
resorts—Environmental aspects—Colorado. 2. Skis and
skiing—Environmental aspects—Colorado. 3. Skis and
skiing—Economic aspects—Colorado. I. Title.
GV854.5.C6C55 2012
796.9309788—dc23
                                        2012016527

British Library Cataloguing-in-Publication Data is available.

Printed in the United States of America

10 9 8 7 6 5 4 3 2 1

The paper used in this publication is recycled and contains
30 percent postconsumer waste. It is acid free and meets the
minimum requirements of the American National Standard
for Permanence of Paper for Printed Library Materials
Z39.48–1992.

To Hal, because I promised to one day return the favor

And to Leisl, always

CONTENTS

ACKNOWLEDGMENTS

This book began on a hike along the Continental Divide. Reaching the middle of a saddle between two peaks, I decided to take a break and sit down alongside the trail for a drink of water and a handful of trail mix. Looking westward, I began to ponder Winter Park Ski Resort lying directly across the Fraser Valley from my vantage point along the Divide. A mere hour's drive from Denver and the Front Range, Winter Park is among the most popular ski resorts within Colorado, pumping millions of tourist dollars into the local economy every year. Taking a few sips of water from my canteen, I came to the sudden realization that while the ski resort was the area's primary economic motor, it constituted a rather small portion of the thousands of acres of surrounding national forest, making skiing a much more valuable commodity than either timber or grazing. It was with this insight that I began exploring what broader environmental, political, and social obligations both the U.S. Forest Service and resort operators have in developing ski resorts on national forests throughout the state, and what the changing visions of these obligations can tell us about our public lands.

So many have helped me in my explorations. Yet, like most authors, I will most undoubtedly fail to remember everyone. To those not mentioned here, I apologize and deeply thank you for your time and contributions. Saying that, I wish to give a special word of thanks to my two mentors. Andy Kirk guided me through my dissertation at UNLV and pushed me to look beyond the simple explanation of history and be innovative in both my scholarship and my methodology. As I enter the profession, I aspire to emulate his original approach to history as well as his overwhelming generosity, sense of adventure, and love of the American West. I also wish to give special thanks to Hal Rothman. Hal hired me as his graduate assistant the first day I set foot on UNLV's campus, a position that I held for the next four years, working on projects as diverse as the history of the National Park Service's fire policy to the downfall of the mob in Las Vegas. During that time, Hal taught me a tremendous amount about history and writing, but more importantly he taught me about being generous with your time, true to your friends, solid in your convictions, and that history is a contact sport so you better buckle your chinstrap.

I am particularly thankful to my editor Ranjit Arab, whose patience in shepherding the book through the publication process often went well beyond the call of duty. His vision and insightful comments helped steer me through the often treacherous waters of being a first-time author. My sincere thanks to my reviewers, John Wright and Annie Gilbert Coleman, whose close readings and insightful criticisms better focused and tightened the book. David Wrobel, David Tanenhaus, David Hassenzahl, Elizabeth Fraterrigo, Tim Farnham, and Elizabeth White Nelson all read several versions of this manuscript at various stages. Lincoln Bramwell offered sage counsel throughout the process, providing invaluable advice at pivotal moments. Bill Philpott and Duke Ritchie each helped enormously in the early stages of writing. Seth Masia, Ben Doone, John Fry, and Edward Brannon all graciously answered my questions over the phone and via e-mail. Sara Dant and Mark Harvey assisted with a particularly thorny question over the role of Interstate 70 and the Wilderness Act of 1964. Erik Martin, Ted Farwell, Richard Lamm, and Mark Mobley all gave their time to answer questions on their roles in a wide range of events. A Summer Award from BYU's Charles Redd Center helped fund some of the early research for the book, while a USDA Forest Service Scholar-in-Residence Fellowship provided invaluable writing time at Grey Towers National Historic Site in Milford, Pennsylvania. Bob, Anna, Hanna, and Tucker Bond let me crash in their basement while I spent a summer digging through the Denver Public Library's archives. And Justin Henderson and Ann Eggers graciously provided me a place to stay in Vail for a summer during the beginning of this project.

No book is written without the help of archivists and I have been blessed to work with some of the best. In particular, I wish to thank Ann Brown, Claudia Jensen, Coi Drummond-Gehrig, and Ellen Zazzarino of Denver Public Library's Western History and Genealogy Archive. Enough cannot be said of the DPL's staff, all of whom often went well beyond boundaries of their jobs to find materials and even offered suggestions that later proved instrumental in the book. Cheryl Oakes at the Forest History Society Archives answered my many questions, both over the phone and via e-mail, and provided vital documents on the Forest Service's management of Colorado ski resorts at the last minute. Patricia Pfeiffer often opened the door of the Colorado Ski Museum and Hall of Fame Resource Center as well as answered numerous questions.

And Keith Schrum helped tremendously by giving me access to the Richard Lamm papers in the Colorado Historical Society's library.

Finally I wish to thank my family, without whose support I could not have completed this book. My wife, Leisl, who suffered me getting up at five every morning to write, yet always had an encouraging word at the right moment. And my parents, who raised my brother, sister, and me to always work hard and to follow our dreams, even when others think them folly, thanks for raising us in such an amazing place. To each of you, and the countless others I failed to mention here, thank you.

COLORADO

POWDER KEG

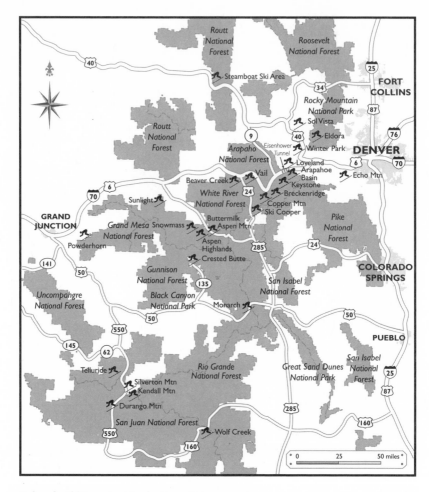

Colorado Ski Resorts. Map by Gerry Krieg.

In the frigid early morning hours of October 19, 1998, William Rodgers raced along the snow-covered ridgeline of Vail Ski Resort setting fires. In a matter of minutes, flames engulfed six buildings across the mountain, including the resort's aging patrol headquarters and opulent Two Elks Lodge. Having set the blazes, the thirty-three-year-old radical environmental activist, known to his friends as "Avalon," made his way to the bottom of the mountain where his fellow Earth Liberation Front (ELF) member Chelsea Gerlach waited nervously behind the wheel of her truck. Gerlach later recalled during an interview from prison, "I waited 10 minutes, then 20. After a half-hour, as I was wondering if I should leave, Avalon appeared. He just walked up to the truck and got inside. He said two things: He said he was injured. And that the action was successful."[1] With Rodgers safely in the passenger's seat, the two immediately drove east to Denver, stopping off at a city library to check on how to best treat Rodgers's sore Achilles tendon, and to e-mail a communiqué taking responsibility for the arsons, motivated, they claimed, by the U.S. Forest Service's approval of Vail's proposed 885-acre Category III expansion into the upper basin of the Two Elks River drainage. Federal and state wildlife biologists and environmental activists had long maintained that the development would disturb the habitat of the endangered Canada lynx. Rodgers and Gerlach's e-mail proclaimed that "putting profits ahead of Colorado's wildlife will not be tolerated," and warned, "We will be back if this greedy corporation continues to trespass into wild and unroaded areas."[2]

Lying just south of Vail's Back Bowls, the Two Elks Roadless Area includes roughly 1,000 acres of lodgepole pine– and aspen-covered mountain terrain ideal for skiing, a fact that had not escaped Vail's cofounder Pete Seibert, who had included the area in the resort's original permit request in 1960. Yet, while the Two Elks Area's open glades and moderate northern-facing slopes held immense promise for skiing, it also remained the prime habitat of several species including the endangered Canada lynx. Roughly twice the size of a house cat, the elusive predator became the cause célèbre in a debate over the expansion of Vail as critics of the ski resort and Forest Service officials argued over whether or not the lynx existed in the area, and if the animal did, what possible impacts the ski resort's expansion would have on it. Listed as endangered by the Colorado Department of Wildlife, the last confirmed sighting of a Canada lynx in the state had been in 1973, fueling skeptics' questions on whether the cat existed in the area at all. But beyond the more charismatic lynx, the Two Elks Roadless Area was also the prime calving grounds of one of Colorado's largest elk herds as well as a key watershed for the Eagle River, which provided water for the small community of Minturn just down valley from Vail Ski Resort.[3] Category III's critics cast further doubt on the need for the nation's largest ski resort to add any further terrain by pointing to Vail Resorts' planned development of the 5,000-acre Gillman property adjacent to the Two Elks Area as evidence that the expansion was more about real estate than it was about skiing.

Vail Resorts officials responded to such claims by stating that the expansion was merely the completion of the resort's 1986 Master Plan created in conjunction with the U.S. Forest Service, and that all impacts on wildlife would be mitigated. Both the Forest Service and the resort asserted that the expansion was necessary to meet growing public demand for skiing in the state. But several environmental organizations, hunters, and even the Colorado Division of Wildlife countered that there was no such evidence of public need and that skier numbers had, in fact, flattened over the previous decade.[4] State biologists also contended that the Forest Service had failed to properly study the impacts of the ski resort expansion on the Two Elks' wildlife, further souring the relationship between the two agencies. As the Forest Service forged ahead with its environmental impact study of the expansion, an intensive letter-writing campaign, public demonstrations, and websites sought to halt the study and bring an end to the corporate ski giant's real estate speculation. The failure of such measures led a group of environmental groups including Colorado Wild and the Colorado Environmental Coalition to file suit, seeking a court injunction to halt Vail's expansion. Nevertheless, on October 14, 1998, the U.S. 10th Circuit Court denied the coalition's request, giving Vail the green light to begin construction. Five days later, William Rodgers made his mad dash in the predawn light, setting fire to six buildings and drawing the nation's attention to the unfolding conflict over the expansion of the nation's largest ski resort and the elusive lynx.

A palpable tension filled the air throughout the Vail Valley in the days immediately following the arsons as speculation over who set the blazes became the central topic of conversation among locals. Vail Resorts had plenty of enemies after all. Some suggested that former employees, bitter at being fired by the resort, had sought revenge by setting the fires. Others accused Vail Resorts, Inc., the ski resort's owners, of burning down the outdated Ski Patrol Headquarters, Two Elks Lodge, and other structures in order to collect on the insurance. However, few put much credence in such conspiracy theories. Rather, the majority of the area's residents pointed at a small group of protestors camped just outside the neighboring town of Minturn as the likely culprits.[5] But as news of Gerlach and Rodger's e-mail spread, shock soon turned to anger as local residents learned the full extent of the fire's damages. "Whoever did this attacked the livelihood of every man, woman, and child in the valley," enraged Vail resident Jonathan Staufer told CBS News reporters.[6] Attention quickly focused on the Earth Liberation Front (ELF). Few had ever heard of the shadowy extremist group prior to the arsons. Causing an estimated $12 million in damages, the Vail arsons marked a significant escalation in the group's use of violence as a means to halt what they believed to be consumerist society's destruction of the planet's biosphere. But such tactics proved counterproductive in the case of Vail, recasting the ski resort as the victim as opposed to a greedy corporation exploiting public lands in order to increase its profit margin. Governor Roy Romer declared the arsons "an act of terrorism."[7] Others agreed, including the FBI, who had labeled the ELF the single largest domestic terrorist organization in the United States.

Mainstream environmental organizations moved quickly to condemn the arsons, seeking to distance themselves from the incident, but the damage had already been done. "The fires really hurt. They turned Vail into a victim, and environmental groups lost a lot of progress on the issue of ski area expansions," recalled Rocky Smith, former director of the Colorado Environmental Coalition, on the aftermath of the arsons and their impacts on public opinion.[8] At the same time, Vail officials moved in to exploit the swell of public sympathy. "Don't let the bastards get you down," Vail Resorts president Andy Daily implored a crowd of resort employees and locals at a public meeting following the arsons—earning a rowdy round of applause.[9] Aired on national nightly news programs, images of the smoldering Two Elks Lodge atop the ski area underscored Vail's victim status by striking at Americans' fears of limitations when it came to their enjoyment of their public lands and the sanctity of private property.

The most notorious act of "eco-terrorism" in American history, the Vail arsons were the just the latest, and most violent, protest against the development of an ever-larger corporate-operated ski resort on America's national forests. For much of the latter half of the twentieth century, the development of ski resorts in Colorado's share of national forests locked resort operators, skiers and snowboarders, environmental activists, and the Forest Service into fiercely divisive political debates over the impacts of ski resorts on rural communities and the role of public lands in an ever-changing American West. The total acreage of ski resorts, which represent the most intensive commercial use of public lands for recreational use, is a significantly small portion of national forest lands, constituting less than one-tenth of 1 percent of all national forests. Yet, ski resorts have had a disproportionate amount of influence over local and regional economies, identities, and environments, especially along Colorado's Interstate 70 corridor through the Rocky Mountains, the subject of this book. Beyond displacing wildlife and impacting watersheds, ski resorts such as Vail have created tremendous booms in speculative real estate development, turning once rural communities into sprawling urban corridors. Responsible for the management of all national forests, the Forest Service has long promoted the construction of ski resorts, believing, perhaps rightly, that such facilities meet Americans' demand for the recreational access to their public lands. However, the agency's collusion with private interests in developing and then operating ever-larger ski resorts does raise significant questions over the management of public lands, such as what constitutes the greatest good when it comes to public lands, and moreover, is it even possible for a profit-driven model of land management to be successful when the goal is to provide access to all?

Such questions trace their roots back to the late nineteenth century, when the West's vast public lands were no longer just seen as sources of raw materials, but became valued instead for the ways they benefitted Americans' leisurely pursuits—if not their overall quality of life. By the late 1920s and into the 1930s, traditional western extractive industries such as mining, timber, and cattle were soon joined, and later eclipsed, by service-based industries such as telecommunications, information technology, and tourism.[10] Following World War II, Americans' measurement of economic well-being was delineated less by quantity of goods and more by services and amenities.[11] In this new, postindustrial West, mountains became more valuable as ski resorts than rangeland, fundamentally changing the nature of public land management and underlining the inherent problem of privatization of public lands by corporate interests—namely, that all too often profits took precedence over broader environmental and social concerns.

Outdoor recreation played a small role in the management of the nation's public lands at the onset of the twentieth century, particularly its national forests. However, within decades, the combination of Americans' increasing leisure time, westward migration, and access to automobiles led millions into their national forests to picnic, sightsee, camp, fish, and ski. This trend continued following World War II, as pent-up consumer demand and growing affluence fueled a boom in outdoor recreation across the West, home to the majority of the nation's public lands. As millions of Americans fell in love with their national forests, parks, and beaches, they grew increasingly uneasy with the nation's growing pollution, suburban sprawl into open spaces, and extractive industries. While the West's growing number of urban and suburban recreationalists often viewed extractive industries such as logging and mining as anathema, many soon found that their recreational desires inflicted an equal if not greater impact on the very places they wished to save from the chainsaw and bulldozer.[12] Such realizations led to further questioning over the costs of recreation on public lands and the Forest Service's role in promoting recreational development and use.

A vital part of the West's tourism industry, outdoor recreation grew into a pressing issue in most national forests, particularly national forests adjacent to western "boom town" areas where recreation became a dominant use early in the century. Few recreational activities embodied this trend more than downhill skiing. As early as the 1920s, the sport's rapid rise in popularity forced the Forest Service to begin constructing small rope-tow ski operations throughout the region. Within a decade, the federal agency came to realize that it would not have the capital or manpower to manage what was quickly becoming a thriving industry, so it turned instead to private interests to develop and operate ever-larger ski areas. By the 1950s, the West's population boom combined with a growing national affluence to drive skiing's popularity to new heights, and ski areas soon transformed into ski resorts, causing further development of national forests and raising the question of private ownership of public lands. With the popular rise of middle-class, quality-of-life environmentalism throughout America, ski resorts became targets of increasing criticism for their impact on wildlife and water quality and their role in the growth of rural mountain communities. This in turn shaped politics in western states such as Colorado, pitting pro-growth boosters against a diverse number of Coloradoans worried about the state's rapid pace of change and its impacts on their quality of life.

Increasingly reliant on private corporations to operate the ski resorts within Colorado, the Forest Service struggled to balance the public's growing demand for more skiing with ski resort owners' demands for greater profits. At the same time, the agency also had to consider widespread concerns over the consequences of the development of ski resorts on both public lands and their surrounding communities. These disparate constituencies, each with a differing vision for the national forests, embodied the increasingly contested nature of public lands management throughout the century—where skiers and snowboarders flocked to the resorts that offered the most terrain and best amenities but remained concerned over such resorts' impacts on wildlife, air quality, and rural growth. Resort operators, meanwhile, embraced free-market ideals in order to bolster profits while promoting environmental sustainability, and land managers fought amongst themselves over the meanings of scientific studies. Such seemingly inherent contradictions lie at the heart of the history of Colorado's ski industry and illuminate the Forest Service's long-running difficulty in grappling with the West's ever-evolving economics, politics, and growing population.

Today, downhill skiing is the basis for the economies of many of the Intermountain West's mountain communities. According to the National Ski Areas Association (NSAA), by 2000 U.S. ski resorts hosted, on average, 52 million skier days annually. Ski resorts within the Rocky Mountain region (Montana, Idaho, Wyoming, Utah, Colorado, and New Mexico) ranked number one in skier numbers, attracting 20 million skier days per season. Of those, Colorado was by far the most popular, hosting more than half of the region's skier visits, with Utah ranking a distant second.[13] Such numbers translate into jobs and economic opportunities for each state, none more so than Colorado. The state's more than two dozen ski resorts, combined with ample winter mountain snows and easy access for Denver's large metropolitan population, combine to create a thriving ski industry that adds billions to the state's economy. Colorado Ski Country USA, the Colorado ski industry's trade association, determined that in 2004 alone, Colorado's ski industry generated nearly 31,000 jobs and constituted a third of Colorado's $7 billion tourist economy. "That says communities and ancillary businesses directly benefit from resort efforts to attract more folks and increase visitation," asserted Rob Pearlman, president and CEO of Colorado Ski Country USA, on the importance of skiing to the state.[14]

Industry critics counter that focusing on such economic windfalls ignores the tremendous environmental and social costs of ski resorts. In his jeremiad *Downhill Slide: Why the Corporate Ski Industry Is Bad for Skiing, Ski Towns, and the Environment*, journalist and vocal critic of the corporate-run ski industry Hal Clifford asserted that "skiing is no longer an end into itself for those looking to profit from it; instead [it] has transformed into a come-hither amenity to sell real estate."[15] Published four years after the Vail arsons, Clifford's attack on corporate ski companies mirrored those of other environmental groups such as the Ski Area Citizens' Coalition, Save Our Canyons, and the Sierra Nevada Alliance. Each argues that the wedding of skiing and real estate development has transformed once rural western mountain towns into sprawling resort communities, causing unanticipated and uncontrollable changes to both the environment and the identity of such places.

Vail Ski Resort is a prime example. As the single largest resort in the United States, Vail sprawls over 5,000 acres of the White River National Forest and includes thirty-one ski lifts, four lodges, and 193 trails. The resort pumps millions of gallons of water onto its slopes as man-made snow every fall and hosts more than 1 million skier and snowboarder visits a year. Such intensive development has dramatically impacted the local wildlife, vegetation, and water quality. But these impacts are often secondary to the development of real estate sprawling "down valley" along Interstate 70 from the ski resort. Critics like Clifford assert that the tremendous environmental and social costs of this combination of growth and the development of thousands of acres of national forests for skiing often far outweigh their benefits by displacing wildlife, degrading air and water quality, and transforming rural mountain communities into amenity-based colonies, causing rampant growth and forever transforming local cultures for ill.[16]

The cycle of conflict over ski resorts began with the advent of the automobile age, as national forests, particularly those abutting burgeoning western metropolises, became favorite playgrounds for hundreds of thousands of people. Driven by the nation's growing affluence and urbanization, skiing continued growing in popularity in the decades immediately following World War II, evolving from a minor recreational activity into a major industry in the region following the war. In Colorado, lift ticket sales jumped from 204,640 in 1955 to more than 5 million by 1970, a trend that continued to a greater or lesser extent throughout the rest of the century. The construction of Arapahoe Basin and Loveland Basin ski areas in the late 1940s sparked a twenty-year boom in the development of ski resorts throughout the state, which culminated in the opening of Vail and Breckenridge during the 1960s. As ski areas transformed into ski resorts, complete with lodging, restaurants, and real estate, they further drove the urbanization of the state's once isolated rural communities. Such growth was particularly dramatic along the newly constructed Interstate 70 as it passed through the Colorado Rockies, linking the state's Western Slope with its growing Front Range. Mounting concerns over the impacts of the growth on Colorado's environment began to emerge, setting the stage for the controversy over Denver's selection as the host of the 1976 Winter Olympic Games.[17]

Changing economic and regulatory realities facing the ski industry during the 1980s brought on a period of industry consolidation, creating what has been best described as an arms race among ski resorts over who could provide the most terrain, fastest chairlifts, and most extravagant amenities to attract the largest market share of skiers. With a climate that favored industry consolidation, Vail Resorts decided in the mid-1990s to move forward with its planned Category III expansion. Critics claimed it was just the latest example of the ski industry placing its profits ahead of wildlife and other environmental concerns. But this was no typical development. To many environmentalists, it came to represent all that was wrong with Colorado's unchecked ski industry. News of the proposed development not only affected Coloradoans but caught the attention of national and international environmental groups, as well. Beyond the Colorado borders, William Rodgers was paying close attention to the battle. It would not be long before he tried to take matters into his own hands, setting Vail Ski Resort ablaze that fateful October morning.

I

A month after winning his second term as Denver's mayor in 1910, Robert W. Speer stood before a small crowd at the city's YMCA and presented his vision of Denver's future. Looking forward, he saw tree-lined boulevards, neighborhoods with open vistas of snow-capped Rocky Mountains, and dozens of parks, the crown jewel of which being a large park in the city's nearby foothills where "the masses could spend happy days and feel that some of the grandeurs of the Rocky Mountains belong to them."[1] The idea of a mountain park quickly took hold, and by the following summer, three separate civic committees had formed in order to pursue the creation of not just a single park, but an entire system of mountain parks. Composed mostly of local business interests and politicians, the three groups combined their efforts in 1912 under the auspices of the powerful Mountain Parks Committee of the Commercial Bodies. In its first report on the need for the creation of an expansive park system throughout Denver's nearby mountains, the new committee asserted that the future of the city, if not the state, lay westward in the towering peaks that divided Colorado, proclaiming that the construction of a system of parks was "Denver's chance to open a gateway into the mountains, and take the lead in making Colorado more attractive to tourists than Switzerland."[2]

Denver experienced remarkable growth during Mayor Speer's first years in office, its population more than doubling between 1900 and 1910, causing the city to struggle to keep up with demand for sewers, water, and other amenities. Faced with escalating problems caused by the city's growth, Speer struck deals with local businesses allowing them to create monopolies in exchange for annual payments he then used toward the beautification of the city's parks and streets. An early proponent of the City Beautiful Movement, the mayor oversaw the construction of multiple city improvement projects including the building of Denver's Civic Center, the City Auditorium, the planting of hundreds of trees along city streets, the expansion of both the Denver Zoo and the Museum of Nature and Science, and, of course, the construction of the mountain parks. Through such public projects, Speer sought to transform Denver from a small regional hub into a vibrant and modern metropolis equal to any within the nation.[3]

Convinced of the vision set out by Speer and the Mountain Parks Committee, Denver voters overwhelmingly passed a special mill levy increase to finance the purchase of land in the city's western foothills for new parks, beginning with the immediate acquisition of 1,200 acres surrounding Genesee Mountain. Bergen Park followed three years later, with Starbuck Park a year after that. The parks continued to grow in popularity during the interwar era as the city added another eight parks, including Red Rocks Park, which later featured Red Rocks Amphitheater. Within a decade, Denver's mountain parks were drawing nearly half a million visitors annually. But as the mountain parks appeared a smashing success, they failed in attracting the tourists hoped for. As the editors of the city's monthly magazine *Municipal Facts* unhappily noted in 1918, "Although there was an enormous increase in the number of machines and people entering the Denver Mountain Parks, there was a decrease in the number of out-of-state cars." City officials estimated that only 24 percent of all automobiles passing through mountain parks were registered out-of-state. The majority of park's visitors were Denver residents, not the tourists that city businesses had hoped to attract, turning the mountain hinterlands into the city's playground—a trend that continued through the rest of the century.[4]

Having passed its tax increase to fund the creation of a mountain parks system, in the spring of 1913 the city of Denver hired the Olmsted Brothers Landscape Firm to design its new mountain park system. Following in their famous father Frederick Law Olmsted's footsteps, John Charles and his half-brother Frederick Law Olmsted Jr. were already renowned for their roles in the early twentieth century's City Beautiful Movement. Author of arguably the key sentence within the future Nation Park Service Organic Act of 1916, which declared that the purpose of all national parks was to preserve the scenery and historic integrity of the parks for the enjoyment of all Americans, Frederick Law Olmsted Jr. believed that all city parks needed to frame nature to help foster civic virtue and a greater appreciation of nature's wonders.[5] In Denver, Olmsted found a raw canvas on which to paint his vision of a modern city, complete with parks and boulevards framing the city's majestic western mountains. After surveying the potential of constructing parks in the city's nearby mountains, Olmsted concluded "the district most suitable for a mountain park system west of Denver lies south of Clear Creek, east of the Pike National Forest, and north of the southern limits of the Bear Creek and Turkey Creek watersheds. The relative value to the city of such tracts is in part determined by the natural charm and fitness of each, and in part by the relative ease with which they may be reached."[6] The true value of the region, he asserted, came from its relative proximity to the city's population and its natural beauty, the combination of which made it the ideal leisure grounds for local residents and out-of-state tourists alike. Olmsted quickly laid out plans for Denver's burgeoning mountain parks, including scenic drives up Lookout Mountain, picnic spots complete with pavilions, automotive campgrounds, and miles of maintained hiking trails, providing a blueprint for one of the most expansive city park systems in the country.

As Denver developed its mountain parks, millions of Americans were flooding into their public lands, parks, and beaches, in what Forest Service Chief Henry Graves identified as "a widespread and spontaneous movement for outdoor recreation."[7] Fueled by increased leisure time, growing middle-class affluence, and an emergent national automobile culture, outdoor recreation blossomed during the era. Americans, especially the nation's swelling urban population, came to prize their national forests not only for their material worth, but increasingly for their recreational appeal. Between 1916 and 1922, national forest visitation grew from an estimated 2.4 million people to 6.2 million, the majority of which occurred in forests near the West's rapidly expanding cities such as Denver.[8] Yet, the Forest Service struggled with the nation's increasing demands for recreation. Many within the agency deemed recreation a minor use of national forests, holding a much lower commercial value than timber and grazing. While such views held sway within the agency, a handful of foresters began asserting that recreation did in fact have a place within the national forests. Pointing to the obvious fact that people were flocking to national forests in ever-greater numbers, men such as Chief

Graves and later the Forest Service's first recreational engineer, Arthur Car-hart, argued that recreation was a commodity that could not only be measured by total numbers of visitors, but more importantly in dollars and cents. Yet, the Forest Service was slow to embrace recreation as a legitimate use of the public lands under its care. Like Denver's creation of its mountain parks, the federal agency's acceptance of recreation as an increasingly important use of national forests marked its growing importance in the commercial development of public lands, a sea change that would dramatically affect the future economic development of Colorado's rural mountains—and the Forest Service's management of the state's vast national forests.

The nation's "spontaneous movement for outdoor recreation" fatefully coincided with the growing popularity of skiing. Long a method of travel and play in Colorado's small mountain communities, skiing blossomed in popularity throughout the state beginning in the early decades of the century. Winter carnivals in rural mountain towns attracted hundreds of spectators as early as 1911. Introduced by Scandinavian immigrants, ski jumping drew thousands to watch as young men flew hundreds of feet through the air after launching off of what seemed impossibly steep slopes. Such competitions soon attracted Denverites to the snow-covered hills of Genesee Park, where in 1920, the newly formed Denver Ski Club leased ten acres and built a ski jump, hosting the Nation Ski Tournament of America championship the following winter. Thousands of Denverites quickly took up the sport, swelling the ranks of the Denver Ski Club and crowding Mount Genesee's single ski trail. The park remained a popular ski spot for a decade, holding the national championships a second time in 1927, but Genesee's popularity began to wane within years of hosting the national championships due to inconsistent snows and limited facilities. At the same time, the construction of larger ski areas, such as that on the summit of nearby Berthoud Pass, began to draw greater numbers of skiers deeper into Colorado's Rocky Mountains, solidifying the sport's place in the state's culture and emergent tourist economy.[9]

Skiing, in one form or another, is as old as human settlement of Northern Eurasia. Archeologists have excavated ancient skis dating back to 2500 B.C.E. out of peat bogs in the arctic regions of Scandinavia, northern Russia, and China and found cave drawings depicting men and women standing on long skis. But while skiing has existed for centuries, it remained a rather primitive winter activity until the mid-nineteenth century when Norwegian skier Sondre Norheim introduced a new binding composed of a traditional

Two women skiers at Genesee Mountain Park, 1920s. Photograph courtesy Denver Public Library, Western History Collection, Ford Optical, Z-3097.

toe strap and a band of twisted roots that held the skier's heel in place. The new technology allowed greater levels of control and helped popularize skiing throughout Scandinavia and Europe. However, the sport remained little known outside of Scandinavia until the turn of the century, when Austrian schoolteacher Mathias Zdarsky published his groundbreaking treatise on ski equipment, Lilienfeld Skilauftechnik [Lilienfeld Ski Technique]. The new techniques outlined in his book taught European skiers how to descend down difficult terrain by using controlled maneuvers based on the stem turn, which used a single pole that was dragged through the snow for braking, balance, and leverage. Zdarsky's Lilienfeld Ski Technique remained the standard until 1910 when fellow Austrian Hannes Schneider introduced what became known as the Arlberg technique. Based in part upon the Lilienfeld turn, the Arlberg technique eliminated the stem altogether in favor of a pure parallel turn. Appealing to greater numbers of novice skiers, particularly British and American tourists, because of its speed and relative ease in learning, the new technique revolutionized skiing and made it more available to a wider public. Within a decade, thousands of Europeans and Americans were schussing down snow-covered slopes using the Arlberg technique.[10]

Skiing made its way to the United States in the mid-nineteenth century. Initially arriving in New England and the Great Lakes region, the sport migrated west with the discovery of gold first in California and later in Colorado, as thousands sought to find their fortune in the region's rocky creeks and rugged placer mines. In both the California Sierra and Colorado Rockies, men such as Snowshoe Thompson and Father John Dyer became renowned for their heroic exploits on skis delivering mail to isolated mountain communities during the 1850s and 1860s. Skiing remained a relatively isolated mode of travel throughout the West until the beginning of the twentieth century, when the region's urban residents soon took up the sport as recreation. Famous as the Flying Norseman in the Barnum and Bailey Circus, Norwegian immigrant Carl Howelson helped introduce ski jumping to Colorado, organizing the state's first winter carnival in the mountain town of Hot Sulphur Springs in the winter of 1911, which attracted hundreds of Denver residents to the rural mountain community. Soon other Colorado mountain towns stretching from Grand Lake to Crested Butte joined Hot Sulphur Spring in hosting ski jumping competitions hoping to attract not only competitors, but tourists and their money.[11]

By the 1920s, skiing was quickly evolving into a popular winter recreational activity. Winter carnivals and competitions continued to draw thousands of spectators, but thousands more were taking up downhill skiing, leading to the construction of hundreds of small rope-tow service ski hills throughout the country. As skiing grew in popularity, and more Americans bought cars, more began exploring ever further into their nearby mountains for deeper snow and better terrain. Such explorations reflected outdoor recreation's rising popularity throughout the United States, a phenomenon that was drawing millions of Americans into their vast public lands to ski, hunt, camp, and sightsee. Initially resistant to recreationalist's demands for greater access and better facilities, by the late 1930s the Forest Service began promoting the development of ever-larger ski areas within national forests. Yet, such an embrace did not come easily; the struggles over recreation racked the agency throughout the first half of the twentieth century as it wrestled over recreation's place in managing the nation's forests.[12]

In the years prior to World War I, the Forest Service viewed recreation as a secondary use of national forests, ranking it well below grazing and timber. The reasons for the agency's disregard of recreation were threefold. First, few Americans owned automobiles before the mid-1910s, limiting overall access to national forests. The railroad played a central role in the period's recreational development by linking the nation's urban populations with far-flung national parks such as Yellowstone and Glacier National Parks, as well as resorts and spas.[13] But rail travel remained largely out of reach for the majority of Americans at the beginning of the century, causing most to find recreational outlets closer to home in city parks, public beaches, or even amusement parks. The boom in automobile ownership following the war, along with the improvement of roads across the country, opened the nation's hinterlands to millions of Americans. Seemingly overnight, thousands of middle-class tourists and their automobiles descended upon their national forests and national parks in unprecedented numbers.

The second reason for the Forest Service's disregard of recreation was its own internal culture. The agency's progressive founders had strongly felt that its sole purpose was the efficient management of the nation's forests and grasslands for timber and grazing. This emphasis on scientific management and silviculture created a mentality within the agency that promoted timber production and grazing above all else. Divided into regional districts,

Forest Service district managers enjoyed the freedom to meet local needs free of Washington bureaucracy—a rare power in the growing federal largess of the era. Such autonomy stemmed from Forest Service Chief Gifford Pinchot's belief that delegating day-to-day decisions to district managers would enable him to focus on broader political issues. Even following Pinchot's dismissal from the agency in 1910 for insubordination, the Forest Service remained largely decentralized until well into the 1950s, dramatically shaping the agency's culture and management of the vast public lands under its care.

But more importantly, when it came to recreation's place as a priority within the Forest Service, many, if not most, foresters stressed that the economic importance of timber and grazing far outweighed that of recreation, and that providing recreational development would take away from the agency's primary objective of providing sustainable forestry and grazing on the nation's public lands. Moreover, the Transfer Act of 1905, which moved the Forest Service and the National Forests from the Department of Interior to the Department of Agriculture, mandated "that all money received from the sale of any products or the use of any lands or resources of said forest shall be . . . available . . . for the protection, administration, and extension of the Federal forest reserves."[14] Under the act, the Forest Service charged fees in order to fund grazing and timber operations, and perhaps more importantly, managed the use of national forests by both industries. While timber and grazing brought in revenue, helping fund the agency, most within the Forest Service believed that recreation would provide a modest income to the agency at best, a significant issue as it relied on fees to cover portions of its budget.[15]

It is hardly surprising, then, that recreation was held in such low esteem within the Forest Service as most rangers were trained either in horticulture by eastern universities or drawn from logging operations, relegating recreation as an inconsequential priority within the agency. But following the Allies' victory in World War I, an increasing number of foresters and forest supervisors came to question such biases as millions of recreationalists continued to pour into the national forests. To study recreation's economic potential and offer some solutions, the agency hired landscape architect Frank Waugh in 1917 to tour the Forest Service's scattered districts. Waugh produced a comprehensive report entitled *Recreation Uses on the National Forests* on the status of the National Forest's campgrounds, picnic areas, and other recreational facilities. In it, he disputed claims that recreation was economically nonviable, asserting instead, "in general terms it appears that the recreation use of

National Forests has a very substantial commercial value, and that recreation stands clearly as one of the major Forest utilities." Using an admittedly rather crude formulation, he concluded that recreational use of national forests was worth an estimated $7.5 million annually. Such a figure, Waugh believed, made it a worthy endeavor for the agency to pursue.[16]

Even without such economic arguments, the Forest Service could not ignore the reality of millions of Americans pouring into their national forests every year. By 1921, Forest Service Chief William Greeley declared recreation a major use of national forests as an estimated 6 million Americans were visiting their national forests annually.[17] While continuing to focus on timber and grazing, even regional foresters gradually began to see the importance of not only controlling the public's use of national forest lands, but also fostering its growth as a new constituency. The question remained, how would the Forest Service meet the public's growing demand for recreation? Unlike the National Park Service, few within the Forest Service had any experience with recreational planning. Moreover, the few recreational facilities that did exist within the national forests were often underdeveloped, underfunded, or under regulated. The National Park Service, on the other hand, relied on a large number of landscape architects who were busily laying out plans for roads, campgrounds, and villages within the national parks to attract visitors. The national parks also had a well-established concessioner system that allowed monopolies to operate hotels, restaurants, and other facilities within parks.[18] In comparison, the Forest Service only had architect Waugh on a part-time consulting basis. The passage of the Term Permit Act in 1915 did provide some guidance to the agency by allowing individuals to apply for permits to build lodges and cabins in national forests. Capital raised by these permits soon became the sole source of funding for recreational planning, privileging those who could afford to lease land from the government over those who simply wished to spend the day outdoors in the woods. But with limited funding and no internal mandate to provide for the public's recreational access, the Forest Service remained far behind its younger sibling.[19]

However, a handful within the agency, including Assistant Forester Edward A. Sherman, who in 1916 wrote two articles promoting recreational management, concluded that the agency needed to hire its own landscape architect in order to confront the growing recreational demands within the western national forests, and, in Sherman's opinion, slow the National Park Service's growing desire to take over all planning and management of recreation on all public lands.[20] The outbreak of World War I in Europe kept Sherman and the Forest Service from moving forward with such plans for another three years, until, in 1919, the agency hired Arthur Carhart as its first landscape architect.

Few have had as significant an impact in promoting recreation and regional planning within the Forest Service than Carhart. During his short but influential tenure with the agency, Carhart tirelessly championed recreation's place within the Forest Service, often butting up against the agency's entrenched timber and grazing culture and Congress's reluctance to adequately fund recreational development within the national forests. As a trained landscape architect, he believed in the need for broader planning efforts in order to best meet the public's interests in managing the national forests, a view not always appreciated by others within the Forest Service, who resented his assertion that recreation held an important role in not only providing for the public good, but in preserving the natural beauty of many national forests. Carhart's career with the Forest Service began inauspiciously, when, in 1919, he met with Edward Sherman to discuss the agency's need for a landscape architect. Unlike the nascent National Park Service, the Forest Service had no landscape architects at the time, a fact Sherman hoped to correct. Even though Sherman saw a need for a man with Carhart's talents, he had had no place to send the young landscape architect. And so for several months after the meeting, Carhart returned home to Iowa until finally, in March 1919, Assistant Regional Forester Carl Stahl offered Carhart an undefined job within the Rocky Mountain Office in Denver and an annual salary of $1,800.[21]

On his arrival in Denver, Carhart, like Olmsted a decade earlier, quickly identified the city's surrounding foothills as ideal for recreational development, writing, "it will be reasonable to say that Denver, in spite of the fact that she has at the present time the excellent foothill parks, is in actual need of a place where her citizens, both laboring class and of the more well to do can go for an extended outing at a reasonable price."[22] What Denver and the surrounding mountain region needed was a comprehensive recreational plan integrating the mountain parks with the millions of acres of national forests, Carhart argued, which would link the nearby national forests with the urban population's recreational needs. Located some thirty miles west of Denver, the 14,000-foot Mount Evans offered Carhart his first opportunity to put such aspirations to work. Denver boosters had long pointed to the region surrounding Mount Evans's wild scenic beauty, as well as its relative proximity to the city, as an ideal setting for a national park. The peak had attracted tourists as early as the 1870s, but with few roads and no facilities, Mount Evans remained largely isolated from the outside world despite its relative proximity to the city. By comparison, Rocky Mountain National Park (RMNP) was more than twice as far from Denver, and yet attracted thousands of visitors every summer, many of whom made a circular tour from the city, over the park's Fall River Road and back to Denver in a day-long drive. "At that time we had a very active Tourist Bureau in Denver dedicated to holding tourists in the city as long as possible by any reasonable means that would trap them here," recalled Carhart on the city's promotion of RMNP as tourist destination. Due to RMNP's popularity, Denver boosters hoped to develop a second national park within driving distance of the city to bolster its budding tourism industry. "This proposition was being hard-driven to get another tourist attraction in the city of Denver and provide for a circle trip out of town with a return at night."[23] To members of Denver's chamber of commerce, Mount Evans appeared a logical choice for the state's second national park.

Carhart agreed with the city's business interests that Mount Evans offered fantastic potential as a tourist draw. On his first assignment for the Forest Service, he spent several weeks surveying the peak and its surrounding area. Noting in his preliminary report that, as a rule, the state's mountains were the primary objective of most visitors, Carhart pointed out that "no adequate road system taps this area, but with the establishment of roads, the Mount Evans Recreation Area will be the most accessible mountainous district for several hundred thousand inhabitants of Denver and the millions in the territory east of this city." With the completion of the narrow road to the summit of the peak, which the city had begun constructing the year prior, Carhart asserted the Mount Evans area would "be a continuation in effect of her present excellent Mountain Park System." He suggested the construction of three residential centers, the most important along Owlshead Creek on the eastern side of the mountain, which would house no fewer than eight hundred people at any one time.[24] The Denver Chamber of Commerce was thrilled by Carhart's idea of developing the area but was hesitant in supporting government-built villages that would compete with the city's own lodging and tourist industries. Likewise, the Forest Service never acted on Carhart's plan believing it to be too ambitious an undertaking, and so the Mount Evans region remained undeveloped for several decades. Despite his failure to secure needed support to develop Mount Evans, Carhart learned a valuable lesson on the important recreational link between national forests and urban populations, a lesson he would build upon over the next three years.

Following the completion of his work on Mount Evans, Carhart was assigned to survey and write a development plan for Trapper's Lake in the White River National Forest. A small natural lake surrounded by the Flat Top Mountains, Trapper's Lake's beauty, as well as its remoteness and good fishing, had drawn dozens of permit requests by outdoorsmen to build cabins along its shore. Carhart spent much of July scouting the alpine lake, laying out cabin sites on its shoreline and hiking the surrounding region. During his survey work, he met Paul Rainey and William McFadden, who were staying at a friend's cabin near the lake for the month fishing. The two welcomed Carhart's company in the evenings, often staying up well into the night discussing the Forest Service's plans to develop Trapper's Lake. Both Rainey and McFadden argued that the construction of cabins along the lake's shoreline would effectively privatize the lake, shutting out those not lucky enough to secure a permit from the Forest Service. Their nightly arguments swayed Carhart, who upon returning to Denver began drafting a plan placing all cabin sites far back from the shoreline in order to preserve the lake's natural beauty for all to enjoy. The proposed plan infuriated the few permit holders who wished to have their cabins on the lake's shore. But Stahl agreed with Carhart's argument that such development would effectively shut off the lake to other visitors, and the assistant regional forester signed off on restricting development along the shoreline.

Stahl's approval of Carhart's plan for Trapper's Lake reflected a growing unease within the Forest Service over the rampant commercialization of national forests by private interests. Although the agency fully approved the development of recreational facilities such as summer cabins, lodges, and campgrounds within national forests and was increasingly dependent upon fees produced from such developments, a handful of foresters such as Carhart began questioning the exclusive nature of the agency's permit system when it came to providing recreational opportunities for all rather than the few. Reflecting on Trapper's Lake a year after submitting his plan, Carhart wrote, "Left to themselves, hundreds of people will settle on summer home sites on the edge of the lake." Such development, he argued, would lead to the eventual destruction of the very beauty that the permit holders sought to possess. "Individuals naturally desire to help themselves to the best they can

obtain regardless of others. This very greed undirected defeats its own purpose in a location of this kind by destroying the very qualities which the individual locates his house on the shore of a lake." The only way to preserve such
scenic areas, Carhart asserted, was for the Forest Service to preserve them for
all rather than the few. He concluded, "There is an absolute moral obligation on the part of the Forest Service to return not to a small group but to the
whole nation the greatest value possible from every resource. The aesthetic
values are no exception."[25] Although such assertions built upon the Forest
Service's ideal of the greatest good, they ran counter to the agency's internal culture, which sought the fullest utilization of every forest as timber and
rangeland. What Carhart identified in his plan for Trapper's Lake was Americans' growing recreational appetite and desire for wilderness preservation. A
pragmatist, Carhart understood the imperative to provide the public adequate
recreational access, but endeavored to do so in a manner that preserved the
very scenery that recreationalists sought when venturing out into the mountains, rivers, and forests. While he strongly believed that outdoor recreation
played a crucial role in individual and social stability, he also understood the
problematic consumerist relationship most Americans had with nature, an
awareness he shared most notability with Assistant District Forester Aldo
Leopold.

A graduate of Yale's Forestry School, Leopold had joined the Forest Service
in 1909 and was assigned to the agency's Region 3 office in the New Mexico
and Arizona Territory. He quickly rose through the ranks, and after a brief
stint with the Albuquerque Chamber of Commerce became the supervisor for
the Carson National Forest. While he later became famously known for his
advocacy for the preservation of wild places and his formation of a land ethic
that moved beyond the Progressive utilitarian ethos to a broader understanding of nature and man's place in it, like Carhart, Leopold had grown gravely
concerned over the commercial exploitation of national forests for recreation
early on. In 1916, Leopold and Tusayan National Forest Director Don Johnston were assigned to visit the southern rim of the Grand Canyon and report
on the area's overall condition. As a national monument managed by the
Forest Service, the canyon's southern rim had become an increasingly popular destination for motor tourists. Leopold and Johnston found the monument overridden with commercial enterprises, makeshift camping sites, and
trash. The chaos of the south rim appalled both men, leading them to argue
in their final report for strict regulation and zoning to guide the commercial

development and preservation of the Grand Canyon's scenic beauty, an ideal that ran counter to many economic interests in Arizona at the time. As historian Paul Sutter notes, the same phenomena Leopold and Johnston observed in the south rim had manifested across much of the West's national forests, leading many foresters to promote the permitting of recreational development among a smaller number of commercial interests, never believing that recreation would grow to rival timber as the largest use of the region's national forests.[26]

Three years after his visit to the Grand Canyon, Leopold traveled to Denver to discuss recreation's role within the Forest Service with Carhart over dinner at the city's famous Brown Palace. Carhart had just completed his report on Trapper's Lake and begun to gain attention throughout the Forest Service for his insistence on recreation's place and the need for stricter planning within the national forests, contentions that had attracted Leopold's attention. No transcript of the meeting was taken, but following their conversation, Carhart penned a several-page memorandum recounting the two men's discussion of the need to both preserve natural beauty and provide adequate recreational access. "The Forest Service, it seems to me, is obligated to make the greatest return from the total forests to the people of the Nation that is possible. This, the Forest Service had endeavored to do in the case of timber utilization, grazing, watershed protection and other activities," wrote Carhart. "There is, however, a great wealth of recreational facilities and scenic values within the Forests, which have not been so utilized, and at the present time the Service is face to face with a question of big policies, big plans, and big utilization for the values and areas." However, while Carhart asserted that the Forest Service should further embrace recreational development and "big plans," he also called for the preservation of scenic values and the limiting of development so that all could enjoy the national forests rather than a select few lucky enough to secure a Term Permit from the government. "There is no question in my mind but that there is a definite point in different types of country where man made structures should be stopped. How best to arrive at a definition of this point, or how best to come to a decision on these areas to be preserved is a question with me."[27] Such a line of reasoning fell more in line with Leopold's growing concerns over the development of national forests for recreation, particularly the construction of roads to facilitate automobile recreation.

Unlike Carhart, Leopold was less inclined to fully embrace recreation as a means by which to preserve nature. While he agreed that recreation provided the highest use in certain areas, Leopold also believed that some forests should simply be left untouched. Writing in 1921, he asserted that the growing conflict between recreational use and wilderness was emerging as perhaps the Forest Service's most pressing issue, stating, "Lamentations over this or that favorite vacation ground being 'spoiled by tourists' are becoming more and more frequent. Very evidently we have here the old conflict between preservation and use, long since an issue with respect to timber, water power, and other purely economic resources, but just now coming to be an issue with respect to recreation."[28] Whereas Carhart would continue to promote the idea of recreational development as a higher economic use of national forests, preserving them from extractive industries, Leopold viewed recreation not as a panacea, but as yet another potential exploitive use of national forests that held the same potentially negative impacts of industries such as timber, mining, and grazing. These two views, recreation use versus preservation, continued to shape the debate over the place and degree of recreational use within the Forest Service through the rest of the century.[29]

Within months of completing the Trapper's Lake plan and meeting with Leopold, Carhart convinced District Forester Stahl, Stahl's assistant, and the supervisor of the San Isabel National Forest in central Colorado to create a recreational management plan for the forest near Pueblo, Colorado. Written in 1919, the "General Working Plan Recreational Development of the San Isabel National Forest Colorado" marked the first attempt by the Forest Service to outline broader goals for managing recreational use within a national forest. The wide-ranging plan outlined campgrounds, trails, and roads, all meant to allow recreationalists greater access to the forest while at the same time preserving the forest's wilderness regions. Explaining the need for such broad visions of recreational planning, Carhart wrote, "This is not really a new field development here or elsewhere applied to the Forest but rather a recognition of the fact that must be directly related to other development and the group made up of camp, summer home block, hotel, trail system and other lesser parts of any large area plan must have direct connection with development and plans for other near by like sections."[30]

Believing that the San Isabel Plan was "bound to be a model for other like plans that will inevitably follow," Carhart sought to expand the idea of recreational planning beyond small projects, such as Trapper's Lake, to create larger regional plans that integrated all recreational uses from highly developed resorts to backcountry wilderness camping. "National Forests are of so great an extent and the problems varied that the planning of recreational uses on any scale in proportion to the site of the problem leaves that realm of playground planning, camp planning or the planning of subdivisions blocks for summer homes and enters the field of regional planning," he wrote.[31] It was a singularly important observation; by 1920, pressures had only increased on the Forest Service to manage an ever-wider array of uses. Timber and grazing remained king within the agency, while recreation's place remained ill defined, despite its growing popularity. The election of Warren Harding as President intensified demands that the Forest Service increase timber sales in order to bolster revenues, casting recreation as an ill-defined, and thus secondary use of the national forests. This emphasis further strained the relationship between the Forest Service and the National Park Service over the highest use of public lands and would eventually lead to Carhart's untimely departure from the Forest Service.

But it was in the northern boundary waters of Minnesota, not in the Colorado Rockies, where Carhart found his greatest challenge as the Forest Service's recreational engineer. In the summer of 1919, the young forester spent several weeks exploring the Boundary Waters by canoe. He became enamored with the forest's vast lakes, abundant wildlife, and scenic beauty. Like Trapper's Lake, dozens had applied for permits to construct seasonal cabins in some of the forest's more scenic spots. And once again, rather than allow the development of campgrounds, lodges, and other "urban conditions" into one of the last untouched networks of lakes, bogs, and boreal forests in the United States, Carhart expressed his desire to preserve the forest's vast system of lakes and wild lands, writing in his preliminary plan, "the preservation and protection of all those things that are of values great enough to sacrifice a certain amount of economic return so there may be a greater total return from the aesthetic qualities."[32] To Carhart, the Boundary Waters area was too special to allow development and argued that doing so would degrade the region's long-term value as wilderness for its irreplaceable flora and fauna. But rather than act on his thoughts concerning the Superior National Forest, for the next two years the plan sat on a shelf in his office as he continued to develop his ideas on recreational planning and preservation.

After what he later called "a period of seasoning and maturing," Carhart returned to his preliminary draft two years later and refined the original report's themes of regional planning and wilderness preservation.[33] Writing in the introduction of the final plan he noted, "The various areas of outdoor territory offering the opportunity for touch with nature must be so handled that thus necessity will not be impaired but rather will be protected and developed in a proper manner. All governmentally owned lands, capable of offering the needed association with nature, must be considered in this system."[34] Among the first calls for the preservation of wilderness, the Superior National Forest Plan reflected a growing, albeit small, push to set aside scenic and wild lands throughout the nation. Unlike the wilderness movement of the postwar era, interwar preservationists such as Carhart defined wilderness not just as places valuable for their aesthetics and ecological importance, but as places valuable for their recreational opportunities. The combination of wilderness preservation and recreation was a natural extension of the Forest Service's own culture of placing an economic value on forests in order to best manage them. If, like timber and grazing, national forests such as the Superior National Forest held an intrinsic value for recreation, then, Carhart argued, recreational use should be placed on equal footing in the management of all national forests. This equality then provided a more balanced and effective management of the national forests. But such ideas ran counter to the Forest Service's institutional thinking, and so failed to gain widespread acceptance.

As he worked on the Superior Forest Plan, Carhart penned a brief article in the City of Denver's magazine, *Municipal Facts Monthly*. In it, he asserted, "Recreation is a market commodity. It is sold every day in the amusement field. It costs so much per hour to buy a seat in a movie house. It takes so much more to see and hear grand opera. In the outdoor field it takes so much membership dues to field clubs, country clubs, and golf clubs." Therefore, "So long as recreation is a product then there must be some sort of plant to manufacture it."[35] For Denver, Carhart argued that such a "plant" would be comprised of a vast "Recreational Fan" that swept outward from Denver with the city's mountain parks at its center and Mount Evans just beyond. The remainder of the fan included the Glacier Region of the Colorado National Forest and the RMNP to the north, the Pike National Forest to the south, and the Arapahoe National Forest to the west. Like the Mountain Parks Committee a dozen years before, Carhart portrayed Denver as the gateway to a vast recreational empire that assured "Denver the envied position of being the 'Playground City of America.'" Doing so would provide Denver with "a group of magnificent playgrounds" that would attract tourists and improve residents' quality of life.[36]

In truth, Carhart's recreational fan expressed what was naturally occurring in the mountains west of Denver. Increasing numbers of Front Range residents and tourists were already enjoying Denver's Mountain Parks and the Pike and Arapahoe National Forests during this period. Outing groups such as the Colorado Mountain Club had begun to organize hiking trips throughout the state's mountains. Improvements to mountain roads and highways further attracted visitors to places like RMNP, Grand Lake, Red Feather, and Squaw Pass. Carhart's recreational fan was not merely a means to attract visitors to the region, it also helped ensure the development of national forests in the best possible manner. The recreational fan was to be a master plan of sorts in which recreational development was steered to both ensure the preservation of wilderness and allow the development of needed facilities. Such an assertion once again challenged the Forest Service's long-held institutional beliefs that recreation held no intrinsic values and could not be managed as a commodity. Carhart rejected this premise, correctly identifying the economic value of recreation, and argued for its management as a commodity by citing its twin benefits of economic development and wilderness preservation.

By his second year with the Forest Service, Carhart was growing increasingly frustrated over his beliefs that the agency was resistant to his ideas on planning and recreation. Events came to a head over Regional Forest Supervisor E. A. Sherman's rejection of Carhart's proposed plan to preserve the Superior National Forest's Boundary Water's for recreational use, instead approving the construction of two roads through the forest principally for fire control.[37] The decision incensed Carhart, who had become resentful over what he saw as both the Forest Service and Congress's continued reluctance to face recreation's growing role within nation forests. Although Sherman and others agreed with Carhart that recreation was a pressing issue, they contended that the agency needed to remain focused on timber and fire suppression. Funding also became a major point of contention between Carhart and the rest of the Forest Service. Concerned more about the continued production of timber, Congress failed to fund recreational programs within the Forest Service. Rather, fire suppression continued to receive ever-larger appropriations due in large part to the agency's desire to prevent massive conflagrations such as the 1910 fires in Montana. It was not until 1922 that Congress finally set aside a miserly sum of $10,000 for recreational development as opposed to the $50,000 asked for by the Forest Service.[38] Not until the New Deal would the agency receive adequate funding with which to build and maintain enough campgrounds, trails, and lodges to meet the public's needs. Adding to this fact, Carhart remained the only recreational engineer within the agency, a point he continuously brought up with both Sherman and Stahl. He also complained about the resistance to, if not outright disregard for, his plans by many in the agency. Carhart became increasingly outspoken about what he saw as the Forest Service's continued failure to support both him and his work, and after several months of bitter fighting with his superiors he resigned from the agency in 1921. Over the remainder of his life, Carhart remained an ardent proponent of wilderness protection and a champion for outdoor recreation's place within the national forests, opening his own landscape architecture firm, as well as becoming a moderately successful author and founder of the Denver Public Library's Conservation Library before his death in 1978.[39]

At the time of Carhart's resignation from the Forest Service, Colorado's Western Slope remained largely isolated from the growing Front Range. High mountain passes and long winters kept travel between the ever-more urban Front Range and the rural Western Slope to a minimum. What few roads did cross the Continental Divide often were just rough dirt tracks passable only during summer months. But by the end of the century's second decade, both the federal and state governments dramatically increased efforts to further open Colorado's Western Slope by funding the construction of numerous highways and railroads through the state's towering mountain ranges. The construction of new roads opened the mountains to further economic development, particularly tourism. As the development of Denver's Mountain Parks had demonstrated, the automobile played a central role in the state's burgeoning tourist industry. Beyond connecting Denver and other Front Range communities to places like Estes Park, Red Feather, and Mount Evans, few tourists ventured west of the Continental Divide due in large part to the limited number of adequate roads that crossed the mountains. Funded by state tax dollars, the Fall River Road within RMNP solved the problem of automobile access within the newly created national park, attracting nearly a quarter of a million visitors during the first year of its operation. Yet, the road's popularity diminished over the next decade, as many drivers feared its steep grades and tight corners, causing park officials to consider a new road through the park. The result was the federally funded Trailridge Road, opened in 1933 and crossing the Continental Divide at 12,183 feet above sea

Actual map of recreational fan in *Denver's Municipal Facts*. Photograph courtesy Denver Public Library, Western History Collection, Carhart, C352.07 8883D4.

level; the road immediately became Rocky Mountains' primary attraction, allowing tourists to easily drive between the towns of Estes Park and Grand Lake over the highest continuous paved highway in the United States.[40]

The Fall River Road was but one of many road projects undertaken by the state and federal government during the period. In 1918, the Forest Service financed the survey of a "Midland Trail" over Berthoud Pass. Using an earlier

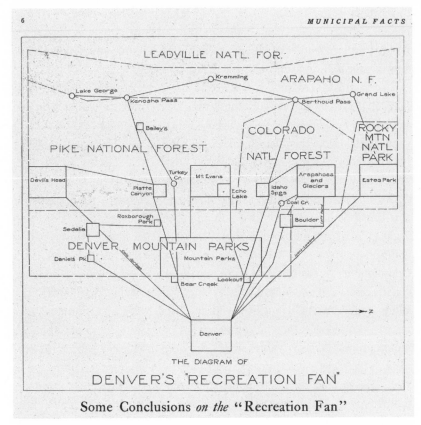

THE DIAGRAM OF

DENVER'S "RECREATION FAN"

Some Conclusions *on the* "Recreation Fan"

Arthur Carhart's recreational fan in *Denver's Municipal Facts*. Photograph courtesy Denver Public Library, Western History Collection, Carhart, C352.07 8883D4.

stage route from the mining communities of Idaho Springs and Empire into the Fraser Valley, Berthoud Pass remained a harrowing journey over the Continental Divide at the beginning of the century. Agreeing on the pass's promise as an ideal route between the Front Range and Middle Park, the Forest Service and state highway department each contributed $110,000 for the construction of a 16-foot-wide dirt road over Berthoud Pass beginning in 1921. Within two years the pass was opened to traffic, making the Fraser Valley and larger Middle Park region a short two-hour drive from Denver. Designated as U.S. Highway 40 in 1925, the pass quickly became the primary route used by most tourists to the region. Still, crossing the Continental Divide at 11,307 feet above sea level, heavy winter snows often closed Berthoud Pass to travelers from late October until early June, if not later. Other mountain passes a shared similar fate, including U.S. Highway 6, which crossed the Divide over Loveland Pass, and Highway 9, which crossed over Hoosier Pass between the mining towns of Breckenridge and Fairplay.[41]

The railroad faced similar challenges crossing Colorado's Rocky Mountains. Bypassed by the Union Pacific and the Denver and Rio Grande railroads, the central Rockies remained isolated until the beginning of the twentieth century when Denver banker David Moffat sunk most of his considerable fortune into establishing a railway between Denver and Salt Lake City. The Denver, Northwestern and Pacific Railroad crested over the Continental Divide via Corona Pass, also known as the Moffat Road. Moffat's sudden death in 1911 threw the Denver, Northwestern and Pacific Railroad into chaos, causing it to be placed into receivership. Two years later it was reformed as the appropriately named Denver and Salt Lake Railroad and resumed operations. Optimistic as to the Moffat Road's future, the newly organized company constructed a $10,000 hotel on the summit of Corona Pass in the belief that summer tourism would quickly pay for the lavish lodge, and continued to lay rail westward to the ranching community of Craig. But like all of Colorado's mountain passes, heavy winter snows and deep drifts often kept trains from making their way over Corona, and once again the railroad fell into debt. By 1920, Denver business interests began advocating for the construction of a tunnel beneath James Peak to solve both the Denver and Salt Lake's continued financial problems and the need for reliable year-round transportation between the Eastern and the Western Slope. Denver politicians introduced a bill to the Colorado state legislature to allocate state tax dollars to construct the six-mile tunnel under the divide, but legislators from Pueblo protested the measure, believing it undermined their own interests in developing a rail link between Pueblo and the western half of the state. The deadlock remained over the issue until a massive flood struck the steel town, causing nearly $30 million in damages and killing at least a hundred people. In the wake of the flood, Pueblo officials asked the state to approve a taxation district to raise funds for flood control. Denver politicians seized upon the opportunity, forcing a compromise, which allowed for the creation of Pueblo's tax district in exchange for their backing of the construction of the tunnel. With its finances set, construction on the Moffat Tunnel began in 1923 and was completed five years later; the new tunnel opened Middle Park and the larger Western Slope to year-round travel.[42]

Winter travel soon changed when, in 1931, the Colorado Department of Highways, asserting that the escalating costs of plowing the pass open every spring surpassed maintaining the road throughout the winter months, announced its plans to maintain U.S. Highway 40 over the Berthoud Pass allowing year-round automobile travel between Clear Creek and Grand Counties.[43] The following year, the *Denver Post* announced the Forest Service's plans to develop a "Ski Mecca" on the pass's summit. "The Forest Service has been at work for more than two years on plans for development of a winter playground in that area," proclaimed the *Post*. "All that is holding up the proposed project is a lack of funds to work with."[44] The Interior Department soon secured Works Progress Administration (WPA) monies to help the Forest Service purchase aging army barracks for use as a temporary warming lodge for the burgeoning "Mecca." Over the next five years Berthoud Pass's popularity grew, and in 1937, a prominent Denver department store, the May Company, financed the installation of a rope tow for the area. No longer having to trudge their way to the top of a ski run, skiers simply skied down, grabbed a hold of the rope, an exercise that often proved much more difficult than it sounded, and were pulled to the top. The new rope tow drew even more skiers to the pass from the Front Range every weekend. "Denver people are suddenly awaking to the fact that within almost an hour's easy drive from the city there lays one of the biggest assets in Colorado—an ideal winter sports center" where "many ardent enthusiasts continue to ski on the receding snow fields until mid-summer," observed a *Rocky Mountain News* reporter on Berthoud's meteoric rise in popularity.[45] Soon after the end of World War II, Berthoud Pass had emerged as one of the most popular ski destinations in Colorado attracting over 20,000 skiers annually.[46]

Berthoud Pass was not the only popular ski destination for Front Range skiers in the central Rockies. Shortly after the Moffat Tunnel's completion in 1928, small bands of Denver skiers began riding the train from the city's Union Station to the tunnel's western portal. There, they would disembark and spend the day skiing on a few roughly cut trails before hopping on the eastbound train later in the afternoon for the ride back home. It was during one of these return trips that a group began bantering around the idea of forming a club "to stimulate interest in proficient ski running as distinguished from ski jumping," and, perhaps more importantly, build a rope tow to pull them up the hill.[47] The idle talk slowly turned serious, and the following summer the group formed the Colorado Arlberg Ski Club. Interest in the club grew slowly at first, but within a couple of winters it became apparent that a more definite organization was necessary if the club were to survive. Among the club's first members was Colorado native and accomplished mountaineer Graeme McGowan. In the spring of 1933, McGowan joined with fellow club members Garret Van Wagenen and Josiah Holland in purchasing the Mary Jane mining claim near the West Portal from a local logger for $1,500. The three formed Portal Resorts, Inc., in the hopes of developing a resort on the site. Soon after, McGowan met with fellow club members and agreed to abandon his commercial plans for the property. Instead, they chose to lease it—and the three buildings he, Van Wagenen and Holland had moved onto the mining claim—to the Arlberg Club, establishing the first permanent ski facility near the West Portal.[48]

Unfortunately for McGowan, who had put a significant amount of his personal time and money into the property, the club often failed to meet its rent, drawing McGowan into increasing debt. Furious over the club's continued failure to pay, McGowan decided to dissolve the company, and after threatening to sue the club, won a small cash settlement with the Arlberg Club taking ownership of the property and new clubhouse. Despite the growing animosity over the development of the club, McGowan remained optimistic about the potential of the area for future development, noting in a letter to the Arlberg Club's secretary H. G. Hodges on his selling the property to the club, "The Mary Jane Placer claim is a valuable piece of ground. This will be very fully appreciated in years to come. An offer of $10,000 was recently refused for the Evan property here. The owner holds it at $25,000. I do not doubt but for that its value will sometime be generally recognized at that or considerably more."[49] McGowan's prediction proved to hold true as skiers from Denver and the rest of the booming communities along Colorado's Front Range continued to flock to the West Portal every winter weekend.[50]

The West Portal's growing popularity as a ski destination soon drew the attention of Denver's Director of City Parks, George Cranmer. Wealthy and well connected, in 1935 he had successfully managed Benjamin Stapleton's mayoral campaign. In repayment, Stapleton appointed Cranmer Denver's Director of City Parks, a position he would hold for the next decade.[51] Cranmer sought to build upon the vision set by Robert Speer by expanding the city's parks system. Often taking advantage of New Deal funding, he directed the construction of Red Rocks Amphitheater, increased the size of Denver Municipal Airport, renamed Stapleton Airport in 1944, and improved dozens of city parks.[52] With an uncannily accurate foresight, Cranmer believed that, as the Denver area continued to grow, so too would the popularity of the region's mountains. An active outdoorsman, he was readily aware of Berthoud Pass's growing popularity, as well as that of Denver's own mountain parks, and concluded that the city needed to build its own ski area in order to provide adequate recreational access for its residents. In addition, such a project would solidify Denver's tourist market. But financing such a project, let alone finding a location close enough to the city with the right mixture of easy access and ample snow, appeared a fairly tall order to fill. Undeterred, Cranmer began searching for his winter park.[53]

His search quickly came to focus on the western portal of the Moffat Tunnel. The area's growing popularity and relative ease of access from Denver by both train and automobile made it highly attractive as a city park, despite its location some sixty miles west of the Denver city limits. After spending a day touring the area with his friends and skiing experts Bob Balch and Otto Schniebs, Cranmer determined the West Portal was indeed the perfect site for his ski area, and quickly set about applying for a permit from the Forest Service. In April of 1938, the Forest Service issued the City of Denver a permit for 6,400 acres to construct and maintain a "winter sports area, including ski courses and trails, ski tows, and appurtenant structures."[54] To the Forest Service, partnering with a municipality such as Denver was ideal; not only did the city have experience managing recreational facilities, but with the help of New Deal programs such as the WPA, Denver seemingly would have little problem financing the development of a new ski area. The partnership would also serve the interests of both the city and the federal agency. Each had a strong desire to expand the commercial development of recreation, particularly downhill skiing, in order to further bolster the state's tourist economy and meet the public's growing demand for recreational development. Struggling economically due to the Depression, Denver city officials saw any opportunity to bolster the city's tax base as a worthy endeavor, even if it was building a ski area sixty miles away. Likewise, the Forest Service sought to encourage the recreational use of the national forests in order to continue to attract visitors, a marked shift in policy from just a prior decade caused largely by the reality of recreation's continued growth, as well as the agency's ongoing battle with the National Park Service over the management of public lands.

News of the Forest Service's approval of Denver's permit thrilled Colorado's skiers. "This brings great joy to the hearts of all the many interested

George Cranmer, former director of Denver City Parks. Photograph courtesy Denver Public Library, Western History Collection, F-24403.

in the development of winter sports in the region. Also, it will help to take care of the ever-increasing crowds at Berthoud Pass, which are becoming difficult to handle; and it will open up a large region of splendid skiing terrain," exclaimed the Colorado Mountain Club.[55] However, not all agreed that the city should be investing in a ski area. *Denver Post* sports writer Jack Carberry attacked the proposed Winter Park as a "playground for the rich," a criticism which held a least a kernel of truth as the majority of the area's supporters came from Denver's elite.[56] Questions also arose on whether the city should build a ski area sixty miles away on the other side of the Continental Divide. Unlike its other mountain parks, it was difficult to argue that Winter Park was near enough to Denver to serve all of the city's residents. Cranmer, however, remained undeterred by such criticisms and pressed forward in building the city's ski area.

Still, funding remained an issue. Even after securing a permit from the Forest Service to begin construction, Denver lacked the needed capital to build Winter Park. Cranmer solved the city's money problems by turning to Colorado's congressional delegation, which in turn secured WPA funds to build two rope tows. Combined with $14,000 from the Denver Chamber of Commerce, the federal dollars solved Winter Park's short-term funding issues.[57] But despite federal and municipal financing, keeping Winter Park opened remained a constant worry. Cranmer cajoled, begged, and pushed city officials, business interests, and railroad officials for money to help pay for the burgeoning ski area, often soliciting contributions, or Winter Sport Subscriptions, varying from $10 to $1,500. Through his tireless letter writing and phone calls, Cranmer kept Winter Park afloat, often promising that one day the ski area would pay for itself and show a profit.[58] He even held in trust the funds raised for the construction of the first two ski tows in his own name until 1942, when they were transferred to the city treasury.[59] Finally, with volunteers helping clear trails, build the two rope tows, and move three aging barracks to the site to be used as warming huts and overnight lodges, Winter Park Ski Area opened to the public in December 1939, marking the emergence of the state's ski industry and its growing economic and cultural importance.

Colorado's remarkable transformation throughout the first half of the twentieth century set the stage for the state's—and the American West's—much larger shifts in the decades following World War II. While the United States' entry into the war brought a brief halt to the development of ski areas within the state, anchored by its wartime industries, Colorado emerged from the war as the preeminent economic power in the Mountain West.[60] Drawn by the promise of work and a better quality of life, millions soon moved to the state, settling mostly along the increasingly metropolitan Front Range. The Forest Service generally embraced recreation as one of its management priorities by the start of the war, though still ranking it lower than timber and grazing. Western postwar urban growth and the nation's rising affluence would fuel the state's emergent ski industry, opening Denver's mountain hinterlands beyond that of both Speer's and Carhart's imagination and presenting the Forest Service a whole new set of challenges as the sport's remarkable growth and economic importance spurred further competition among Colorado's newest ski areas.

2

In the spring of 1947, Denver's city park manager, George Cranmer, angrily wrote Rocky Mountain Regional Forester John W. Spencer demanding that the Forest Service act immediately in financing the construction of more trails at the city's Winter Park ski area. Cranmer condemned the Forest Service's failure to meet the public's growing demand for skiing by failing to provide any funding assistance for the six-year-old ski area. Located some sixty miles from Denver, Winter Park's slopes had become overwhelmed with hundreds of skiers virtually every weekend, and its two aging rope tows had fallen into such disrepair due to a lack of funds that the Forest Service had threatened to revoke the city's permit if nothing was done to improve them. But with its ski area already $59,000 in debt, the city did not have the money needed to pay for the repairs or expand Winter Park's trail system.[1] While sympathetic to Cranmer's plight, Spencer heatedly responded that the Forest Service was well aware of the public's mounting demand for skiing within Colorado, and had, since 1945, cooperated with the City of Denver on the expansion to Winter Park, begun avalanche control on Berthoud Pass, issued permits for both Berthoud Pass and Arapahoe Basin, purchased Cooper Hill from the War Department, arranged for the replacement of the ski shelters on both Berthoud and Loveland Pass, and entered negotiations for the construction of a ski area at Climax outside the town of Leadville all in efforts to meet the rising demand. Other than that initial assistance, Spencer noted, "It is the policy of the Forest Service to give private capital an opportunity to develop ski areas on national forest land under special permits. This results in the creation of new business opportunities . . . while at the same time the best interests of the skiers are protected by the administrative control exercised by the Forest Service."[2] It was now the policy of the Forest Service, he explained, to allow private interests to develop and operate ski areas on national forest lands. It would be up to the City and County of Denver to raise the needed capital to expand Winter Park as its operator, not the federal government.

The Forest Service's refusal to provide any further funding, and Cranmer's subsequent retirement in 1947, brought about a new chapter in Winter Park's story. Alarmed by the ski area's worsening financial condition and the Forest Service's threat to revoke the city's permit, Denver banker and long-time Arlberg Club member Alan Phipps approached Denver's new mayor, Quig Newton, with a proposal to set up a nonprofit board to run the ski area similar to that already running the city's natural history museum and botanical gardens. Pointing out the fact that the ski area's rope tows were becoming too dangerous to use, Phipps easily convinced Newton of the need for a separate entity to run Denver's ski area, and, in 1950, Phipps and a group of Denver business leaders formed the Winter Park Recreation Associates (WPRA). Led by a fifteen-member volunteer board, the nonprofit organization agreed to manage Winter Park, plowing all profits garnered from ticket sales and concessions back into the ski area. Such an arrangement allowed the city to remain the owner, while effectively making Winter Park a privately run operation, an arrangement that would have long-term implications for both the city of Denver and Winter Park.

Faced with the necessity of turning a profit in order to remain open, the WPRA began investing in the ski area's facilities. The first order of business was the replacement of the ski area's two rope tows. "I concluded that the rope tow was perhaps the most dangerous piece of equipment there was, and we set out to retire them just as quickly as possible," the WPRA's first executive director, Steve Bradley, later recalled.[3] The danger of rope tows lay in the fact that they run constantly, and unless a skier quickly grabbed on to the rapidly moving rope and then remained standing, the skier could quickly, and often violently, be jerked to the ground. In addition, long hair or loose clothing could be potentially caught in the tow's pulley system, seriously injuring or even killing those unlucky enough to be not paying attention. T-bars, on the other hand, allowed skiers, individually or in pairs, to grab hold of a long T-shaped bar suspended from a cable and rest on the crossbar while riding uphill. Such an improvement kept skiers away from the cable, reducing the possibility of losing a favorite jacket or limb and allowing lift operators to more effectively help skiers load and unload. Introduced years later, ski lifts would improve upon the T-bar concept by attaching chairs to the cables and elevating them off the ground. Both chairlifts and T-bars remain in use at most ski resorts today, carrying thousands of skiers and snowboarders to the top of their favorite runs with greater speed and capacity. With money raised by Phipps and others, Bradley tore down the ski area's dangerous rope tows and replaced them with more modern T-bar tows. He also added terrain by expanding Winter Park's trail system further up the mountain. And over the next decade the WPRA continued to develop Winter Park, expanding the parking lot, introducing trail grooming with the invention of the Bradley Packer—named after Bradley—and replacing the old barracks that had served as the area's lodge with the much larger and more comfortable Balcony House in efforts to accommodate the ever-growing numbers of skiers. By the mid-1960s, Winter Park added six new ski lifts, the on-mountain restaurant Snoasis, and hundreds of acres of new trails, all of which continued to attract greater numbers of skiers.[4]

Winter Park's transformation from a small rope tow operation to a thriving ski area embodied the emergence of Colorado's modern ski industry in the postwar era. Already an increasingly popular winter sport in Colorado prior to the war, downhill skiing's popularity exploded immediately following the Allied victories in Europe and the Pacific. Skier numbers jumped a remarkable 75 percent statewide in the two years following the war, inundating Colorado's handful of ski areas.[5] Such rapid growth was not unique to Colorado. Pent-up demand for travel combined with a growing national affluence in drawing millions of Americans into their national parks, national forests, and other public lands. Nationwide, national forest visitation grew from 7.5 million visits in 1944 to over 21 million by 1947 and showed no signs of slowing.[6] Recreation quickly became the dominant use of many national forests in western states such as Colorado—a fact many within the agency, including Spencer, continued to argue that the Forest Service must face.[7] But downhill skiing presented a particularly thorny problem for the agency in terms of meeting public demand. While immediately following the war the Forest Service funneled as much capital and manpower as it could afford towards improving new ski areas, it simply did not have enough of either to meet

Base of Winter Park Ski area between 1940 and 1950. Photograph courtesy Denver Public Library, Western History Collection, E. T. Bollinger Collection, X-14188.

growing demand. In order to solve the problem of providing both adequate access to skiing and the needed capital to build and operate new ski areas, the Forest Service took a page out of its management of timber and grazing and, in essence, privatized the industry by issuing permits to private operators to develop and then operate ski areas on national forests without any financial support from the agency.[8]

Although the Forest Service's embrace of the private sector appeared to solve the problem of meeting the public's growing demand for downhill skiing, it quickly presented new challenges to the agency's ability to regulate a rapidly emergent ski industry that generated millions of dollars in profits. As skiing became a commodity, and ski areas grew into capital-intensive enterprises following the war, the sport grew into a major industry in mountainous states like Colorado, pumping millions of dollars into local and state economies, and rural mountain communities transformed into recreational colonies increasingly more reliant on tourism and real estate than traditional extractive industries. As skiing became an increasingly profitable venture, permit requests by hopeful developers wishing to get into the new amenity bonanza swamped regional Forest Service offices. In Colorado, the agency quickly found itself at odds with developers over the pace of permit approvals and the Forest Service's policy ensuring fair competition among the growing number of ski areas. This became a particular problem with the proposed construction of Vail Ski Resort. The model of a modern ski resort, Vail combined the development of a massive ski area with real estate. Such resorts promised enormous economic boons to their investors, and to Colorado's thriving tourism economy, but the investment of so much wealth created enormous pressures on the Forest Service to allow the construction of new resorts throughout the state along with ensuring the solvency of those resorts already in existence. Desiring to meet the public's seemingly insatiable thirst for skiing, the agency often endorsed the development of newer larger ski resorts, but then struggled to keep up with the ski industry's mercurial pace of growth.

The influx of private capital was not the only factor in the emergence of Colorado's modern ski industry. With only a handful of narrow highways crossing the Continental Divide, Colorado's Western Slope remained largely isolated from the rest of the state. Despite the efforts of the state's highway division to keep open many mountain passes during the winter months, avalanches and heavy storms often closed roads for days or weeks. Only two highways passed through the state's central mountains—U.S. Highway 6 and U.S. Highway 40, greatly limiting the access to the state's Western Slope. The federal government's announcement of its intention to build an interstate highway system in 1956 appeared to be the answer to the region's relative remoteness and lack of development. Although the highway was initially deemed unnecessary and too difficult to build, state boosters, including politicians, business interests, and ski areas, successfully lobbied the Eisenhower administration to extend Interstate 70 through the Rockies, creating an urban corridor that stretched through the Colorado Rockies from the metropolitan Front Range to the agricultural and mining community of Grand Junction, which bolstered the growth of Colorado's ski industry.[9]

However, the early story of Interstate 70 was not one of development, but rather political struggle. With millions of dollars at stake, local and state boosters fought countless political battles on first securing the extension of the interstate through the Western Slope and then on its route through the mountains. The decision where to build the interstate proved to be life or death to the rural mountain communities hoping to secure their piece of the bonanza of tourist dollars the highway promised to bring. Those towns located near the interstate understood that the highway would provide seemingly limitless opportunities, while those too far away would follow the fate of so many rural communities across the nation after the construction of the interstate highway system and would simply fade into memory. Yet, many Coloradoans also began voicing fears over the proposed construction of the sixteen-mile Red Buffalo tunnel under the Gore Range–Eagles Nest Primitive Area, soon designated the Eagles Nest Wilderness. A broad coalition of conservationist organizations concerned over the tunnel's impacts on the primitive area, along with environmental costs of the state's rapid pace of growth, joined forces opposing the tunnel's construction, launching the modern environmental movement within Colorado.

Long before the construction of Interstate 70, those within the Forest Service recognized the importance of highway access in the development of new ski areas, a recognition that helped build Colorado's ski industry. In a 1931 survey of the White River National Forest, the Forest Service identified both the eastern side of Loveland Pass and a small watershed on the pass's western side known as Arapahoe Basin as ideal for future ski areas. Both enjoyed easy access via U.S. Highway 6 and ample snow, much like Berthoud Pass. Yet, it would be another five years before a small rope tow was built on Loveland's eastern slope. The small operation slowly grew in popularity, changing its name to Loveland Ski Tow Inc. in 1945 and adding three more tows by the mid-1950s, imaginatively named A, B, C, and D. Over the next decade, Loveland Ski Area built three more chairlifts beginning in 1948, and following the prudent naming of the area's original four rope tows, the new lifts were called, of course, 1, 2, 3, and 4.[10] But as the eastern slope of Loveland Pass developed, the potential of Arapahoe Basin captured the imagination of Regional Forest Service Ranger W. "Slim" Davis. Pointing to the basin's combination of high elevation, north-facing exposure, and access directly off Highway 6 in 1941, Davis laid out plans for a ski area in the basin that included several short runs and a rope tow. Lamentably, the United States' entry into World War II derailed Davis's vision of developing Arapahoe Basin. Yet the idea remained, and in the months following the defeat of Japan, Denver's Chamber of Commerce begin exploring the possibility of opening a ski resort within easy proximity of the city, perhaps looking to replicate the success of Winter Park Ski Area, and hired U.S. Army 10th Mountain Division veterans Lawrence "Larry" Jump and Frederick "Sandy" Schauffler to locate a suitable site to build a ski area. Briefly scouting the mountains along Highway 6, the two men came across Arapahoe Basin. Like Davis before them, Jump and Schauffler quickly identified the area's fantastic potential for skiing and soon recruited former Olympic medalist Dick Durrance, ski manufacturer Thor Groswold, and former Penn State forestry professor Max Dercum to form Arapahoe Basin Inc. and begin the process of securing the financing and permits need to build a ski area.[11]

Forest Service officials welcomed the construction of a new ski area in the state. In response to Dercum's inquiry on the agency's willingness to support the development of a ski area at Arapahoe Basin, Regional Forester John Spencer, the same forester Denver's city parks manager George Cranmer later attacked for not doing enough to promote skiing in Colorado, wrote "I feel personally that a development of the type you propose is badly needed, and you are invited to give us further details."[12] Given downhill skiing's remarkable growth in popularity, the Forest Service concluded that more ski areas would be needed to satisfy increasing demand. "Since there are no indications that this meteoric increase in winter recreational use is beginning to level off," noted Ranger W. S. Davis in the May 18, 1947, edition of the *Forest Service New Bulletin*, "the national forests in the Rocky Mountain region are making preparations to accommodate an even greater number of people next season."[13] Arapahoe Basin, along with neighboring Loveland Basin, seemed likely solutions in meeting the public's demand for more skiing. And that following winter, Arapahoe Basin opened to the public.

Despite the Forest Service's optimism, the new ski area struggled in its first years of operation as a lack of parking and adequate facilities kept many skiers away. Those who did visit the new ski area often came away with tales of traffic tickets, inadequate facilities, and frightening rope tow rides up the mountain. Parking in particular became a constant source of frustration for Arapahoe Basin's owners. The Colorado Department of Highways refused to plow the snow far enough back for skiers to park safely alongside the highway, leaving many skiers no choice but to park virtually on the highway, risking either a ticket from the state highway patrol or getting stuck in the ditch. It was not until the eventual construction of a larger parking lot area some years later that the fight between the Colorado highway patrol and the ski area over parking ended.[14] But beyond its parking and other infrastructure problems, Arapahoe Basin faced serious financial problems caused in large part by its lack of management. Jump failed to raise sufficient funds to improve the area's deficient rope tows, lodge, and parking lots, which in turn kept many potential customers away. This failure to attract adequate numbers of skiers to turn a profit caused Schauffler to sell his share of the business in 1949. Jump did all he could to combat such stories, often writing Forest Service officials to demand help for the small ski area, repeatedly pointing out that Arapahoe Basin did not share the same luxury of public funding as early areas had. Reluctant to become involved in the operation of a private business and no longer willing to spend public dollars for the development of a ski area, the Forest Service retained its hands-off approach with Arapahoe Basin. The agency's lack of overt support, combined with Arapahoe Basin's continued operation in the red, infuriated Jump, who believed that the Forest Service had a vested interest in securing the ski area's long-term financial stability.

Jump's frustrations with the Forest Service's lack of help soared when, in 1951, the Forest Service approved the construction of a new chairlift for neighboring Loveland Ski Area, renamed from Loveland Basin three years prior. On hearing the news, Jump immediately wrote in protest to Regional Forester Edward Cliff, "In 1946 when Arapahoe Basin, Inc. was organized to construct two chairlifts on Loveland Pass, Forest Service officials stated that there would need to be a far greater need for the approval of any additional lifts. On this basis we undertook to raise the necessary capital to make all the required improvements at a time when there were no public funds (unlike competing areas) to help with such facilities as parking areas, toilets, shelters, etc." He continued, saying that despite careful management and attention to costs and expenses, "only now can [we] see a possible small profit under existing conditions." Jump concluded the letter by stating, "A chairlift at Loveland Basin would be ruinous to our business we are convinced, and would create serious stockholder reaction which conceivably could lead to bankruptcy."[15] To Jump, Arapahoe Basin's continued financial struggles suggested that there was no true need for another ski area in the state, let alone one mere miles away from an already established area struggling to attract adequate numbers of skiers—his logic being, then, that Arapahoe Basin's struggles in attracting skiers had little to nothing to do with its location or management, but rather a lack of consumer demand. Therefore, the construction or expansion of any ski area, such as that proposed at neighboring Loveland Basin, could only be justified when skier numbers reached a point where all existing ski areas were operating at capacity and thus in the black.

Clearly annoyed by the continued squabbling over Arapahoe Basin's failure to gain profitability, Cliff responded to Jump that "any new develop-ments at an established area could not be disapproved on the basis of objec-tions by a competing area."[16] It was not the Forest Service's responsibility, Cliff argued, to ensure the profitability of any ski area by limiting the develop-ment of its competition. Competitiveness among ski resorts such as Arapa-hoe Basin and Loveland was quickly becoming an increasingly thorny issue for the Forest Service. By allowing the private development of ski resorts in national forests, the federal agency had sought to meet public demand in the best and most cost-effective manner possible. But private interests were not always the same as the public's. Ski area operators often held very differ-ent priorities than the Forest Service in terms of maximizing their profits by maintaining a healthy share of the skier market. Such demands led to com-plicated questions for the agency. What if, as in the case of Arapahoe Basin, a ski area struggled financially? Was it within the Forest Service's power, or interest, to limit competition in order to ensure that the ski area remained open and solvent? This option protected the public's interests by limiting the development of national forest lands by limiting recreational use, but hurt consumers who desired lower ticket prices and better service potentially cre-ated by increased competition. However, if the Forest Service allowed market forces to determine the success or failure of a ski area what would happen if an area failed? Who would become responsible for the abandoned ski lifts, trails, and buildings left behind? Could the agency allow the national forests, the public's lands, to become pockmarked with abandoned ski areas? Such questions lay heavily on the minds of Forest Service officials in forests where competition among a burgeoning number of ski areas was growing increas-ingly fierce like those in Colorado.[17]

The answer became, in part, to closely regulate not only the number of ski areas issued permits but to ensure those who were issued permits were economically solvent enough to survive. To say the least, such efforts proved contentious. Nowhere was this more apparent than within the White River National Forest. Already home to a handful of the state's most popular ski areas, including Aspen, by the late 1950s, private developers were inundat-ing the White River's office with permit requests to build Colorado's next ski area. Fearing future conflicts over competition and ski area solvency, such as had occurred with Arapahoe Basin, in 1959 White River National Forest of-ficials initiated a policy of "staging-in" new ski areas in order to meet the growing public demand and also ensure fair competition among established

Entrance to Vail on U.S. Highway 6, 1961. Photograph courtesy Denver Public Library, Western History Collection, Box 2 (Mt. Sniktau notebook), WH1304.

ski areas. This practice allowed for the development of new ski areas within the White River National Forest only after all existing areas had achieved financial stability and met public demand. White River foresters concluded that they had the responsibility both to meet the public's need for recreational access and to closely manage the development and use of the forest. But while such a policy appeared straightforward on paper, in application it became the primary point of contention in the development of Vail—Colorado's largest—and arguably most iconic—ski resort.

The story of Vail's founding is often told as myth. After a seven-hour climb through waist-deep snow, friends Pete Seibert and Earl Eaton stood on the summit of a relatively nondescript, and unnamed, mountain overlooking the Two Elks Creek drainage. "Beneath the brilliant blue sky we slowly turned in a circle and saw perfect ski terrain no matter which direction we faced," Seibert reminisced a half-century later on the moment. "We looked at each other and realized what we both knew for certain: This was it!"[18] With rolling, mellow terrain, abundant snow, easy access via U.S. Highway 6, an incredible view of the Gore Mountains to the north, and deep bowls to the south, the two men concluded that the unnamed mountain was the perfect site for Colorado's next ski area; all that was needed was to build it. Four years later, Vail Ski Resort opened as North America's largest ski resort, with more than 4,000 acres of skiable terrain served by the state's only gondola, three chairlifts, and a handful of buildings at the base of the mountain. "It is difficult to believe, but three winters ago there was no Vail," *Sports Illustrated* journalist Fred Smith wrote in 1964 of Vail's rapid development. "Never in the history of U.S. skiing has a bare mountain leaped in such a short time into the four-star category of ski resorts."[19] Vail's seemingly overnight emergence both physically and in America's consciousness epitomized the modern gold rush in recreation and real estate seizing the American West in the decades following World War II. Its faux Bavarian architecture and narrow pedestrian lanes that wandered ever so circuitously to the Vista Bahn ski lift felt like the Austrian Alps to many visitors. Like Aspen and Sun Valley before, Vail's cachet attracted the rich, the famous, as well as those who wanted to see the rich and the famous.[20] But Vail's success was far from certain that day that Seibert and Eaton stood atop their nameless peak and envisioned ski runs crowded with people on its slopes running down the front of the mountain.

Many within White River National Forest considered the proposed development of a ski area the size of Vail overambitious, excessively expensive, and possibly unnecessary. In his initial survey of Vail Mountain, White River's supervisory forester and resident ski expert Paul Hauk agreed with Seibert and Eaton on the mountain's potential, but noted that the development of another ski resort in the area posed some problems regarding the White River National Forest's newly instituted "staging-in" policy. With applications for at least four other proposed ski areas ahead of Vail's, most of which were near existing towns, as well as Vail's uncertain finances, Hauk denied the Vail investors' request for a permit to begin construction, arguing that there was no immediate need for another ski area of Vail's size in the region, and suggested that Seibert and fellow investors shore up their balance sheet before reapplying for a permit in another two to four years. Seibert rejected Hauk's advice, countering that the Forest Service was simply protecting Aspen's monopoly, setting off a two-year fight over the Forest Service's granting Vail the permits needed to begin construction.[21]

Few men became as synonymous with skiing in Colorado in the half century following World War II than Pete Seibert. Seibert had fallen in love with skiing as a young boy when his father moved the family to New Hampshire. There, young Seibert grew into one of the region's better junior ski racers. At

Pete Seibert, co-founder of Vail
Ski Resort. Photograph courtesy
Denver Public Library, Western
History Collection, Box 2 (slide
1), WH1304.

age nineteen, he joined the celebrated 10th Mountain Division and traveled
west for the first time to Colorado and Camp Hale. Like many 10th Mountain
veterans, Seibert became infatuated with Colorado's towering mountains and
vowed to return after the war.[22] After recovering from wounds he suffered in
Italy, Seibert returned to Colorado, eventually finding work as a mountain
manager at Loveland Ski Area. It was there that he met Earl Eaton.[23]

A Colorado native, Earl Eaton dropped out of high school to work in the
Civilian Conservation Corps in the 1930s. After serving as an engineer in
the army he returned home to work in the molybdenum mines near Leadville before moving to Aspen to work as a ski patroller. Like Seibert, Eaton
grew enamored with the idea of one day opening his own ski resort, having
fallen in love with skiing and spending his winters working as a ski instructor. But it was uranium, not powder, that led Eaton to discover his ski area.[24]
It was while prospecting for uranium in 1954 that Eaton stumbled upon the
Two Elks Creek drainage above the town of Minturn. He quickly realized that
the area's open bowls and spectacular views were ideal for skiing. Eaton's

dreams of developing the mountain remained just that until three years later when he met Seibert at Loveland. After listening to Eaton's description of the unnamed mountain on the western side of Vail Pass, Seibert agreed to the fateful climb.[25]

Convinced they had found their mountain, Eaton and Seibert sought help purchasing enough land to build the ski area. Seibert contacted Richard Fowler, a lawyer from Denver whom he had met while working in Aspen. Fowler readily agreed to join Seibert and Eaton in attempting to build a ski resort and suggested hiring the services of Denver real estate appraiser John Conway to help purchase the necessary land for the resort. Intrigued about the possibility of developing a ski resort from the ground up, Conway soon joined the venture, and the four men quickly began looking for land on which to develop a resort village. Two criteria were critical: any property needed to lie adjacent to the national forest on which the mountain sat, and it needed to have easy access from U.S. Highway 6. This limited the hunt to properties within the Vail Valley. Only a handful of small cattle ranches lay within the rural valley at the western base of Vail Pass, including the 500-acre Hanson ranch. Identifying the ranch as the ideal location for their future resort, Conway approached owner John Hanson about buying the property. Hanson declined to sell at first, suspicious as to why four investors would want to buy the ranch. But over the following year Conway continued to stop in and visit the rancher, building a friendship with Hanson and his younger son. Conway's patience finally paid off in the fall of 1958 when Hanson accepted an offer of $110 per acre.[26]

With the property for the resort village secured, Seibert, Eaton, Conway, and Fowler pressed forward searching for investors to help finance the development of that resort. Seibert next approached George Caulkins, believing the successful oilman and avid skier a likely candidate to invest in the venture. A longtime friend of Seibert, Caulkins agreed to tour the property but remained skeptical of the idea of building a new ski resort so far from any established town. But Seibert persisted, and in 1959, finally convinced Caulkins to invest. Jack Tweedy, Fowler's law partner, soon joined the group, and the six formed Vail Corporation Inc. Retaining 50 percent of the new corporation for themselves, the group then sold the remaining half of the corporation to twenty investors comprised of lawyers, architects, oilmen, skiers, and even an executive with Time Inc. The new corporation promised to build the largest ski area in the United States and develop a 230-acre base village comprised of residential, commercial, and recreational use. "Its primary appeal will be to the skier who would patronize Aspen or Sun Valley for winter vacations. Skiers from the East, Midwest, and Southwestern states will find it more accessible than either. Its proximity to Denver will make it desirable as a weekend ski resort. Its diverse terrain and superior snow conditions will attract substantial numbers of one-day skiers from Denver, Colorado Springs, and their suburbs," promised the promotional investment brochure. Such an ambitious plan sought to change the very nature of the ski industry by linking real estate with the development of a truly enormous ski area.[27]

Before breaking ground on the new resort, the fledgling corporation's first order of business was to secure a permit from the Forest Service. While the agency's White River office had initially offered encouragement on the potential of Vail as a ski area, by 1960 White River officials grew increasingly reluctant to grant Vail's developers a permit to begin construction. One reason for the Forest Service's reluctance was, despite the corporation's long list of investors, Vail remained on rather unstable financial ground. Unwilling to allow the construction of a ski resort without solid assurances that once the trails were cut and the lifts were in place the new resort would have enough capital to remain open, the agency suggested that Vail hold off on submitting a permit application until its finances were in order. White River National Forest policy also stood in the way of Vail's gaining the necessary permits.

The Forest Service's point man on ski resorts within Colorado's White River National Forest was twenty-year Forest Service veteran Paul Hauk. As the lead on recreation within the White River National Forest, Hauk also enjoyed broad control over the day-to-day operations of ski areas within the forest. Through the late 1970s, the White River District office regulated virtually every aspect of every ski resort within the forest, from the total acreage of each resort to lift ticket prices. With such wide-ranging power, the agency believed it could meet its mandate to both provide adequate recreational opportunity to the public while protecting fragile ecosystems. So, when Seibert and Eaton walked into the Glenwood Office seeking a permit to begin construction of their ski resort, Hauk remained solely in charge of the development of skiing in his corner of Colorado.

After touring the Two Elks drainage with Eaton and Seibert, Hauk reported, "I would venture to say that Seibert might resign his job at Loveland

Basin and start promoting the financial backing which for him, with all his contacts would not be too difficult."[28] Hauk agreed that the area possessed greater potential and variety of terrain than Aspen, especially when the mountain's expansive back bowls were added, and voiced support for the development of the mountain in his initial report. Yet, he also noted a few unfavorable factors that might cause the venture's failure. The first was the cost of the private land on which the base village would sit. With the majority of the land in the valley floor lying in the hands of private ranches, once word got out that investors were interested in purchasing land, property values would skyrocket, making any venture extremely expensive. Second was the simple price of developing a ski area of such a size. Costs of building ski lifts and trails along with an entire village from scratch could potentially grow into the hundreds of millions of dollars, Hauk reasoned. And without any firm financial backing, which Vail's investors could not provide at the time, the Forest Service was uncomfortable granting a permit for such an extensive venture.

Money was not the only problem in the way of Seibert and Eaton gaining a permit to develop the ski resort. Concerned about the rising number of requests for permits for ski area development, in 1959 the White River National Forest announced a Master Plan aimed at managing the development of new ski resorts within the forest. Concluding that Colorado needed at least two new chairlifts a year just to keep up with skiing's rate of growth in the state, White River Forest officials argued that a systematic approach to ski resort development was needed to head off any potential economic collapses at ski resorts within the forest. Under the plan, priority was given to allowing existing ski resorts to become economically secure before allowing the construction of any new resort. White River officials worried about allowing too many ski resorts to be developed within the forest, oversaturating the market, and causing future potential economic harm. In order to solve this issue, the plan identified two major growth areas, or "zones of influence," for skiing within the forest.[29] The first centered on the area surrounding Aspen, and included Aspen, Buttermilk, Ski Sunlight, and Snowmass. The second included the numerous ski resorts in the mountains closer to Denver and the Front Range. Within each zone the Forest Service would allow the development of new ski resorts based on public need and economic feasibility. The plan also included the survey of potential sites with target dates by which ski developments would be needed. To Hauk and others within the White River National Forest Office, the plan made sense: they feared that if public demand for new

Paul Hauk surveying Vail, 1958. Photograph courtesy Denver Public Library, Western History Collection, Box 2 (photo 4), QH1304.

ski resorts slowed, they would be left holding the bag financially on any failed ski resort and believed that they could manage ski resort development sensibly by systematically regulating the development of new resorts.

Like all other commercial uses of national forests, the Forest Service relied primarily on private initiative for the initial planning of ski areas. Prior to passage of the Ski Area Permit Act of 1986, which combined the Forest Service's two-permit system, the agency required developers of any potential ski resort to demonstrate the suitability of the proposed area for skiing and the long-term economic sustainability of the operation. After determining that an area was suitable and economically viable, the Forest Service then issued a special-use permit allowing for the construction of all ski trails, buildings, and ski lifts on national forest property. Following construction of the area, the Forest Service then issued two types of special-use permits, one annual and one term permit. Annual permits often covered all commercial facilities such as rental shops and restaurants, while term permits covered all national forest lands used for trails. As denoted by their title, annual permits were renewed every year, while term permits lasted thirty years provided the permit holder continued to comply with the permit requirement and pay the requisite fees as outlined in the Term Permit Act of 1915. The Forest Service initially set fees as a flat percentage of total ticket sales, but with the rapid expansion of recreational use of the national forests during the 1950s, the agency adopted a graduated fee system based upon the combination of a ski resort's gross receipts and assets. As a ski area's sales increased in relation to its assets, its annual fees rose. Conversely, if sales decreased, so too did the area's fees. The idea was to maximize both investments in ski resorts by their owners, thus meeting the public's need for recreation and the shareholders' desire for profits, while ensuring the Forest Service received adequate revenues from the lease without bankrupting the permit holders.[30]

Vail's permit application immediately ran afoul of the White River's "step-in" policy. A day after submitting their application for a permit, ignoring Hauk's concerns over costs, Eaton and Seibert sat down with Hauk and White River Recreational Forester Charles McConnell for a two-hour meeting to discuss the Forest Service's issues surrounding Vail's application. Citing the White River policy, Hauk contended that there was no real public need at the time for the development of a new ski area and that the Forest Service had an obligation to existing areas, particularly Aspen and Aspen Highlands, allowing them to complete their own developments and become profitable before permitting any new ski areas within the White River National Forest. To Seibert and Eaton the Forest Service's "obligation" appeared more as favoritism than sound policy. Incensed by what they saw as the agency's protection of Aspen and its sister ski areas Aspen Highlands and Buttermilk, Vail's board filed a twenty-one-page appeal with the agency, noting that there was, in fact, a large public need for another ski resort in the region and that the decision by Hauk and others was "arbitrary, capricious, and an abuse of discretion."[31]

Nevertheless, the Forest Service remained reluctant on making any decision on Vail's permit application for the next several months. Frustrated, Vail's investors appealed to Congressman Wayne Aspinall and Senator Gordon Allott to intercede on their behalf. As chairman of the House Committee on Interior and Insular Affairs, which had jurisdiction over the Forest Service's budget, Senator Aspinall's interest in the matter carried significant weight, especially when it involved a pressing economic issue in his home district. Similarly, as a member of the Senate Interior Committee, Senator Allott was an ardent pro-growth advocate who used his position on the interior committee to promote federal projects within Colorado. Both the senator and congressman wrote the White River National Forest Office inquiring as to the reasons why Vail had not been issued a permit, mentioning the potential economic growth such a resort would bring to the area. District Forester Donald Clark responded that the problem of issuing Vail a permit was more one of timing than of feasibility, pointing out the Forest Service's policy of phasing in ski resorts according to public demand. In spite of the agency's policy, Aspinall and Allott's intercession soon led to a negotiated agreement between the Forest Service and Vail's partners, allowing for the issuance of a conditional permit with the understanding that the new resort would not open until 1963 or 1964. Citing the fact that the corporation had not raised the prerequisite $2 million to ensure Vail's solvency, Forest Supervisor E. H. Mason argued that the delay in opening the resort would not overly inconvenience the applicants. Mason reiterated to Seibert and Eaton, "However, since we have never given you any encouragement regarding a permit and as discussed with you on May 12, we are disapproving your application for the conditional permit that would allow you to be in operation by November 1961."[32]

Despite their victory in securing a conditional permit, Vail's board of directors continued to press for an earlier opening date. But the corporation's lack of funding remained an obstacle. Vail's board of directors had used the $100,000 raised by the initial sale of stock to conduct a feasibility study on the concomitant construction of both a ski area and village, which estimated the cost of construction of the ski area, village, and golf course to be roughly $1.4 million, well within the board's fund-raising ability. Concluding that it was possible to build the ski resort and village simultaneously, the board then sought the necessary funds. Their first stop was the First National Bank of Denver. Securing a loan for $500,000 from the bank, Seibert, who had become the board's president, and Caulkins set off on a cross-country tour to raise the remaining capital. The pair managed to raise only an additional $1 million, well short of the required $2 million mark set by the Forest Service. Unable to secure a loan without a permit, Vail's investors approached the Forest Service with a proposal that reduced the required on-hand cash from $2 million to the $1.4 million mark in order to meet the loan requirements and avoid a public sale of stock.[33]

Negotiations over the amount of ready cash resulted in the Forest Service accepting the $1.4 million figure and Vail scaling back its plans for a much larger, and expensive, gondola to a smaller four-person Bell gondola from the village to mid-mountain. With the financing issue settled, the Forest Service issued the final term and annual permits for the ski resort in January

1962, granting Vail access to a total of 6,470 acres, 3,900 of which was designated for future expansion. Reorganized as Vail Associates Ltd., the group of investors quickly moved forward building their resort. Construction crews began putting in the utilities for the village that spring, and after a furious summer of construction, Colorado's newest ski resort took form and opened to the public in December.[34]

Three years after Seibert and Eaton submitted their first permit application to the White River National Forest office, the Wichita, Kansas–based Rounds and Porter Lumber Company announced plans to develop a ski resort above the former mining community of Breckenridge. One of the most successful mining regions in Colorado during the 1859 gold rush, the mountain town's population had dwindled below 400, with many expecting the community to soon become a ghost town.[35] The announcement of the development of a ski resort came as welcome news to locals looking to save their town by jumping on Colorado's latest "gold rush." But the proposed development of Breckenridge Ski Area once again brought the issue of the Forest Service's regulating the development of ski resorts into focus. Ironically, this time the protest against the development of a new resort came from Vail Associates, who had just won their battle with the Forest Service over the agency's reluctance in awarding Vail a permit based upon the White River National Forest's policy of only allowing the development of new resorts after existing resorts within the forest achieved some measure of solvency and skier numbers demanded it. Vail's board members argued that the development of a nearby ski resort within the same forest at the same time would critically hurt Vail's competitiveness and sought to block Breckenridge's permit. White River officials ridiculed the Vail group's obvious hypocrisy on the matter and simply ignored their protests. Despite this, Vail Associates' attempt to block the Forest Service's approval of Breckenridge underlined the increasingly high stakes and risks involved in the development of ski resorts. Backed by solid investors, the proposed resort threatened to seriously damage Vail's ability to establish itself as the premier ski resort within the state, if not the region. But faced with continued growth in skier numbers, and willing to work with developers backed by sufficient funds, the Forest Service was more than happy to work with Rounds and Porter in developing a new ski resort.

Founded in 1859, the town of Breckenridge followed a path similar to most western boomtowns during the nineteenth century, one with strong ties to the history of skiing within Colorado. The discovery of gold along the banks of the Blue River had drawn thousands to the area seeking their fortune in the surrounding streams and hillsides. Within a year of its foundation, Breckenridge quickly became one of the largest towns in the Rocky Mountains, attracting thousands, Father John L. Dyer among them. An itinerant preacher from Ohio, Dyer moved to Breckenridge to build a church in 1862. There, he became known as much for his exploits on twelve-foot-long wooden skis as for his sermons, traveling between Breckenridge, Alma, and Leadville for twenty years on his "Norwegian snowshoes" in order to minister to the isolated mountain communities.[36] As the gold played out by the end of the nineteenth century, Breckenridge began to fade. Locals continued to eke out a living by mining what little ore was left, logging, and ranching. Still, skiing remained a part of the town's culture. During World War II, the principal of the local elementary school and former Winter Park Ski Patroller, John Bailey, installed and operated a short rope tow on the outskirts of Breckenridge on cemetery hill. A graduate of Brown University, Bailey would later become mayor of nearby Dillon. Still, it was not until the paving of U.S. Highway 9 in the mid-1950s that tourists rediscovered the old mining town and its surrounding mountains.

One of those was timber magnate Ralph "Bill" Rounds, who after visiting Breckenridge in 1958 fell in love with the mountain town and surrounding mountains. Believing the area an ideal setting for a ski resort along the lines of Aspen, where he and his family had vacationed for years, Rounds established the Summit County Development Corporation (SCDC) to develop a ski resort on nearby Peak 8, one of ten mountain peaks that make up the Tenmile Range along the Continental Divide. Rising to an elevation of 12,987 feet above sea level and looming directly above the town of Breckenridge, most of Peak 8 lies above timberline, exposing it to high winds and somewhat limiting its skiing potential. Undeterred by warnings about the peak's exposure, Rounds and fellow developers Claude Martin and Bill Starks contacted the Forest Service for a feasibility survey of the mountain's potential for skiing. After exploring the mountain, Hauk noted the issues facing any ski area with limited trees to protect skiers from fierce mountain winds. But after discussing Round's plans for the mountain and base resort, Hauk gave the SCDC his tentative go-ahead to apply for a permit.[37]

On hearing news of SCDC's application, Seibert sent a terse letter to the White River office protesting the prospect of the opening of another resort during the same season in which his Vail Associates had hoped to start on the construction of Vail. Seibert argued that Vail should be permitted at least a year of operation to secure its financial stability before the Forest Service allowed any other new area. The opening of another ski resort during the same year would harm both Vail and Breckenridge's ability to attract adequate numbers of skiers and would be highly damaging to Vail's ability in securing further investment.[38] In a sadly ironic twist, Seibert's argument was virtually the same made by Hauk just a year prior on withholding Vail's permit in order to ensure Aspen and Aspen Highland's solvency, a point made by the Forest Service after receiving Seibert's note of protest. To solve the problem, Hauk and Seibert met in Aspen to discuss the concerns. After hearing Seibert's arguments for a delay in authorizing Breckenridge's permit, Hauk replied that Seibert could expect no sympathy from the White River National Forest in view of the "all for competition" and antitrust law arguments Vail had used in its permit appeal. "My personal opinion, as mentioned to Bill Rounds late in December at Aspen, was that the Vail Corporation had no grounds for objecting since Vail is not an operating or existing area and it does not have a final permit in any sense of the word," Hauk later wrote about Vail's complaint over the Forest Service's decision to issue a permit to Breckenridge's developers. Hauk also pointed out the fact that while Vail was still struggling to find investors, the SCDC had sufficient assets to immediately develop both Peak 1 and Peak 8.[39] Seibert conceded Hauk's arguments, and the matter appeared resolved, but within a month tempers flared once again when Vail Associates refused Hauk's request to write a letter supporting the SCDC's application for a special-use permit, a necessary requirement for all special permits.[40]

This time, Vail Associates protested the SCDC's proposed development of a base village on land adjacent to the national forest, a model Vail itself had created. In what must be the most incongruous correspondence concerning the development of ski resorts in national forests, Vail Associates board member John Tweedy wrote White River Forest Supervisor Henry Tiedemann that "the installation of this type of equipment on its own land would enable its owners to advertise the winter recreational potential as a stimulant for real estate sales without making the Public Domain for the Forest Service a part of their promotion." Tweedy continued, "we believe this matter is of sufficient importance to ourselves, to the Forest Service, and to the general public to justify our intervention in this matter."[41] Such a development, he argued, would not be subject to the Forest Service's oversight, and would thus greatly affect orderly future planning of ski areas throughout Colorado and the West.

Both Hauk and Tiedemann rejected this argument outright, believing it to be nothing more than a delaying tactic by Vail Associates in order to buy more time to get Vail opened.[42] As Forest Service employee Henry Harrison drolly observed, "You can be sure Vail Pass [Associates] is more directly concerned with competition than [its] high sounding ideals."[43]

In the meantime, Breckenridge mayor Frank Brown contacted Senators Allott and John Carroll and Congressman Aspinall asking for their help in expediting the Forest Service's approval of a special-use permit for the construction of the ski resort. Pointing to the proposed ski resort's proximity to both Denver and Pueblo, Brown argued that the new resort would be a much-needed "Family Ski Area" as opposed to Vail, which was selling itself more as a destination resort. Finally, in March 1961, the SCDC submitted an application for a special-use permit. Facing pressure from the Forest Service, both senators, and Congressman Aspinall, Vail Associates withdrew its protest, and construction of the new resort began.

Breckenridge Ski Area opened the following winter with one double lift, a single T-bar, and a base shelter and restaurant. Like Vail would nine months later, the new ski resort grew quickly in popularity.[44] And within a couple years of opening, it became apparent Breckenridge would need to expand to serve its increasing numbers of visitors. In 1967, White River District Rangers Paul Wachter and Mike Penfold organized a Forest Service team to review the skiing potential of the slopes on the southern face of adjacent Peak 9. Concluding the site was sufficient for skiing, the Forest Service approved Breckenridge's expansion. In 1969, Breckenridge Ski Area opened several hundred more acres to skiing, all accessible by three lifts and three T-bars. The following summer, real estate developer Dan Fowler announced his plans to develop a $52 million resort near the base of Peak 9, beginning with the construction of 160 condominiums. Additionally, Aspen Ski Company, owners of Aspen Ski Mountain, Buttermilk, Aspen Highlands, and Snowmass, revealed its plans to purchase the entire Breckenridge Ski Area and add another two lifts and 200 acres to the area.[45]

Vail and Breckenridge's opening corresponded with the beginning of construction of Interstate 70 through Colorado's Rockies. More than the development of either ski resort, the extension of I-70 through the state marked a turning point in Colorado's development. With greater access to the rapidly growing population along the Front Range, ski resorts along I-70's corridor flourished. Allowing unprecedented access, the new highway opened the

Aerial photograph of Breckenridge Ski Resort. Photograph courtesy Denver Public Library, Western History Collection, Paul Hauk Collection, WH-1304.

state's largely isolated Western Slope to development, creating an urban corridor that would stretch from the metropolitan Front Range to the booming community of Grand Junction. However, the construction of Interstate 70 did not come without its challenges. Initially rejected as too difficult to build by the federal government, state boosters and politicians launched an intense lobbying campaign to secure the interstate. Understanding the potential economic impact, ski resorts and rural mountain communities joined in the effort with the hopes of gaining greater access to the Front Range and national tourist markets. But, the expansion of Interstate 70 through Colorado also marked the first significant environmental protest against growth within the state when conservation groups joined together to oppose the construction of the sixteen-mile Red Buffalo Tunnel under the Eagles Nest Primitive Area, foreshadowing looming fights over the environmental and social consequences of Colorado's seemingly unbridled growth.

Colorado's desires for a transmountain highway grew in earnest during the 1940s, when state politicians began lobbying the Truman Administration for the construction of a highway through the Rocky Mountains in hopes of opening the Western Slope to further economic development. Despite their efforts, Colorado's boosters failed in convincing the federal government of the necessity to build a highway through the Rockies. Federal officials had long argued constructing such a highway over the Continental Divide would prove far too expensive and difficult to build. Indeed, in 1940, the Public Roads Administration's study on a nationwide system of highways failed to even mention the possibility of building a highway through Colorado's mountains. This line of reasoning continued with the drafting of the Federal Highway Act in 1956, which called for the construction of two interstate highways within Colorado. The first, designated Interstate 25, would run from north to south along the Front Range, while the second, Interstate 70, would stretch across the eastern half of the state from the Kansas state line to its terminus in Denver. Upset at hearing Congress's decision to terminate Interstate 70 in Denver, thus isolating the state's Western Slope, Colorado politicians and businessmen demanded the extension of Interstate 70 over the Continental Divide and into southern Utah. Citing the difficulty and expense of such a highway, as well as the Utah Road Commission's opposition to the construction of an interstate in the southern part of the Beehive State, federal officials refused Colorado's request. Yet, Colorado's demands for a transmountain highway did not fade. Led by men such as Colorado governor Edwin Johnson and chairman of Denver-based Mortgage Investments Company Aksel Nielsen, state boosters redoubled their efforts to extend Interstate 70 from Denver, over the Continental Divide, and into Utah.[46]

Colorado's most ardent lobbyist for the construction of an interstate highway through the state's mountains was its governor, Edwin "Big Ed" Johnson. Reelected as Colorado governor in 1955 after serving three terms as a U.S. senator, Johnson was an untiring advocate for the state's business interests and saw the extension of Interstate 70 as paramount for Colorado's economic future. Pointing to the importance of such a highway to the economic development of the state's isolated Western Slope and its natural resources, he pressured members of Congress, Federal Highway Administration officials, and President Dwight Eisenhower himself in efforts to secure the interstate's extension. As Johnson worked from the governor's office, businessman and Colorado booster Aksel Nielsen used his personal and political ties with President Eisenhower to press the case for Colorado's mountain interstate. Nielsen and the President often fished on Nielsen's ranch in the Fraser Valley near Winter Park Ski Area. Nielsen pressed the necessity of completing I-70 across the state to Eisenhower during the president's visits to the mountain valley, often citing the region's beauty and potential for tourism.

But even with Johnson and Nielsen's efforts, Colorado failed to win the political support needed to extend Interstate 70 westward when Congress declined to add the sought-after miles in the final version of the Federal Highway Act of 1956. Undeterred, state boosters continued to lobby for a transmountain interstate, and within a year earned the Eisenhower administration's backing. With the president's assistance, a bill extending Interstate 70 some 547 miles from Denver and the Front Range over the Continental Divide, across southern Utah, to join Interstate 15 near Cove Fort, Utah, passed through Congress and onto Eisenhower's desk.[47]

With federal approval to extend Interstate 70 through Colorado, one important question remained—what route would it take? To many within the state, it appeared that the new interstate should follow one of the two U.S. highways that already traversed Colorado's mountain region. Both were narrow two-lane roads that wound over high mountain passes reaching over 10,000 feet in elevation, making winter travel treacherous. Heavy snows and avalanches often closed either highway for days despite the state highway department's best efforts to keep both open throughout the winter.[48] At first blush, neither route appeared more promising than the other, setting off a hotly contested debate over the advantages and shortcomings of each proposed route that raged over the next two years and ended in deadlock. Compromise proved impossible as most Western Slope communities sought to ensure that they would enjoy the significant economic windfall that would most certainly follow the interstate's construction. With the decision stuck in a quagmire of local and state politics, in 1959 the state hired the E. Lionel Pavlo engineering firm from New York to study the issue and identify the best path for the interstate through the Rockies. The firm examined eight possible routes over the next year, each roughly following either Highway 40 or Highway 6. Disregarding six of the eight as unfeasible due to either cost or geologic difficulties, the engineering firm identified two routes as the best options for construction of the new highway. The first, designated Route B, roughly followed Highway 40 crossing through a tunnel under Stanley Mountain, thus bypassing Berthoud Pass, through the Fraser Valley past Winter Park Ski Area, then following along the Colorado River to the small town of Wolcott near the new Vail Ski Resort. The second route, named Route H, followed the southerly Highway 6, first crossing the divide through a tunnel at Straight Creek adjacent to Loveland Pass, then through the town of Dillon before either crossing Vail Pass or passing through a tunnel under the Gore

Range. Citing that "cost estimates for final route studied indicate a decided advantage in favor of Study Route H," the firm declared that Route B would cost an estimated $133,410,000 while Route H would only cost $78,050,000. Based largely upon the differences in costs the report recommended the more southerly Route H to Colorado's highway engineers in charge of building the new interstate.[49]

Following the Pavlo Report's recommendations, the Colorado Department of Highways began conducting its own study of the proposed route. Publishing their report in 1963, state engineers agreed with the firm's conclusion on the suitability of the southern route with one small exception. Rather than following Highway 6 over Vail Pass, which required the construction of a steep switchback on the eastern side of the pass, the Colorado Department of Highways requested permission from the Forest Service to route the interstate through the Gore Range–Eagles Nest Primitive Area across Red Buffalo Pass. Instead of building over the pass, state engineers proposed the construction of a sixteen-mile tunnel under Red Buffalo Pass, arguing that it would not require the difficult construction of a switchback and appeared to have a favorable benefit-cost ratio. Federal officials, particularly Secretary of Agriculture Orville L. Freeman, were skeptical of such a plan and asked for the state to provide more specifics on the costs, environmental impacts, and engineering specifications. In 1966, the state submitted a revised report based on data collected by the state highway engineer and in August, the Federal Highway Administration approved Route H, including the Red Buffalo Tunnel, pending a public hearing.[50] But the decision to construct a sixteen-and-a-half-mile-long tunnel under a federally designated primitive area, soon to become a wilderness area, swiftly became the center of a controversy over the construction of the interstate, as well as the legal definition of wilderness.

With the announcement of the state's selection of the southerly route for the new interstate, concerns immediately arose over the proposed construction of the Red Buffalo Tunnel on the region's local economies. Local newspapers ran angst-ridden editorials warning of impending ruin if the state followed through with its plans to build the tunnel under the Gore Range–Eagles Nest Primitive Area. "Unless the truly phenomenal happens, Interstate 70 is going to substantially by-pass the High Country in its path through the mountains by boring under them in the now famous and commonly called 'Buffalo Red Mountain' route," wrote the Summit County Journal's editor on the disaster that awaited the mountain town if the tunnel was built.[51] Such

Town of Vail, early 1960s. Photograph courtesy Denver Public Library, Paul Hauk Collection, WH-1304.

fears of being bypassed by the interstate led many business owners in Summit, Lake, and Eagle counties, the three counties most dependent on tourism dollars and affected by the proposed tunnel, to write letters to Governor John Love and the Colorado Highway Department's chief engineer, Chas Shumate, imploring them to step in and halt the tunnel's construction. Breckenridge business owner Edward Emrich wrote, "Obviously the interstate cannot pass through or near every town in the state. But when it is possible to follow existing highways, as it has been so far, at a lower construction cost and without appreciably higher mileage, it seems to me that the Department of Highways has some duty to consider the welfare of communities whose very existence has to this point been solely based upon highway frontage."[52] Officials from Vail agreed with such sentiments, adding their voices to the opposition of Red Buffalo by arguing that the tunnel violated the spirit of the Wilderness Act.[53] It was clear by the end of 1967 that while local communities wanted the interstate they did not want the tunnel.

The communities along the interstate's slated route were not the only opposition to the Red Buffalo Tunnel. Conservation groups objected to the tunnel and the possible routing of the interstate through the Gore Range–Eagles Nest Primitive Area. In a letter to U.S. Senator Peter Dominick, a solid tunnel proponent, Shumate noted that two groups primarily opposed the tunnel.

The first was made up of local politicians and business owners who felt "that the closer the Interstate System can be brought to their communities the more they will benefit," explained Shumate. The second, and probably the more concerned group, was a coalition of various conservation organizations represented by the Colorado Open Space Coordinating Council (COSCC). "Certainly, the effort of these people to preserve the maximum amount of open space is a most commendable one," wrote Shumate. "However, we cannot agree that the construction of the highway through this area will destroy this great natural beauty and area. In fact, it will give millions of Americans the opportunity to see an area which most of them would never have the opportunity to view otherwise."[54] By framing his defense of the Red Buffalo tunnel in terms of preserving open space, Shumate clearly understood the interstate's role in drawing tourists to the region, but failed to comprehend the broader sea change in Coloradoans' views on growth and the environment that the Red Buffalo tunnel was quickly coming to symbolize.

In many ways, the struggle over Red Buffalo reflected broader concerns over the development of the West's public lands and the emergence of the modern environmental movement. Beginning with the controversy over the damming of Echo Park Canyon in Dinosaur National Monument in 1956, many Americans questioned the real impact of commercial development on public lands. Federal and state authorities had long believed in the

Progressive Era ideal of providing the greatest good for the greatest number, an ideal that had meant encouraging the development of natural resources. By the late 1950s, this belief came under attack as a growing number of Americans began to value open space over traditional extractive use. Led by men such as David Brower, Howard Zahniser, and Bob Marshall, groups such as the Sierra Club and the Wilderness Society spearheaded a broad campaign to set aside millions of acres of the public's lands as wilderness, especially in the American West. The passage of the Wilderness Act in 1964 marked the triumph of such groups over industrial interests, as well as the emergence of the environment as a highly contested political issue. By the late 1950s, a nascent environmental movement came to focus on suburban middle class quality-of-life issues such as the preservation of wilderness and open space. Over the next decade the environment grew into one of the most contentious political issues in the country, pitting competing economic interests against one another over issues such as wilderness, clean air, water, and suburban growth.[55]

Resting between Summit and Eagle counties, the rugged Gore Range is among the most inaccessible areas in the state. For this reason, combined with the public's growing desire during the 1930s to preserve some of the more spectacular areas under Forest Service management, the Forest Service had designated the region as the Gore Range–Eagles Nest Primitive Area in 1933. Among the first national forests designated as wilderness following the passage of the Wilderness Act in 1964, the Gore Range became a bargaining chip in the Congressional debate over wilderness. Fearing that designating the entire region wilderness would hinder the potential construction of Interstate 70 through the area, Congress added a caveat to the Wilderness Act, which allowed the Secretary of Agriculture to remove up to 7,000 acres from the southern tip of the Gore Range–Eagles Nest Primitive Area if needed to construct the new interstate.[56]

Following World War II, wilderness became one of the most highly contested environmental issues throughout the American West with opponents arguing that setting aside public lands for wilderness protection undercut rural economies by removing lands from extractive use. Wilderness advocates, on the other hand, argued that the preservation of large sections of public lands provided an important counterpoint to the country's rapidly expanding metropolitan areas and offered protection of fragile ecosystems. Recreation played a centrally important role in the debate over wilderness. As urban recreationalists sought expanded opportunities in the region's vast public lands, many questioned traditional extractive development.[57] In order to protect the nation's national forests from the axe and bulldozer, recreationalists often sided with preservationist groups in backing the creation of wilderness areas. But this alliance was tenuous at best, for recreationalists wanted to use the public's lands for activities while preservationists wish to halt the use of such areas altogether. The Wilderness Act's language held this very contradiction, defining wilderness as an area "where man himself is a visitor who does not remain."[58] The marriage between recreation and preservation formed a potent political alliance that came to oppose traditional extractive uses of the public's lands and helped give rise to environmental groups such as the COSCC during the 1960s but would lead to further conflicts over the use and management of the public's lands in the future.[59]

The potential passage of the interstate through, or underneath, the newly designated Gore Range–Eagles Nest Wilderness Area greatly alarmed conservationists and recreational advocates alike. The most outspoken of these groups was the COSCC. Formed in 1965 under the leadership of longtime activist Ed Hilliard, the COSCC quickly grew from a small group of environmental and recreational organizations into a broad-based coalition of more than twenty-five different organizations with more than 50,000 members, including the Colorado Mountain Club, the Rocky Mountain Chapter of the Sierra Club, and Trout Unlimited. Later renamed the Colorado Environmental Coalition, the COSCC reflected the changing political and cultural tenor within the state. And young activists, including future Colorado governor Richard Lamm, became the backbone of the coalition and began tackling issues such as wilderness and outdoor recreational access throughout the state.[60]

During the public hearing over the Red Buffalo Tunnel held in Frisco in 1966, COSCC Executive Director Roger Hansen argued in a strongly worded statement that the tunnel was an "unwarranted and unjustified invasion of an area soon to be reviewed by Secretary of Agriculture, the President, and Congress for possible inclusion in the National Wilderness Preservation System."[61] The COSCC opposed the tunnel's violation of the spirit of the Wilderness Act by attacking the costs of constructing and maintaining the tunnel, its impacts on the region's tourism industry, and its safety. Hansen took issue with the Colorado Highway Department's argument that the tunnel would save taxpayers roughly $4 million a year. Mountain scenery and recreational access, he argued, were more valuable in the long term to the state's economy than the savings created by constructing the tunnel, savings that only came after taxpayers paid off the tunnel's construction costs. To further underline this point Hansen asked rhetorically, "What dollar value can be assigned to the scenic, wilderness, wildlife, and recreational resources in the Gore Range–Eagle Nest Primitive area that would be destroyed by the proposed highway?"[62] Construction of the interstate over Vail Pass was to be easier and far less costly, he argued. Also, routing the interstate over Vail Pass had the added benefit of keeping the Gore Range–Eagles Nest Wilderness Area intact, allowing for its entire inclusion as a wilderness area in the years to come.

In the end, it was not the protests from environmentalist groups or local business interests that killed the Red Buffalo Tunnel, but simple economics. Colorado Department of Transportation cost estimates for constructing the tunnel hovered around $40 million, while projected costs for building the interstate over Vail Pass were less than half that amount.[63] When faced with the cost difference, Governor Love dropped his support of the tunnel, spelling its end. In May 1967, Secretary of Agriculture Orville Freeman denied the state's request for access through the primitive area, stating in a terse one-page statement, "Through four decades, this Department has maintained that the National Forest Wilderness System should not be invaded—even for important purposes—if there is a feasible alternative."[64] The costs, both economic and environmental, were too high, Freeman believed, for the Department of Agriculture to allow Colorado to build the Red Buffalo Tunnel. With the secretary's denial of the state's request, the Red Buffalo Tunnel died.

Construction on Interstate 70 began in 1971 with the section of highway stretching from Denver to the foot of Loveland Pass. At Loveland Pass, the state began excavating two seven-mile tunnels under the Continental Divide. Weak rock and shifting pressures caused massive delays and cost overruns for both bores. The westbound tunnel, named the Eisenhower Memorial Tunnel after President Dwight Eisenhower, opened in 1973. In an attempt to learn from the mistakes made while drilling the westbound bore, state engineers spent the next five years designing the eastbound tunnel before opening the job to bids. Other miscues and unforeseen mishaps plagued the second bore, causing further delays and cost overruns; the eastbound tunnel, named after former Colorado governor Edwin Johnson, finally opened in 1979. Even so, capacity became an emerging issue as early as the 1980s with weekend traffic often bottlenecked at the tunnels. By the end of the century over 10 million cars and trucks were passing through the Eisenhower and Johnson Tunnels annually, creating massive traffic jams and leading to calls for the widening of Interstate 70. Once again, the state faced the unenviable position of balancing economic and environmental costs against increasing demand for transportation access as Interstate 70 proved unable to meet growing numbers of Front Range residents escaping to the Western Slope to camp, hunt, and ski every weekend.[65]

Anchored by ski resorts such as Vail and Breckenridge, the construction of Interstate 70 opened the Western Slope to unprecedented levels of growth, drawing millions of new visitors into the region's rural communities, transforming the region into a recreational empire that stretched along the newly constructed interstate from the Front Range to the Utah border. Complete with a restaurant, ski shop, lodge, and a growing number of homes, the new Vail resort was a harbinger of Colorado's future. By end of the decade, towns such as Breckenridge, Crested Butte, and Steamboat Springs grew from relatively isolated rural towns reliant on timber, mining, and ranching to burgeoning ski towns. New resort towns such as Vail became the model for future developments combining skiing with real estate and retail, all of which placed further pressure on the Forest Service to both meet public demand in providing for skiing while somehow regulating a burgeoning ski industry focused on increasing its bottom line. The collapse of the White River National Forest's staging-in policy demonstrated the incredible political and economic power the state's ski industry now enjoyed and the difficulties the Forest Service already faced in balancing the public's growing love of skiing with developers' desires for increased profits. At the same time conservationists' concerns over the potent mixture of increased access and increased development were beginning to lead to further struggles over the environment, as highlighted by the struggles over Interstate 70's route through the Colorado mountains. Competitiveness among the state's ski resorts, along with concerns over growth and the environment, would only increase by the decade's end and the selection of Denver to host the 1976 Winter Olympic Games.[66]

3

Colorado's aspiration to host the Winter Games began in the late 1940s when Governor Lee Knous offered to host the 1956 Winter Games both in Aspen and at the Broadmoor Ice Palace outside Colorado Springs. And while the state failed to secure the bid to host the Olympic Games, the idea remained. Seven years later, William Tutt, owner of the Broadmoor Ski Area, and Steve Knowlton, founder of Colorado Ski Country USA, presented a bid to host the 1960 Winter Olympics to the U.S. Olympic Committee (USOC). Once again, Colorado failed to win the nomination, losing out to Squaw Valley. In 1964, a small group of businessmen and state boosters, including Tutt, along with the president and founder of Vail Associates Peter Seibert, publisher of Ski Magazine Merrill Hastings, vice president of the Adolph Coors Company Joseph Coors, and United Airlines executive Donald Fowler, formed the Colorado Olympic Committee to study the economic feasibility of the state hosting the Winter Games.[1]

Soon after forming, the group of business leaders and state politicians announced their intentions to secure the right to host the Winter Games. Holding all of its meetings behind closed doors and forwarding its minutes only to the governor, the committee lobbied USOC officials tirelessly for the next two years to secure the right to be the American nomination, finally receiving the committee's blessing in 1967.[2] Even with the nomination, Colorado's Olympic hopes remained in doubt for two more years, when on the third ballot the International Olympic Committee selected Denver as the host of the 1976 Winter Olympics.

News of Denver's selection shocked most Coloradoans. The Denver Olympic Committee (DOC) had never considered that the majority of the state's residents would be less than excited about the Olympics, believing instead the only issue they would face was finding adequate financing for the Games. Throughout the early 1960s Coloradoans had welcomed the expansion of the state's ski industry with open arms. The opening of Vail, Breckenridge, and Snowmass defined the high-water mark in the development of ski resorts in the state. By drawing increasing numbers of tourists, the state's ski industry pumped millions into the state's economy. Hosting the Winter Olympics appeared a natural extension of Colorado's booming winter tourism industry. But although many Coloradoans welcomed the continued development of the state's tourist economy, especially the development of new ski resorts, Colorado voters grew increasingly disillusioned at what many saw as an elitist organization of business interests making decisions behind closed doors, decisions that greatly affected the economies and environments of their communities throughout the state, the most outrageous examples being the selection of Evergreen as the host site for the Nordic and bobsledding events, to which the DOC's public relations director asserted, "Evergreen is just going to have to eat it."[3] Such arrogance and lack of transparency reinforced Olympic opponents' growing assertions that the Games were little more than a ruse by the state's hotel, airline, ski resort, and banking industries carried on the backs of the state's taxpayers, all of which led to a backlash against both the Olympics and the development of new ski resorts in the state that would redefine Colorado's politics and make the development of new ski resorts synonymous with fears over unbridled growth.[4]

Nonetheless, for many within Colorado's ski industry, the Winter Olympics offered the perfect opportunity to both showcase the state's ski resorts and leverage the Games to develop a new long-term resort. In its winning bid to the International Olympic Committee to host the Games, the Denver Organizing Committee promoted such a strategy, promising, "Every plan for new facilities for the 1976 Winter Olympic Games involves consideration of both after-use and the highest quality possible for effectively staging the Games. The Denver Committee of Candidature has determined that no new facilities will be proposed that will not serve the recreational interest of Denver after

1976."[5] No other sport represented this ideal more than skiing. By the 1960s, downhill skiing had emerged as the signature Olympic event attracting millions of spectators both live and on television. With an ever-growing number of ski resorts, Colorado sought to further cement its reputation as one of the premier ski destinations in the world by hosting the Winter Olympics and displaying itself to the millions of spectators and television viewers who would watch as the world's best skiers raced with Colorado's Rocky Mountains as the backdrop. Such publicity would, it was hoped, draw the same viewers to the state's slopes long after the embers from the Olympic torch faded.

Like Colorado's ski industry, the Forest Service also hoped to use the Olympics as a means to meet the growing demand for skiing within the state. The federal agency was an integral part of Denver's Olympic organizing efforts due in large part to the fact that any alpine venue would most likely be developed on national forest land requiring the Forest Service's approval. And where Colorado's ski resorts viewed the Olympics as a means to attract tourists and bolster business, the Forest Service saw the Olympics as an opportunity to develop a new resort within the state to meet skiing's growing popularity. Even with the opening of nine new resorts between 1961 and 1969, the sport's continued growth combined with its institutionalization within the Forest Service necessitated that more ski resorts be opened in the coming decade. This alliance between the ski industry and the Forest Service during the Olympic debate raised the concerns of anti-Olympic critics that the agency was colluding with the state's business interests in furthering growth and development rather than protecting the state's natural beauty and resources. Moreover, the Winter Olympics forged a wide range of complex social and economic issues facing Colorado—and the nation as a whole—into a single issue: the environmental costs of growth.

By the end of the 1960s in America, middle-class anxieties over issues such as clean air, clean water, and open space redefined environmental politics, moving them away from their preservationist roots towards broader quality-of-life issues. Postwar affluence had radically changed Americans' perception of themselves and the world around them. Many found themselves living in the nation's rapidly expanding suburbs, so that by the 1970 census, more Americans lived in the suburbs than in cities. New technologies saved time and provided the majority of Americans a higher standard of living than any other people in history. But there were environmental costs to this growing affluence and ever-greater standard of living. A mounting unease over the health costs of chemicals used in products, the pollution of lakes, rivers, and streams, and the overrunning of national parks and forests by recreationalists were among the long list of issues Americans worried about when it came to the environment. Secretary of the Interior Stewart Udall captured these sentiments in his book *The Quiet Crisis*, writing in the introduction, "We stand today poised on a pinnacle of wealth and power, yet we live in a land of vanishing beauty, of increasing ugliness, of shrinking open space and of an overall environment that is diminished daily by pollution and noise and blight. This, in brief, is the quiet conservation crisis."[6] Other books on environmental issues, most notably Rachel Carson's *Silent Spring* and Paul Ehrlich's *The Population Bomb*, became national best-sellers, further fueling concerns about the effects of pesticides and continued growth. The passage of the Wilderness Act in 1964 in part embodied this desire to protect the nation's most beautiful lands. Words such as smog and sprawl entered the American lexicon as suburbs expanded ever further outward and Americans became ever more reliant on the automobile. Environmental catastrophe became front-page news when events such as the Santa Barbara oil spill in California and Cuyahoga River fire in Ohio, both in 1969, captivated American audiences, many of whom feared that such calamities could, and most likely would, occur in their hometowns.[7] Such quality-of-life concerns drove the passage of environmental legislation such as the National Environmental Policy Act of 1970, the creation of the Environmental Protection Agency, the Clean Air Act of 1972, and the Endangered Species Act of 1973—each signed into law by the politically astute Richard Nixon.[8]

In western cities such as Denver, Portland, Seattle, Austin, Vancouver, and Omaha, concerns over the environmental impacts of the region's breakneck growth transformed local and regional politics. Fueled by World War II's military buildup, the postwar defense industry, and tourism, the West's metropolitan population more than doubled between 1940 and 1960. While this growth brought increased wealth, the pace at which it occurred unsettled many westerners, who watched as rural landscapes quickly transformed into sprawling housing developments and four-lane highways. Such worries led to a political and cultural backlash throughout much of the region, giving rise to antigrowth activism and quality-of-life politics. Led by suburban middle-class professionals, the movement blended environmental concerns and social concerns with 1960s antiwar activism and postwar prosperity in opposing established municipal and regional growth coalitions that sought continued growth in order to ensure economic prosperity and stability. Such growth, quality-of-life activists and politicians argued, lay at the center of the West's larger environmental and social problems, from air pollution caused by the growing numbers of commuters to the abandonment of the inner city and the loss of open space such as viewsheds and recreational spaces. As millions of Americans moved to western states such as California, Oregon, and Colorado in the decades following World War II to enjoy the region's clean air, vast federal lands, and economic opportunities, by the late 1960s, many of these residents believed that too many people were moving in and the gate should be closed behind them in order to maintain their own quality of life.[9]

While often identified with suburban liberals, quality-of-life politics was neither liberal nor conservative. Rather, it was a broader reaction to fears about the impacts of the nation's seemingly out-of-control growth and constant barrage of environmental disasters that led many Americans to call for a reining in of suburban sprawl, industrial pollution, and preservation of open space. At the same time, many middle-class voters also demanded increased access to the public's lands, cheaper energy, and consumerist lifestyles.[10] Such seemingly contradictory desires recast the role of the environment in American politics as a quality-of-life issue synonymous with access to cheap consumer goods. Unlike the divisiveness of the civil rights movement, or later the women's rights and gay rights movements, the environmental movement appeared to many at the beginning of the 1960s as a common concern to all Americans. After all, who wanted their children swimming in polluted rivers or building sand castles on oil-covered beaches? By the end of the decade environmental concerns joined the civil rights, women's rights, and gay rights movements as a part of the nation's emergent culture wars, a wedge issue that combined concerns over pollution, open space, and consumer goods.[11]

In Colorado, rapid growth had brought prosperity to the state, but by the mid-1960s increasing numbers of the state's residents began to question its long-term benefits. In 1965, a venomous, albeit short, fight over the proposed routing of Interstate 70 through a sixteen-mile tunnel under the Gore Range–Eagles Nest Primitive Area in order to open the Western Slope to development, particularly ski resorts, marked the beginning of a broad political and cultural shift. Attacking the tunnel's violation of the spirit, if not the law, of the Wilderness Act, as well as the further degradation of the state's mountain beauty, a coalition of environmental and recreational organizations formed the Colorado Open Space Coordinating Council (COSCC) in opposition to the tunnel.[12] The council's victory, helped in large part by the proposed tunnel's massive costs, vaulted concerns over growth and the environment to the forefront of the state's political agenda. By the end of the decade, Colorado's population had grown to 1.7 million people, a million more than just prior to the war.[13] While many of these newcomers settled along the Front Range, the state's rural mountains also shared in the growth, causing many within the state to grumble over their perceived loss of lifestyle. Many longtime residents pointed directly at the state's tourist industry as one of the main culprits in Colorado's population boom. "The trouble with tourists," wrote *Denver Post* columnist Tom Gaven, "is that having looked around, many wish to return."[14] Ski towns like Aspen, Breckenridge, and Vail swelled as thousands of young ski bums, affluent second homeowners, and those looking for a better life moved in. Longtime locals grew resentful of newcomers and the changes they brought to the state, fueling growing opposition to the state's business and political leaders who promoted a gospel of growth as the means to create jobs, profits, and tax revenues.

Colorado's postwar population boom, along with the decision to extend Interstate 70 over the Continental Divide, transformed Colorado's once-isolated western mountain communities into budding resort communities. Often anchored by bustling ski resorts, these mountain towns attracted thousands of new residents looking to escape for a few years or perhaps settle down. "It is the freedom of it. You know you could just come here and live a good life and do what you wanted to do. Ski all day, party all night, do a little work in between," explained longtime Fraser Valley resident and former Winter Park Ski Resort vice president Gary McGraw.[15] Drawn by the promise of a lifestyle enjoying the outdoors, freedom, and economic opportunity, thousands like McGraw moved to Colorado's sprawling suburbs and mountain towns throughout the decade. Such growth further spurred the state's economy as tourism grew into a multimillion-dollar-a-year industry in Colorado, driving everything from lift ticket sales to real estate development.

The fight to bring the 1976 Winter Olympics to Denver helped unite disparate groups, each concerned over different aspects of the Games, into a broader political coalition that embodied the antigrowth, anti-Olympic fervor of the period, as well as the growing importance of environmental issues in state and national politics. Urban minority groups feared the Games would lead to their eviction from their neighborhoods and were among the first to call out for more transparency by the organizing committee on the development and cost of Olympic venues. Rural residents of the mountain communities of Evergreen and Indian Hills rose in opposition to the Games when they discovered that their backyards, literally in some cases, were to become the sites for the Nordic and bobsledding events. Many Coloradoans focused on the potential costs of the Games, believing that they would cost Colorado taxpayers millions. Lastly, in the spring of 1972, a small band of political activists, along with Democratic state representatives Bob Jackson and Richard Lamm, formed the Citizens for Colorado's Future (CCF). Uniting the various anti-Olympic forces, the CCF led the eventual successful defeat of the Denver Winter Olympic Games and helped form a broad-based political coalition that propelled Lamm into the governor's office as well as brought the environment to the forefront of state politics.

Despite this growing opposition, the efforts to bring the Winter Games to Denver continued to gain momentum. Upon winning the nomination from the U.S. Olympic Committee (USOC), the organizing committee reorganized as the Denver Olympic Committee (DOC) to sell Denver to the International Olympic Committee (IOC). The new committee represented some of the state's most prominent business leaders and politicians, including many of the same members who had helped secure the national nomination. For the next four years after winning the bid to host the 1976 Winter Games, the committee hid its work from most Coloradoans, holding all of its meetings behind closed doors and forwarding its minutes only to the governor. The committee believed that the state's residents would easily embrace the idea of hosting the Olympics and that any release of information was unnecessary. Equating their interests with the good of the state, the DOC failed to even consider that many Coloradoans might oppose hosting the Games.[16] The Olympics, they reasoned, would be good for the state's overall financial interests. Once Coloradoans saw these benefits, they would jump onto the Olympic bandwagon. Such hubris proved to be the undoing of the Denver Olympics as the taxpayers questioned the logic of paying for the construction of Olympic facilities that benefited business interests at the cost to the state's economy and environment.

Over the next three years, Denver officials wooed IOC members, presenting Denver as the ideal city in which to host the Winter Games—close to the mountains, with established sporting facilities, an international airport, and more than enough hotel rooms to host the world. However, in 1970 most IOC members still believed that the Winter Games could be held at a compact site such as Squaw Valley, ignoring the glaringly obvious fact that the French village of Grenoble had barely accommodated all thirty-seven countries with their 1,293 athletes and countless spectators and members of the media during the 1968 Winter Games.[17] Hosting increasing numbers of athletes, press, and spectators, as well as providing adequate sites for events as diverse as alpine skiing, bobsledding, and ice-skating meant that the Winter Olympics needed to be held on a regional scale rather than in the smaller sites the IOC members favored. Realizing the IOC's desire for a more compact Olympics, Denver officials sold the sprawling western city as a quaint metropolis in the Colorado Rockies. The IOC bought the "magnificent piece of salesmanship," and in 1970 Denver became the host city for the 1976 Winter Olympic Games, beating out Sion, Switzerland, on the third ballot.[18]

As the world celebrated the conclusion of the 1972 Sapporo Winter Olympic Games in the Makomanai Indoor Stadium, the scoreboard above them jubilantly announced "We Meet Again in Denver '76." Believing that the Games would bring international attention, and with it considerable economic windfalls, cities around the world fiercely competed for the privilege to host the Olympics. Colorado's lieutenant governor Mark Hogan had argued that very point in defending the state's quest for the Olympics, telling reporters in 1969, "The influx of Olympic visitors, plus a continued flow prompted by the exposure given the host city will be a benefit to all facets of business in the state."[19] What was good for the state's tourist economy, Hogan and other Olympic proponents reasoned, would be good for the state. But by the late 1960s an increasing number of Coloradoans questioned the benefits of Colorado's booming tourist industry, particularly the continued development of new ski resorts, and the growth that it wrought. To Colorado voters, the Olympic Games sounded less like an economic opportunity and more like a multimillion-dollar snow job meant to line the pockets of real estate and resort developers with taxpayer money. Colorado State Representative Richard Lamm, who would ride anti-Olympic sentiment into the governor's office, perhaps best captured this sentiment, calling the Olympics little more than "rich man's games paid for by poor man's taxes."[20]

News of Denver winning the Olympics came as a shock to many Coloradoans, especially those who discovered that their neighborhoods had been slated as Olympic venues. When residents of the mountain communities of Evergreen and Indian Hills learned that their towns were the proposed sites for the bobsledding, cross-country skiing, and Nordic jumping events, they quickly rose in protest, but found little sympathy and even less information from the organizing committee. This breakdown in communication further infuriated the affluent mountain communities. Located just thirty miles west of Denver and its surrounding suburbs, Evergreen had become a commuter community by the late 1960s, attracting hundreds who worked in the sprawling metropolis below but wished to live in a bucolic mountain setting. The proposed development of Olympic facilities was seen by many of the area's residents as an unwanted invasion of their mountain hideouts—a perception the DOC failed to realize until the news had leaked and the political damage was done. "The plans were conceptual," explained Ted Farwell, who became the focus of locals' ire over the proposed development of ski trails and parking lots in their backyards.[21] As technical director for the planning and design of all Olympic venues in 1970, Farwell became the target of locals' frustrations over the DOC's communication failures. The three-time Olympian and former National Collegiate Athletic Association ski champion for the University of Denver had worked for much of the previous decade for Sno-Engineering assessing the potential viability of ski resorts in both New England and Colorado. After working for seven years in New Hampshire, he and his wife moved to Evergreen in 1968 to open up a western office for the firm. Two years later the DOC hired Farwell to oversee the planning and design of the Nordic skiing, ice-skating, and alpine skiing venues. While a strong proponent of the Denver Games, Farwell often found himself at odds with the organizing committee over issues of design and site selection. Many on the DOC believed that the specifics of site selection and costs did not matter in the short term as long as Denver secured the Olympics; any issues concerning site design could be dealt with afterwards. Farwell believed that he could fix any issues within the different venues, particularly the alpine events, as they arrived, but with little political pull and even less authority, his efforts proved doomed from the beginning.

Concerned over their property values and the long-term environmental impacts of the infrastructure needed to host thousands of spectators tromping through their communities, and angry at the DOC's cavalier responses to their questions, Evergreen and Indian Hills residents soon organized the grassroots group Protect Our Mountain Home (POME) in order to fight the selection of their communities as Olympic venues. Led by Indian Hills resident and retired University of Denver law professor Vance Dittman, POME began a campaign to remove the Olympics from their backyards. Area residents did not necessarily oppose the Games; they simply feared that bringing the Olympics to the Evergreen area would create too much growth in the town and surrounding area, eroding its quite rural character through the clearing of hundreds of acres of trees in order to make room for the construction of luge, bobsled, cross-country skiing, and ski jump facilities, all of which would leave behind massive "white elephant" athletic facilities that would permanently change Evergreen's character, turning the suburban community into a tourist destination. "We don't want to keep people out of here," stated Dittman in an interview with the magazine *The National Observer*, "but we are just like a theater. When all the seats are sold, they don't keep selling tickets and putting people on your lap. We are sold out."[22] Dittman's response reflected the growing middle-class not-in-my-backyard sentiments within Colorado that came to define the struggle against the Olympics, as well as future conflicts over the development of ski resorts throughout the state. Such sentiments arose from increasing fears that the state's frenetic pace of growth was quickly eroding Coloradoans' quality of life, causing many to wish to close the rhetorical gate behind them in order to preserve the state's character. This despite the fact that many of the state's residents had only recently arrived in Colorado, often drawn by Colorado's beauty, promise of clean air, and recreational opportunities—the very same things Olympic boosters hoped to sell in attracting tourists. Dittman and his fellow Evergreen and Indian Springs residents desired to preserve their home's quite rural character, halting the crass commercialism and unbridled growth they associated with the Olympic Games. To do so, they soon seized upon the DOC's apparent failure in planning and the area's lack of snow as reasons to stop the development of acres of new parking lots, miles of cross-country trails, and other Olympic facilities in their backyard.[23]

Located in the foothills west of Denver, Evergreen's simple dearth of adequate snowfall made it a poor choice for the cross-country skiing events. Less than five inches of snow had fallen annually in the area since 1963.[24] When DOC officials suggested the use of snow-making machines to compensate for this lack of snowfall, POME members questioned the amount of water needed to produce enough manmade snow to hold the events. Other problems, including the leveling of hillsides to build parking lots, the construction of a four-lane highway, and the proposed biathlon course, which required competitors to "ski right through Evergreen High School and Wilmont Elementary School," led POME members to argue that hosting any event in Evergreen was "completely out of the question in every respect."[25] After several unsatisfying meetings with DOC officials, in which organizers either did not know the answers to or simply refused to answer locals' questions, POME embarked on a letter-writing campaign. Most letter writers argued against the destruction of the area's natural beauty. "The very thought of thousands of our beautiful evergreens being destroyed, Bear Creek re-routed and practically covered to make way for a gigantic ski jump, Evergreen Lake and our municipal golf course being taken away from us, helicopter pads and parking lots, an interchange of roads and highways, television cables and poles everywhere, plus all of the other scars such events will inevitably leave, makes me ill," wrote Evergreen local Lolo Wright to Governor John Love, protesting the area's selection.[26] Another letter to Love from an Evergreen resident took on a more plaintive tone, asking the Governor to help preserve the area's rural character and local residents' quality of life. "Please, try to see our point. Many people are moving and more have planned to do so. Our mountains here will be ruined for open community living [here]. We look to you to protect our investments and way of life by urging the selection of one of the more appropriate alternate sites like Winter Park or Steamboat Springs."[27] The battle between Evergreen residents and the DOC gained national media attention when *Newsweek* published a story entitled "Nevergreen" on the fight over the area's selection as an Olympic venue. In a letter to State Senator Harry Locke, the chairman of the Senate Joint Budget Committee, Dittman explained, "Such sports facilities will degrade the whole community environment as a place to live, and will have no reasonable after-use in the Denver Mountain Parks and will require maintenance beyond that now available from the city and county of Denver."[28]

The DOC finally relented to POME's protests during its meeting in Sapporo, Japan, and agreed to relocate the cross-country and jumping events. While it was apparent that the DOC needed to relocate the Nordic venues, there remained another question. A DOC report had concluded that "the scope of a modern Olympics with an official party of over 15,000 requires facilities of a major city. The practical compromise . . . is to select competition sites within logical commuting distance of housing facilities." Any new cross-country site needed to be at or below 7,800 feet in elevation, leaving only three potential sites—Steamboat Springs, Buffalo Creek, and Indian Park. Like Evergreen, Buffalo Creek and Indian Park had questionable snowfall, leaving only Steamboat. IOC officials reluctantly agreed to the selection

of Steamboat, which lay 160 miles west of Denver, only after the DOC promised to use aircraft to shuttle athletes and Olympic officials between Denver
and the resort town.[29] The move of the Nordic events to Steamboat opened
the door for holding alpine events on the Western Slope and marked the turning point in the debate over the Olympics. Now, not only was the secrecy surrounding the Olympics an issue, but the effect Olympic development would
have on Colorado's mountain communities also became a source of concern.

In western states such as Colorado, these concerns translated into conflicts over the issue of growth. Led by Governor Love, Colorado looked to
seize the economic benefits of growth with its "Sell Colorado" campaign beginning in the early 1960s.[30] For Love, the idea of growth itself appeared a
win-win situation. New residents, drawn to the state by its beauty and promise of economic opportunities, received the quality of life they sought, and
Colorado's economy blossomed. But the specter of the unbridled growth of
Southern California led many Coloradoans to call for, as a popular bumper
sticker of the time put it, an end to the "Los Angelization" of Colorado.[31] John
Denver's 1972 hit "Rocky Mountain High" reflected the contrary sentiments
of both longtime and newly arrived Coloradoans. A recent transplant to Aspen himself, the bespectacled folksinger happily crooned of the quiet beauty
of his new life in the Colorado Rockies while lamenting, "Why they try to tear
the mountains down to bring in a couple more / More people, more scars
upon the land."[32]

Such contrasting sentiments defined how many Coloradoans viewed their
state. While many had moved to the state because of its beauty and opportunity, like Denver, they lamented the changes that economic growth and a
growing population brought with them. Such apprehensions over the impact
of unbridled growth lay at the heart of the emerging debates over the Denver Winter Olympic Games, playing out in the site selection for the alpine
events.[33]

In 1967, Aspen Ski Resort board member and chairman of the Colorado
Olympic Committee site selection committee George "Parry" Robinson
asked the White River National Forest's resident skiing expert, Paul Hauk, to
join the selection committee in identifying a site at which to host the alpine
events.[34] Hauk was the ideal choice for the task. After becoming Supervisory
Forester in Charge of Recreation and Lands for the White River National Forest in 1957, he had conducted over fifty feasibility studies on the potential of
various mountains for the development of skiing throughout Colorado, New

Mexico, and Arizona. Hauk also was no stranger to the Olympic Games. In 1960, he had served as a member of the avalanche control team at the Squaw Valley Winter Olympic Games. But beyond Hauk's résumé, it was necessary to involve the Forest Service in developing any mountain site within the state as most likely any Olympic venue would be located within the White River National Forest; in fact, the Forest Service hoped to use the Olympics to develop another long-term ski resort within the White River National Forest—to be operated by a private party and satisfy the Forest Service's need to meet public demand.

Composed of ski industry insiders, including Vail Associates president Pete Seibert, the selection committee faced significant challenges in locating an acceptable site to host the men and women's alpine event. During the committee's first meeting in March, Robinson pointed out the essential features needed for any venue: adequate vertical feet, good snow conditions, and close proximity to Denver. Such requirements greatly limited the number of potential sites by excluding much of Colorado's Western Slope, home to the majority of the state's ski resorts. Proximity remained an overriding concern on the selection for the signature Olympic alpine event, the men and women's downhill. Few established ski resorts had the sufficient mixture of vertical feet and steepness to hold the speed event in which racers raced down a steep and windy course for just over two minutes. In facing these concerns, committee member and *Skiing Magazine* publisher Merrill Hastings noted that the USOC nomination, if Colorado won it, would not obligate the committee to any one site until the official IOC bid. Other committee members questioned hosting the downhill at the same mountain as the slalom and giant slalom events. The meeting ended with the decision to have Hauk and Earl Eaton further investigate potential sites and report to the committee at the next meeting. The following month, Hauk made a slide presentation of several potential venues, including Mount Sniktau, Independence Mountain, and Copper Mountain. Believing that the U.S. Ski Association would never agree on an Eastern Slope site, and citing concerns over proximity, the committee voted Copper Mountain as the primary site with Vail as the alternate.[35]

Located at the junction of U.S. Highways 6 and 91, Copper Mountain had long been a favorite of Hauk's. "I recognized the skiing potential at Copper in 1952 when I became district ranger at Dillon," wrote Hauk in his history of the resort.[36] In 1954, he had suggested the development of Copper for skiing to Regional Forester Dave Nordwall, but despite Hauk's recommendations, the mountain stayed undeveloped. That remained true until 1969 when the Righter family, heirs to the McCormick farm equipment fortune, requested a permit to develop a ski area on the mountain. The family's interest stemmed from the mountain's potential and its selection as an Olympic venue as well as the construction of Interstate 70, which would pass by the base of the mountain. The Forest Service awarded the family permits to develop 3,180 acres as a ski resort in August 1971, but financial delays kept Copper Mountain from opening until the 1972–1973 ski season. The resort became an instant favorite of Front Range skiers, who simply drove up the newly completed Interstate 70 to the base of the ski area. In 1977, Copper hosted the World Alpine Championships, the first international competition held in Colorado since the 1950 World Championships in Aspen.[37]

The selection of Copper Mountain as the Olympic venue got the DOC into trouble when USOC officials voiced their fear that its distance from Denver would hurt the city's bid. Desiring to keep alpine events within an hour's drive of Denver and meet the required vertical feet needed to hold the downhill, the DOC quickly chose Mount Sniktau, a 13,000-foot, windswept peak adjacent to Loveland Ski Area on the Continental Divide, believing that any technical issues could be resolved after Denver won the bid to host the Games.[38] As was the organizing committee's practice, the selection of Sniktau remained hidden from the public, including the owners of Loveland Ski Area, which DOC officials slated as the site for the slalom events. Ironically, Loveland's owner, Bob Murri, learned of the selection of his ski area and the neighboring mountain for the slalom races on the radio. Surprised on hearing the news, Murri pointed out the obvious problem with the DOC's assertion of the commercial viability of a ski area on Mount Sniktau. Noting the peak's lack of snow and windswept summit, he told reporters, "I certainly don't think any private enterprise would want to go in there [Mount Sniktau] and put in the total package."[39] While Mount Sniktau met the IOC's standards as a venue in terms of height and location, it lacked the adequate snowfall and long-term viability as a ski resort as required by the Forest Service.

By the summer of 1971, it became apparent to both the organizing committee and the Forest Service that Mount Sniktau's failings were too many to overcome. Several alternate venues emerged, including, once again, Copper Mountain, along with Independence Mountain, Harrison Creek, Aspen, Catamount Ski Resort near Steamboat Springs, and Vail Associate's proposed Beaver Creek Resort. Some held promise as viable ski resorts following the

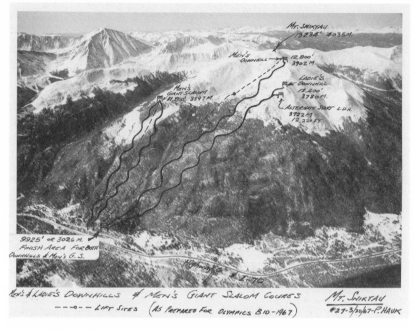

Proposed layout of Olympic Downhill Course on Mount Snikatu. Photograph courtesy Denver Public Library, Western History Collection, Paul Hauk Collection, WH-1304.

Games but did not meet the criteria needed for an Olympic downhill, while others offered ideal terrain for downhill course but were too extreme for intermediate skiers, negating their long-term viability. The Forest Service and the DOC each formed separate committees to investigate all of the proposed sites, with the agency focusing primarily on its goal of establishing a resort with good after-use potential and the organizing committee worried about a site to effectively stage the Olympic downhill events. Yet, both groups failed in responding to mounting public criticism over the environmental impacts of building another ski resort. To mollify such environmental concerns, in January 1972 the DOC formed a third planning board to evaluate the environmental impacts of each proposed site. All three groups reached different conclusions on which site best met the need for an environmentally sensitive, Olympic-caliber venue with long-term viability as a resort. Mount Sniktau lacked long-term viability as a commercial resort. Established resorts such as Keystone solved the environmental issue as they already had developed the facilities needed to host the world. The Environmental Planning board's preferred site, the proposed Mount Catamount near Steamboat Springs, was near the Nordic events, but ran into opposition by the DOC executive board's preference of Vail Associates' Beaver Creek project over strenuous objections from many inside and outside of the organizing committee. Consequently, the selection of the alpine events venue became highly politicized.[40]

In order to decide which proposed site best fit the Forest Service's requirements, Regional Forester William Lucas appointed a Blue Ribbon Team of the agency's leading skiing experts, including Hauk and the White River National Forest's newly hired ski resort planning specialist, Erik Martin, to assess the design issues, environmental concerns, and mitigation options for each site within the White River National Forest. After months of study, the team presented an ambitious proposal of developing thousands of acres of national forest stretching from the top of Vail Pass west to Beaver Creek, including Grouse Mountain above the rural town of Minturn. The proposed ski resort, or resorts, sought to mimic European-style resorts that spanned across several different mountains, each linked by dozens of ski lifts with multiple base villages. The key to this idea was the development of Grouse Mountain, which lay between Vail Ski Resort and Minturn. In presenting the project, Martin told attendees of a public meeting in Vail on the selection of an Olympic site, "Development of Grouse Mountain for alpine skiing would allow optimum use of a very unique recreation resource on National Forest System lands." Such a development required "at least twenty ski lifts" to optimize use of the skiing terrain.[41]

One obstacle stood in the way of Martin's vision—the opposition of residents living in the small town of Minturn. Settled in the 1880s, the feisty rural town had resisted becoming another resort community following the opening of Vail Ski Resort a decade prior, preferring to retain its rural way of life. To Martin and others both within the Forest Service and the ski industry, such decisions made little economic sense. "Minturn residents have the potential to own the most expensive and envied ski-to real estate in Eagle County; or remain isolated on a dusty pot-holed service road with little opportunity for retail sales or real estate gains for the next fifty years after the Olympics and the interstate highway are completed," concluded Martin in his remarks on the potential of developing Grouse Mountain and linking Vail Pass with the Beaver Creek area.[42] Martin's argument for the development of such an expansive ski resort encapsulated the larger debate over the Winter Olympics. While the Forest Service and Denver Organizing Committee viewed the development of a new ski resort as an economic boon for the state, residents of the affected communities often times did not. Rather, they viewed the growth promised by the Olympics as a threat to their very way of life. For Minturn, the development of a mega-resort would have brought massive changes, including significant population growth, increased costs of living, higher property values, and a loss of local identity.

In response to mounting pressures by environmental groups, the DOC formed another commission of environmental experts known as the Planning Board in January to review the proposed alpine sites in terms of their environmental impacts on the land and surrounding communities. In its final report, the group ranked Mount Catamount near Steamboat Springs first due to its suitability for the men and women's downhill event and its proximity to Steamboat, which was already the site of the Nordic events. The board ranked the Beaver Creek site last, citing that the development of a ski resort under the guise of the Winter Olympics "would invite the most trouble" for the Olympic Committee.[43] In addition, board members feared the political ramifications of selecting a third venue. In a memo to fellow Planning Board members Bob Pringle and George Robinson, Carl DeTemple relayed that Bud Little had told Merrill Hastings that if the Olympic Committee selected any other sites except Sniktau or Copper Mountain, they were "in for trouble," and that in fact "[IOC President] Avery Brundage may institute action to switch the Games" over the DOC's apparent inability to select an agreeable venue for the alpine events.[44] Despite the creation of the Planning Board and its subsequent report, DOC officials failed to recognize the increasing importance of environmental issues in the debate over the Olympic Games and instead worried about the IOC's perception of the DOC's clumsy attempts to select adequate event venues.

Along with the political struggle over the selection of a site for the alpine events, articles began appearing in the state's two major newspapers, the *Rocky Mountain News* and *Denver Post*, questioning the mounting price tag of the Games and pointing out the unexpected expenses of past Winter Games. In a six-part series in 1971, *Rocky Mountain News* journalist Richard O'Reilly wrote that previous Winter Olympic host cities had grievously underestimated their overall costs, a failure that had in turn brought higher taxes to area residents and enormous facilities with little after-use potential. The 1960 Squaw Valley Games had cost the State of California thirteen times as much as originally estimated. The city of Grenoble, France, had spent over $250 million on the 1968 Winter Games, and Sapporo, Japan, was in the process of spending anywhere between $750 million to $1.3 billion for the 1972 Winter Games.[45] Such articles, along with the DOC's continued silence on all Olympic matters including costs and site selection, only reaffirmed the beliefs of an increasing number of Coloradoans that the Olympics were more about profit and less about people. The DOC responded that there was no way it could offer the State of Colorado a guarantee that the Olympics would not cost taxpayers. "Whatever that cost might be, we know it will be small in comparison to Olympics which have been hosted by our predecessors. We also know it will be small in comparison to the opportunities presented to the State by the Olympics."[46]

Added to this potent mixture of economics and politics was the IOC's long-running opposition to the commercialization of the Olympic Games, particularly the Winter Olympics. IOC president Avery Brundage had long maintained that the Winter Games were little more than a way for host cities to bolster their tourism industries. Considered an anachronism by his critics, Brundage spent most of his career attacking what he saw as the creeping influence of commercialism into the Olympic movement. This was especially true of downhill skiing, which he believed to be little more than a commercial enterprise promoting ski manufacturers and resorts. At the 1972 Sapporo Winter Olympics, Brundage went on a tirade on the subject, loudly asserting,

> Today, the Olympics Winter Games are still far from universal . . . they are monopolized by only a dozen or so countries and they are difficult to keep amateur. The winter tourist business is so important to some countries that their ski teams have literally become almost government departments and are subsidized accordingly. This is not sport. They [the Olympics] can only be given to large communities which can afford the enormous expense—and they are more likely to be a set of world championships than Olympic Games.[47]

This was certainly true in Colorado where the Winter Olympics were promoted more for the benefit of the state's ski industry than that of the state's citizens.[48]

As the Forest Service and DOC struggled to choose a site for the Olympic alpine events, a small group of Colorado residents began to meet and discuss the environmental and economic consequences of holding the Olympics in Colorado and what they could do to stop it. After a year of informal meetings, the small band incorporated as Citizens for Colorado's Future (CCF) in January 1972 and began campaigning against the Denver Games. The group's first action was publishing an "Olympic Fact Sheet" in the *Denver Post* describing both the economic and environmental costs of the Olympics, including increased air pollution, loss of open space, and the ballooning costs of hosting the Games.[49] The organization quickly followed the fact sheet by circulating a petition protesting the Denver Winter Games to the Sierra Club, Audubon Society, and League of Women Voters. The petition received more than 25,000 signatures, surprising even the members of the CCF. The petition's success indicated that an increasing number of Colorado voters were unsure about the Olympic Games. Seizing upon this uncertainty, the CCF joined forces with other anti-Olympic groups in attacking the DOC's efforts to gain further state and city funding for the Games.

The founders of CCF comprised some of Colorado's leading liberal political activists, including state representative Richard Lamm. After moving to Colorado in 1957, Lamm became heavily involved in the state's nascent environmental movement, merging his passion for Colorado's outdoors with his political ambitions. As a member of the Colorado Open Space Coordinating Council, he had opposed the construction of a tunnel under the proposed Gore Range–Eagles Nest Primitive Area and later fought against the damming of the Grand Canyon, as well as called for greater protection against air and water pollution along the South Platte River, the need for urban renewal within Denver, and the removal of billboards along the state's highways. Inspired by John F. Kennedy's call to political arms, Lamm joined Colorado's Young Democrats in 1963, and three years later, successfully ran for the state legislature, serving as a state representative for eight years. Young, brash, and liberal, Lamm quickly gained the attention of the state's voters by drafting what was then the nation's most liberalized abortion law allowing abortions in cases of rape, incest, fetal deformity, and physical and mental health six years before the Supreme Court's decision on *Roe vs. Wade*. But it was the fight over the Olympics that vaulted the young state legislator to national prominence.[50]

With a groundswell of support, members of the CCF decided to take their concerns directly to the IOC. Pooling their resources, the group sent Estelle Brown, John Parr, and Sam Brown to the IOC's meeting in Sapporo, Japan, during the 1972 Winter Olympic Games. Literally breaking into the room, the three presented the shocked IOC board an eighteen-inch-thick stack of signed petitions along with several letters from state legislators, environmental activists, and property owners opposing the Denver Games. The stunt worked. After having police escort the three activists from the room, the IOC announced the withdrawal of its invitation to Denver to host the 1976 Winter Olympic Games. The news stunned everyone. But before the CCF members could celebrate their victory, the DOC secured an endorsement from President Richard Nixon as well as a special Congressional Resolution from Secretary of the Interior Rogers Clark Morton stating the federal government would ensure the solvency of the Denver Games, and Denver was reinstated as the host city for the 1976 Winter Games.[51]

Undaunted by their failure to stop the Denver Olympics in Sapporo, the CCF quickly changed tactics and launched a petition drive to place a referendum on the November ballot that would create a state constitutional amendment capping the amount of state funding available to pay for the Olympics. The Denver City Council followed suit, placing its own initiative on the same ballot restricting the amount of funding the city could provide for the Games. Governor Love quickly responded to the petition, arguing that any vote on such a measure would be "too late" and needlessly disastrous to DOC planning efforts. Denver Mayor Bill McNichols joined Love in his opposition to both the statewide referendum and the city initiative and gave little credence to polls that showed a popular opposition to the Games.[52] But both Governor Love and Mayor McNichols misjudged Colorado voters' growing anger towards the Games. In July, the CCF presented Colorado's secretary of state Byron Anderson a steamer trunk full of petitions with 77,392 signatures—27,392 more than were needed to place the referendum on the November ballot.[53]

Facing the new political reality, which demanded the consideration of environmental and community concerns, the DOC reorganized under the new name of the Denver Olympic Organizing Committee (DOOC). William Goodwin, president of the Johns-Manville Corporation, replaced Mayor McNichols as chairman of the new board. Carl DeTemple, a former Denver city councilman and lobbyist for the Colorado Association of Commerce and Industry, took over organizing the committee's day-to-day operations. Such changes proved largely cosmetic with the majority of the previous DOC leadership remaining in place. The DOOC continued to promote the economic benefits the Winter Olympics would bring to the state, ignoring the growing skepticism over the real costs of such benefits.[54] The debate over the Olympics

Governor Richard Lamm.
Photograph courtesy Denver
Public Library, Western History
Collection, Z-8948.

raged throughout the summer of 1972, with each side's rhetoric becoming increasingly bombastic. Costs and growth became the two central issues around which the debate revolved. A *Denver Post* article in March quoted De-Temple as stating the Olympics would cost Colorado taxpayers $1.5 million. That number soon ballooned to $5 million, despite additional federal funding. Pointing to the costs of past Winter Olympics, critics argued that such figures would only increase as the Games drew near. DOOC officials argued any economic costs would be largely offset by new tax revenues produced by the Olympics. The CCF responded that even under the most opportunistic of circumstances, revenue predictions would fall far short of actual costs. Citing the DOOC's April 3, 1972, budget, the CCF pointed out that the state government would be responsible for $4.7 million, the city of Denver for $12.7 million, while revenues were estimated only at $10.3 to $15.8 million.[55] These costs could and most likely would increase, argued Olympic opponents. "The Olympics are unimaginable," Lamm told reporters in September. "They are full of economic land mines. I fear, based on Olympic history that costs will far exceed estimates, and the Colorado tax payers will have to pick up the tab."[56] While the issue of costs remained highly contentious throughout the summer, so too were concerns over growth.

In an October 22, 1972, editorial, the editors of the *Denver Post* rhetorically asked, "How can we shroud Colorado from view?" Rejecting the Olympics would not halt growth, they argued. Instead, they suggested Colorado voters should approach the Games as both a challenge and an opportunity: a challenge to solve the major environmental issues facing the state, and an opportunity to promote Colorado's continued prosperity through continued growth.[57] But growth was precisely what Olympic opponents feared. A press release by the Rocky Mountain Chapter of the Sierra Club captured such worries, arguing that "the staging of the 1976 Winter Olympic Games in Colorado will encourage population increase, which will subsequently place a detrimental strain on the resources necessary to sustain life quality within the State of Colorado."[58] The solution to the problem of growth, argued Lamm, was not to "build a wall around Colorado," but instead to institute stronger land use controls rather than always accommodating growth. "One of the first things we do is stop 'selling' Colorado," he wrote in the CCF's newsletter. "Stop the mindless promotion and the Chamber of Commerce boosterism, exemplified by the Olympics, which has so characterized our past policies."[59] To Lamm and other Olympic opponents, the Winter Games were nothing more than the use of taxpayers' money to help fund the state's tourism economy. And nowhere was this more evident than in the emerging fight over the selection of Beaver Creek as the site for the Olympic alpine events.[60]

Disturbed by the relocation of the Nordic events to Steamboat Springs, the IOC demanded that the DOC settle on an adequate site for the alpine events by the Sapporo Winter Games. To do so, the organizing committee appointed a subcommittee to assess and then select a site. But soon after its formation, members of the new subcommittee postponed holding any discussions until after the holidays. Disgusted at the behavior of his fellow committee members, the DOC's technical advisor, Ted Farwell, complained, "Two weeks went by before our first meeting. Two weeks when absolutely nothing was done."[61] Returning from its holiday break, the subcommittee began reading through proposals submitted by ski resorts throughout the state, including Aspen, Snowmass, Steamboat, Copper Mountain, and Vail. Understanding the economic windfall hosting the Olympic events promised, each resort highlighted its strengths, from adequate snowfall to funding. Copper Mountain general partner Charles Lewis wrote that the new resort needed no further financial assistance from the state or federal government to host the alpine events and that environmental impacts would be "nil," due in part to the Forest Service's intensive environmental review. Steamboat executives pointed out the functionality of hosting both the Nordic and alpine events on or near the proposed Catamount Mountain, an argument supported by Farwell. But it was Vail that swayed subcommittee members, persuading them that its Beaver Creek project would meet all Fédération Internationale de Ski (FIS) requirements for an Olympic downhill with an ideal spectator arena as well as a prime location to host the cross-country events, allowing the Nordic skiers to be housed in the same competitors' village. "Our growth plan contemplates developing the Beaver Creek property as an integral part of the total Vail complex. We presently have a timetable for development, which could easily accelerate to stage these events. In addition, the facilities for Alpine skiing would be funded by private funds as designated in our growth plan," wrote Vail Associates president Pete Seibert to the subcommittee's chair, Robert Pringle.[62] After several weeks of deliberations, the subcommittee formally selected Beaver Creek as the official site for the Olympic alpine events and fired Farwell as the DOC's technical director, partially in response to his support of Catamount Mountain as well as his role in the controversy over the selection of Evergreen for the Nordic skiing events.[63]

As early as 1957, Vail founders Seibert and Eaton had played with the idea of developing Beaver Creek. Nestled ten miles west of Vail in a narrow drainage valley ringed by slopes covered in virgin forest, Beaver Creek seemed the perfect site for the development of another ski resort. But two issues stood in the way of Seibert and Eaton's vision. Much of the land needed to develop a base resort was owned by Willis Nottingham, who by all accounts was not too keen on having a ski area just up the valley from his ranch. The second problem was gaining the Forest Service's approval to develop the area for skiing. Early on, the federal agency had determined Beaver Creek suitable for recreational development, but the passage of the National Environmental Policy Act (NEPA) in 1970 changed the way the agency approved the development of new ski resorts on national forest land. The new legislation required the completion of an Environmental Impact Statement (EIS) before approving any project funded by the federal government, located on the public's lands, or in any way falling under the purview of the federal government. Examining all the environmental and cultural impacts of a project, an EIS can take years and add untold expenses to any project—time and expense Vail Associates hoped to forego. Soon after opening Vail Ski Resort in 1962, Seibert began asking Beaver Creek's owner about buying his 2,200-acre ranch at the bottom of the mountain valley. At first Nottingham resisted Seibert's overtures, but as the Eagle Valley continued to grow throughout the decade, the rancher began looking for greener pastures and in 1971 the two men struck a deal and Seibert began planning his next resort.[64]

After buying the Beaver Creek property, Seibert and Vail Associates immediately pressured the DOC for the selection of Beaver Creek as the site for the Olympic alpine events, hoping that its designation would cut some of the red tape in attaining permits from the Forest Service to develop the resort. In January 1972, in a closed-door meeting in Sapporo, Japan, the DOC designated Beaver Creek as the official site of the men and women's alpine events for the 1976 Winter Olympics. Critics immediately decried the selection of Beaver Creek, citing the former organizing committee's prior assessment that Beaver Creek was less attractive than Copper Mountain to host the alpine events because its development would cause much greater environmental and economic impacts on the surrounding area. Several members of the DOC's planning board resigned, outraged over the selection of Beaver Creek. Few believed Vail Associates' assurances that the development of the multimillion-dollar ski resort would have minimal impact on the area's environment, especially after learning that the ski resort's trails would be in a proposed wilderness area. Vail officials had hoped the designation of the area would help expedite Forest Service approval in developing the area, but Forest Service officials declined to make any quick judgment on the site.[65]

Seibert and other Vail Associates officials denied that the selection of Beaver Creek was meant to circumnavigate the Forest Service in gaining a permit to begin construction. But many saw the selection as an obvious ploy by DOC insiders, especially as Vail's Director of Operations Richard Olson was a member of the DOC's board of directors. Before the DOC's selection of Beaver Creek in Japan, Olson had leaked the committee's dilemma to Vail officials, who in turn ordered Olson to "get Vail's plan into high gear."[66] Olson did just that, and with the help of the chairman of the alpine site selection committee George Robinson, sold Beaver Creek to the DOC as the logical choice for the alpine events. Interestingly, as the organizing committee announced its selection of Beaver Creek, specially prepared booklets about Vail printed in three languages were being circulated around Sapporo. To many, including the organizing committee's soon-to-be-fired technical director, Ted Farwell, who was advocating the Steamboat area for both the Nordic and the alpine events, it appeared that the fix was in having the Beaver Creek site selected.[67]

With the purchase of the Nottingham ranch out of the way, only one sticking point remained in starting construction at Beaver Creek. The Forest Service was considering whether to designate the heavily forested slopes on which Vail hoped to build its new resort as a part of the proposed Mount Holy Cross Wilderness Area. Known as Mountain Meadows, the area provided both excellent ski terrain—Forest Service plans had long regarded the area as available for recreational development—as well as an excellent stand of virgin forest. Seibert believed that because the Forest Service had always considered the Mountain Meadows area as open for development, Vail Associates could be certain that the Forest Service would allow the development of the area even before its designation as an Olympic venue. Governor Love seconded this sentiment in a speech before the Colorado General Assembly, stating, "The proposed alpine ski area at Avon, near Vail, is going to be built in the next few years whether Olympic contestants come there or not."[68] Such proclamations seemed premature, as the Forest Service still needed to determine whether to designate Mountain Meadows as wilderness. In order to make such a decision, the agency needed to hold public hearings, produce an environment impact statement, and submit its findings to Washington. The Forest Service's decision on Mountain Meadows came in June. The agency decided not to include the area in the proposed Holy Cross Wilderness, opening the door to the development of Beaver Creek and its use in the Winter Olympics.[69]

However, divisions remained within the forest service over the selection of Beaver Creek for the Olympics. Hauk's choice remained Copper Mountain, but as the agency announced its decision on Mountain Meadows, White River National Forest Regional Forester W. J. Lucas voiced his support of Beaver Creek. In a letter to U.S. Senator Gordon Allott dated June 8, Lucas articulated Beaver Creek's many attributes. "It has excellent potential for after-use in helping to meet the demand for public recreation winter sports, good access from the eastern slope cities via I-70, which is scheduled for completion by 1975, a minimum amount of environmental problems, ample land for base facilities (owned by Vail Associates), excellent terrain for the competitive alpine events, existing or acceptable service facilities, airport, plus available private capital and experience to create the facilities needed for a project of this magnitude."[70] For Lucas and others within the Forest Service, Beaver Creek offered the perfect solution to two problems—the long-term viability of any venue chosen for the Games and private funding. And because the Forest Service's budget remained linked to permit fees collected by the agency,

Beaver Creek would guarantee revenues for both Vail Associates and the Forest Service. Such mutually beneficial relationships between the Forest Service and the timber industry had long drawn fire. Now, with the growing popularity of skiing, the Forest Service looked to harness recreation's economic potential in augmenting its budget.[71]

In November 1972, Colorado voters ended the dream of hosting the Winter Games. While resoundingly reelecting Richard Nixon, and with the war in Vietnam still the primary issue on the minds of voters across the country, Colorado voters passed the two referendums restricting state and city spending on the Olympic Games by a margin of 10,000 votes. The decision of Colorado's voters shocked the world. Previously, no host city had ever rejected the Olympic Games after winning the right to host the international sporting event. DOOC officials bemoaned the defeat and blamed CCF's use of fear tactics in order to convince voters to reject the Olympic Games. "I feel that three of five people who voted against the Olympics did not realize the deep and far reaching implications of what they did and the damage to the state and nation," said DOOC member Neil Allen to reporters.[72] Opponents, jubilant in their victory, argued that the election was the final rejection of the "Sell Colorado" campaign and expressed the desire of Colorado voters for a more sensible attitude toward growth. The day following the election, *Denver Post* columnist Joan Ditmer rhetorically asked if the rejection of the Games was going to save Colorado. "Not unless all of us—those pro and those anti-Olympics plus many more—work towards some positive action in the state," she concluded.[73] Colorado still faced tremendous challenges managing its growth, the economy, and the environment, primarily the development of federal lands within the state by ski resort developers.

With its defeat at the polls, the DOOC faced the task of officially declining the Olympics. On Thursday, November 9, 1972, the DOOC met for the final time to officially dissolve and in doing so decline hosting the 1976 Winter Olympic Games. In a last-minute spasm of desperation, a small group of Olympic supporters won a temporary restraining order preventing the DOOC from notifying the IOC of its dissolution. Arguing that the voters had not rejected the Olympics—they had merely rejected paying for them—the group attempted to win an audience with new IOC president Lord Killanin. Killanin refused the group's pleas and accepted the DOOC's declination of hosting the 1976 Winter Games. Several cities immediately appealed to the IOC for the right to host the 1976 Games, including Lake Placid, the site of the 1932

Winter Olympics, and Squaw Valley, site of the Winter Games in 1960. In the end, the IOC awarded the 1976 Winter Olympic Games to Innsbruck, Austria, which had hosted the 1964 Winter Olympics and which already had the needed facilities in place.[74]

Richard Lamm and fellow anti-Olympic activists attended a raucous victory party the night of the election. "A guy named John Sally hoisted me up to the ceiling," recalled Lamm of the evening, "and said ladies and gentlemen the next Governor of Colorado! I looked around the room, and said you know, he is right."[75] The realization was a surprise to the eight-term state representative. A highly controversial legislator, Lamm had long viewed himself as a political outsider in the state. His sponsorship of a bill that made Colorado the first state to legalize therapeutic abortions, as well as his controversial stances on the environment, had earned Lamm the reputation of a liberal extremist in a rather conservative state not prone to such political rhetoric. But the battle against the Olympics shifted politics in Colorado by creating a broad-based coalition that included antigrowth advocates, environmentalists, ranchers, Latinos, African Americans, fiscal conservatives, and property rights advocates. With Lamm at its head, this alliance of varied interests propelled him into the governor's office in 1975, as well as several other Democrats into state and federal offices following the defeat of the Olympic Games. Long-time U.S. representative and chair of the influential House Interior and Insular Affairs Committee Wayne Aspinall lost in the Democratic primary to the younger and more liberal Alan Merson in 1972. Congressman James McKevitt and Senator Gordon Llewellyn Allott, both Republicans, lost their jobs at the polls that same year. Allott lost to the energetic Patricia Schroeder who went on to represent Colorado's First District for the next twenty-four years. Both Allott and McKevitt's defeats were in large part due to the voters' anti-Olympic sentiments. But voter dissatisfaction came from more than unease over the costs of the Olympic Games; Coloradoans had larger concerns over growth. By 1970, many Coloradoans had become increasingly alarmed over the consequences of the state government's pro-growth policies such as Governor Love's Sell Colorado Campaign and the Olympic Games, leading to a decade of increased state regulation and continued struggles over the development of ski resorts.[76]

Antigrowth forces within the state quickly turned their attention toward the development of the yet-to-be-completed Beaver Creek. After being elected governor, Lamm initially opposed the Forest Service's acceptance of Vail

Associates' application to lease Forest Service lands on which to build Beaver Creek ski area, questioning the environmental and social impacts of the proposed ski resort and the Forest Service's role in furthering development within Colorado. Unable to use the Olympics as cover, Vail Associates spent the next decade fighting both the state and the Forest Service over the construction of its new ski resort. Critics of Beaver Creek voiced worries about the resort's fragmentation of wildlife habitat with the construction of ski trails. In 1974, Director of Colorado Division of Wildlife Jack Grieb wrote Dr. Wil Ulman, the land-use coordinator of the Colorado Land Use Commission, that the construction of Beaver Creek "will all but eliminate the elk herd which winters here."[77] The debate over Beaver Creek continued through the decade, pitting many of the same forces that had fought over the Olympics against each other once again.

Despite the legacy of Colorado voters' rejection of the 1976 Winter Olympic Games, Colorado's Olympic dreams remained. In 1988, a group of Colorado politicians, business interests, and individuals raised $500,000 to finance a Denver/Colorado Olympic Development Committee to make a pitch to the USOC to host the 1998 Games. A full 60 percent of Coloradoans polled at the time stated that they would support hosting the Games, many citing the economic benefits the Olympics offered host cities.[78] Colorado was a markedly different place in 1988 than in 1972. For the first time in years, the state was losing population and, with the collapse of the natural gas industry, was facing yet another economic downturn. The Olympics appeared to be a way to stop Colorado's economic freefall. "We can't afford to see things in black and white terms anymore, antigrowth versus economic development," said Governor Roy Romer, the Democratic governor who succeeded Lamm in 1986. "We've got to have a healthy environment, but we've also got to have a healthy economy." Even Lamm agreed that a Winter Olympics bid might be a good idea. "The people and the times were wrong in 1972," he said. "They may be right in 1989."[79] Colorado failed to win its bid for the 1998 Games, which eventually were awarded to Nagano, Japan, but with over a dozen ski resorts now within a few hours' drive from Denver International Airport, as well as a new modern stadium, sports arena, and convention center, it seems just a matter of time before Colorado hosts a Winter Olympic Games.

4

Following Colorado voters' rejection of the Winter Olympic Games, the public's ire over its perception of the state's unbridled growth quickly shifted to the development of newer, larger, ski resorts across the Western Slope. To environmental groups, the unbridled development of ski resorts on public lands held the same tremendous negative environmental impacts they had halted in the Olympic Games by causing further unchecked growth in once-rural communities throughout the state, if not the entire Mountain West—a truth, they argued, the Forest Service often overlooked when issuing permits for new ski resorts. "It shouldn't be an easy or quick decision. You're talking about permanent commitment of public land that belongs to everybody," argued Rick Applegate, director of the Bozeman-based environmental group the Center for the Public Interest. But many within the ski industry disputed such claims, countering that increasing environmental regulations and federal oversight were in fact pricing them out of business. "You can't just start with a rope tow and 10 years later be a little Vail," responded Gustav Raaum, chairman of Montana's Big Sky Ski Area, to the mounting challenges new ski resorts faced.[1]

Like Raaum, many within Colorado's ski industry adamantly maintained that the Forest Service, plus federal and state regulations—and environmentalists' undue influence on both—were behind the ski industry's mounting economic woes. Furthermore, they argued that while the number of new resorts under development across the country had slowed significantly, particularly in Colorado, skier numbers had in fact continued to grow, demonstrating the need for additional and larger ski resorts.[2] While skier numbers did indeed continue to climb throughout the 1970s, critics argued that unbridled growth of ski resorts was leading to the rampant development of Colorado's Western Slope, gravely impacting the region's water and air quality, wildlife, and wilderness areas. All sides in the debate, from the governor's office to ski industry executives, attacked the Forest Service for being in bed with the opposition.

Selected as the venue for the Olympic alpine events in 1972, Beaver Creek Ski Resort emerged as what Forest Service district ranger Paul Hauk later called "a political football" following the bursting of Colorado's Olympic bubble. The proposed ski resort came to embody the growing state and national backlash against the development of ski resorts, pitting development and preservationist forces against one another in a pitched political battle over the future of the Colorado high country.[3] But while the political wrangling over the development of Beaver Creek dragged on throughout the decade, an intensely bitter fight over another proposed venture, the Marble Ski Resort, briefly took center stage within the state. Opponents of the new ski resort near the former quarry town of Marble argued that the Forest Service had been, from the beginning, "grossly biased in favor of that development."[4] Conversely, Marble's developers seethed at what they believed to be the agency's shifting management policy and deliberate attempt to halt the resort's development. Along with the fight over the Olympic Games, the controversy over the Marble Mountain ski area triggered a sudden increase in the state's scrutiny of new proposals and ways to assess the impacts of major developments and marked a sea change in the public's views of ski resorts and the development of the state's public lands.

Few in Glenwood Springs seemed to take notice of the announcement in the *Glenwood Sage* newspaper in early December of 1963 that a group of investors had bought a sizeable piece of property above the small town of Marble with the hope of developing a ski resort.[5] Such rumors had become all too common throughout the Western Slope by the mid-1960s. Seemingly every ski instructor, bartender, banker, and real estate developer dreamed of striking it rich by opening the state's next Vail or Aspen. Located in the crux of the Crystal Valley in the heart of the Elk Mountains, roughly an hour's drive south of Glenwood Springs, the small town of Marble had had its share of being been the object of such rumors. But this time, it seemed, the rumors proved to be more than just idle gossip when a Denver real estate investment firm, the Oberlander Corp., offered local real estate developer Henry Stroud $375,000 for a 1,500-acre parcel of land on the northern outskirts of the former quarry town. Once home to one of the most productive marble quarries in the nation, producing stone used in both the Tomb of the Unknowns and the Lincoln Memorial, Marble's fortunes—as well as its population—fell following World War II when the marble quarry closed its doors for the final time. By the early 1950s, so few called the town home that most guidebooks listed Marble as a ghost town.[6] Stroud first discovered the former quarry town in the early 1960s and quickly recognized its idyllic mountain setting, relative isolation, and gentle slopes as ideal for the development of a ski resort. Purchasing 1,500 acres north of Marble, he soon began talks with the Oberlander Corp. on selling the property with the idea of building a ski resort along the lines of Vail. The deal collapsed almost as quickly as it started when Stroud failed to provide a suitable title for the property, forcing Oberlander to walk away. However, Stroud remained optimistic about Marble's potential as a ski resort and continued to look for a potential developer.

It took another six years for Stroud to garner interest in Marble, this time by Lee Stubblefield. President of the Colorado Western Development Company, Stubblefield had already begun construction on a $3 million residential development near the small town of Larkspur, south of the Denver metropolitan area, and was excited at the prospect of developing a resort community anchored by a ski area on Colorado's Western Slope.[7] On reaching a tentative agreement with Stroud, the developer sought Forest Service approval for a permit to develop a ski area on the national forest adjacent to the property. Paul Hauk, White River National Forest's resident skiing expert, toured the site, returning with a less-than-favorable appraisal of its potential for skiing. Hauk found that Marble's relative isolation, limited accessibility, and questionable geology made its potential as a ski resort marginal at best.[8] Yet, he reluctantly recommended the development of the area, concluding that the favorable aspects outweighed the unfavorable. In his final report on the area, Hauk reasoned, "The ski area and related development land, when considered in light of the future potential summer use and attractions—wilderness, scenery and water related activities—could, in time, become partially competitive with the Aspen and Vail developments."[9] It appeared that Marble Mountain Resort was well on its way to becoming Colorado's next ski resort.

However, Crystal Creek Valley residents soon began voicing their unease over the construction of a ski resort in their backyard. Most residents living in the valley worried about the potential loss of the area's rural character caused by the construction of the ski resort and believed that the Forest Service was blatantly disregarding their concerns in its review of Marble Mountain. Soon after the Forest Service announced its decision to grant the resort a permit for the 624 acres of adjacent national forest, a vocal group of Crystal Valley residents formed the Crystal Valley Environmental Protection Association (CVEPA) to combat the construction of the resort, arguing that the federal agency had overlooked the resort's impacts on the local elk and deer herds as well as the issues of avalanche control, watershed protection, and the closure of public access to the national forest on roads due to the resort's development, any of which should have prevented the Forest Service from granting the permit.[10] But while the CVEPA voiced concerns over access, erosion, and wildlife, like POME in Evergreen, the group's primary problem with the Forest Service's decision was the agency's failure to address the development that the Marble Ski Area would undoubtedly attract significant growth to the Crystal Valley. "The position of the Forest Service with regard to the Marble Ski Area, Inc., and its application for a permit to use Forest Service land for a ski area has, from the beginning, been grossly biased in favor of that development," CVEPA spokesman J. E. DeVilbiss angrily wrote White River National Forest Regional Forester W. J. Lucas on the Forest Service's failure to account for locals' worries over the potential growth the ski area would bring, demonstrating, they believed, an inherent bias towards development.[11]

It was easy to see how DeVilbiss and other members of the CVEPA had come to this conclusion. Vail had grown from an open pasture to a thriving village in a single decade. In the Fraser Valley, home to Winter Park Ski Resort, rapid population growth had led to the incorporation of the town of Winter Park in 1978, as well as the construction of several unincorporated subdivisions and condominium developments throughout the valley. But of all ski resorts within the state, Aspen symbolized the unbridled growth Western Slope residents feared the most. By 1960, the transformation of the once-rural mining town into a sprawling resort community had squeezed many longtime residents out of Aspen. And the term "Aspenization" came to represent all that was wrong with resort communities—rampant growth, mass commercialism, environmental degradation, and a loss of local character. Members of the CVEPA feared the very same fate awaited Crystal Valley if Marble Ski Area was allowed to open.[12]

Following the group's establishment, members of the CVEPA launched a letter-writing campaign to the Forest Service, denouncing the agency's decision on Marble Mountain as capricious and ill informed and arguing that the resort had been poorly planned and that the agency's actions had led to the "uncontrolled growth" of ski resorts and their adjacent communities throughout the state. In response to one particularly scathing letter from Crystal Valley local, White River National Forest Supervisor Evans wrote, "I do not agree that the area 'has been badly planned' as you [have] stated. My opinion is that the area has more than adequate planning by several consulting firms that have covered all aspects of the project." A strong ski resort proponent, Evans replied to the CVEPA's criticisms by asserting that the main issue was not the "uncontrolled growth" of ski areas, but rather of rural communities outside his jurisdiction. Writing that "the uncontrolled development and subdividing of private land in the mountains that can only be slowed down or controlled by state and county governments," Evans effectively shifted blame from the federal agency to local and state governments.[13] While the Forest Service actively approved the development of ski resorts, Evans refused to take responsibility for the growth such resorts caused in adjoining communities. Rather, he saw such issues as being under the jurisdiction of state and local governments; there was very little the federal agency could do to halt the development of rural western towns. Evans would stress this point again in his decision concerning Beaver Creek. The Forest Service's only mandate, he argued, was to ensure the public's continued use and access to national forest lands, not to regulate growth outside forest boundaries. While legally correct, such assertions only further enraged the CVEPA and other Western Slope residents who believed that the Forest Service was complicit in the over-development of Colorado's Western Slope.

Events at Marble would soon allow the Forest Service a means to reverse such perceptions, when massive mudslides caused by a heavy snowstorm buried many of the ski area's trails and single access road. The public relations fallout over the mudslides highlighted Marble's growing troubles. Frustrated by the resort's continued resistance to heed warnings on the stability of its slopes, as well as a brief fight over forest access through the property, in 1975, the Forest Service rejected Marble Resort's proposed expansion into 600 acres of national forest for environmental and social reasons. In the final draft of the EIS, Supervisor Evans finally yielded to pressure from antigrowth forces and concluded the "expansion at this time will prematurely trigger accelerated development of private land in geologically hazardous areas. Furthermore, it is important to note that this action would not be irreversible. It provides the opportunity for county government, if they desire, to find solutions for the potential social and environmental problems created by the proposed expansion."[14] A victory for the CVEPA and its supporters, the decision signaled the beginning of the end for Marble Ski Area.

Marble Ski Area closed its doors to the public in late 1975, as the resort began to die a slow, and painful, death. Unable to remain open and forced to reimburse investors, the owners soon filed for Chapter 11 bankruptcy; three years later, they were accused of fraud and fined $1.3 million for failing to complete the construction of three roads and a sewer plant on three other development projects in Larkspur, Colorado. The Colorado state attorney's office claimed that the developers also offered lots before the state's approval of the subdivision, which was in violation of state law.[15] Unquestionably, the Forest Service's rejection of the resort's expansion onto national forest lands, combined with the legal and financial problems of its developers, proved too costly to overcome.[16]

While Marble Mountain had suffered from inept, if not outright corrupt, management and poor geological planning, its targeting by local, state, and even national antigrowth forces reflected ski resorts' increasingly controversial role in Colorado politics. Paired with the defeat of the Olympic Games, Marble's failure marked an important transition point in Colorado politics, placing ski resorts, and more broadly the tourism industry, on the defensive within the state. Yet despite the decade's growing economic woes caused by a sluggish national economy, skiing continued to grow in popularity and in terms of sheer numbers throughout the 1970s. However, as the sport grew in popularity so too did Coloradoan's aversion to the development of their rural regions. By successfully linking ski resorts with the Western Slope's development boom, antigrowth forces within the state launched campaigns to slow down, or even halt, the development of mountain communities by opposing further construction of any and all ski resorts.

But even as some wished to check the Western Slope's growth, others continued to promote it, believing it to be a panacea for the state's economic doldrums, which by the mid-1970s were closely linked to the nation's larger energy crisis and rising inflation. Rampant inflation hindered Colorado's economy throughout the decade. Combined with OPEC's Oil Embargo in 1973, Colorado's economy, like that of many other western states, stagnated.

Its languishing economy played no small part in the political battles over growth and ski resorts throughout the state, with opposing sides believing that growth was either a remedy for or a cause of Colorado's declining economic health during the decade. The energy crisis impacted Colorado's economy in matters beyond increasing gasoline costs and inflation. Growing demand for domestic sources of energy made extracting resources a top priority, shifting the nation's interest to a region known as the Green River Formation, stretching from western Colorado to eastern Utah and southern Wyoming. There, petroleum experts believed, trapped in trillions of tons of oil shale, sat more oil than existed under the entire Arabian Peninsula. With the cost of oil more than doubling in a single year, by mid-decade all those tons of oil shale looked like a viable, and profitable, solution to America's energy needs. Energy giant Exxon joined forces with local oil corporation Tosco in building a $5 billion processing plant near the newly constructed town of Parachute, seeking to take advantage of the opportunities oil shale offered. Seemingly overnight, the western Colorado towns of Rifle, Silt, and New Castle turned into boomtowns reminiscent of the gold rushes of the nineteenth century. Both thrilled about the potential economic windfall and yet resentful of the thousands of newcomers flooding their towns, locals grappled with the dramatic rise in the cost of living, which was as great as that found in any of the the state's growing ski resort communities.[17]

Despite its role in bringing thousands of new residents to the Western Slope, the ski industry remained wary of the growing oil shale industry. Some living in the region's resort communities voiced concerns that pollution produced by nearby refineries would turn ski slopes black with ash. Others feared the competition the new energy industry would create in hiring and retaining employees. Notorious for low wages, particularly in menial labor jobs, the ski industry could not hope to compete with oil companies willing to pay much higher wages. "The people may not find working in the energy industry as much fun," Aspen's mayor Herman Edel told reporters, "but it will pay a hell of a lot more, and that's where they're going to go."[18] Governor Lamm remained unconvinced that oil shale development should be at the center of the West Slope's economy. Writing in his 1984 book, *The Angry West*, Lamm attacked the oil shale industry as both bad for the environment and having "the ability to destroy every other economic element around it."[19] Oil shale, he argued, would damage western Colorado's tourism, farming, and ranching industries by poisoning the ground water, turning rural communities

Forest Service Survey photograph of Marble Mountain. Photograph courtesy Denver Public Library, Western History Collection, Paul Hauk Collection, WH-1304.

into bedroom communities for enormous mining operations, and converting much of the Western Slope into a colony of large energy corporations, irrevocably damaging the region's environment and its future.[20]

Oil shale's expansion, and eventual collapse, followed the West's historic boom-and-bust economic pattern. As in previous times of bust, the collapse of the West's energy industry, combined with frustrations over the country's continued economic "malaise," led a growing number of westerners to point at federal environmental and other regulatory acts as the culprits in creating the region's economic problems. Such antiregulation sentiments fed a broad conservative backlash throughout the region, perhaps best symbolized by the so-called Sagebrush Rebellion, which swept across the rural West by the end of the decade and helped shift western politics further to the right. Like the western ranching, timber, and energy industries, ski resort managers increasingly blamed federal and state environmental regulation for their own economic struggles. While many resort managers and investors fully supported protecting the environment on which their livelihood depended, by the mid-1970s a growing number of resorts railed against what they believed to be federal and state government overreach in regulating the development

and operation of ski resorts. Such complaints further strained the relationship between the industry and the Forest Service, as developers pressed for
the continued construction of new ski resorts throughout Colorado as well
as the rest of the country, while antigrowth and environmental activists increased their opposition. Following the rejection of the Denver Games, along
with the eventual collapse of Marble Mountain, the brief struggle over the
implementation of the National Environmental Policy Act (NEPA) in Winter
Park's Mary Jane Expansion, and the similarly brief battle over the proposed
construction of Catamount Resort outside Steamboat Springs, the development of Beaver Creek became the main battleground for this growing political struggle between ski resorts and government regulators.[21]

Despite the Olympic defeat, Colorado's rather sizable growth coalition
continued to press for the further development of the state in order to bolster
its economy. In contrast, antigrowth critics feared that the continued development of ski resorts like Beaver Creek would lead to the urbanization of the
Western Slope and forever change its rural character. "When Beaver Creek
came it seemed to me that we ought to slow down and think about what parts
of Colorado we really wanted to develop for ski areas, and whether or not we
wanted them all along the I-70 corridor," recalled Lamm.[22] Elected governor
in 1974 due in large part to his opposing the Denver Olympic Games and antigrowth rhetoric, Lamm remained the voice of caution over the continued
development of Colorado's Western Slope, believing that a balance must
be struck between growth's promised economic prosperity and the need to
maintain a quality of life that he and so many other Coloradoans wished to
protect.

While antigrowth politicians such as Lamm linked the development of ski
resorts with Colorado's population growth, the Forest Service continued to
foster the development of ski resorts. "If we are to meet 1980 demand, we
have to get this project under way now," White River National Forest Supervisor Thomas Evans explained to a Colorado Land Use Commission in 1974
on why the Forest Service had so readily approved the designation of Beaver
Creek as a winter sports site two years prior.[23] Although few within the state
could argue against skiing's continued popularity, a growing number did believe that the Forest Service should look at other factors in allowing the development of new ski resorts besides ski numbers. The agency conceded that
there was a link between its approval of new ski areas and regional growth,
but continued to contend that problems associated with the urbanization of

rural communities were not under its jurisdiction, but rather that of local and state agencies.

The bitter debate over the Olympics had left mounting concerns over local governments' ability to control the level of growth. Several rural communities throughout the state had unsuspectingly found themselves slated as the venues for Olympic events by the Olympic organizing committee without notice. To keep such incidents from occurring again, in the spring of 1974, the Colorado State Legislature passed two land use bills which placed greater control over the use and planning of public lands into the hands of local and county governments. The Local Government Land Use Control Enabling Act, simply known as HB 1034, gave county governments the power to plan for and regulate the use of land to ensure its orderly use and adequate environmental protection.[24] Correspondingly, the Areas and Activities of State Interest Act, otherwise known as HB 1041, sought to broaden local and state oversight over any land development considered a "matter of public interest," and defined these areas of public interest as mineral resource areas, natural hazard areas, areas containing or having a significant impact upon historical, natural, or archaeological resources of statewide importance, and areas around key facilities in which development may have a material effect upon the key facility or the surrounding community.[25] Both laws amended the 1970 Colorado Land Use Act, establishing the Colorado Land Use Commission (LUC), which oversaw all state government development within Colorado and placed greater control over issues of growth and development in the hands of county governments. Proponents of both acts argued that federal agencies, particularly the Forest Service, had often failed to take local concerns into consideration in regulating the development of private lands adjacent to public lands, which promoted the rampant growth of rural communities near the state's booming ski resorts, a problem hopefully solved with the passage of both HB 1034 and HB 1041.

But local control did not necessarily slow down or even prevent ski resort development. In fact, it often had the opposite effect; proposed ski resorts often gained the approval of rural county governments who desperately needed the tax revenues. In the case of Beaver Creek, Vail Associates quickly acquired the approval from Eagle County's commissioners by promising the new resort would bring the magical mixture of increased tax revenues and jobs. Hungry for increased revenues, Eagle County commissioners embraced growth and its promise of tax revenues and jobs as a way to increase the county's coffers. The problem, however, was that such development quickly became a vicious cycle. The more development counties approved in order to pay for new roads, schools, and other social services, the more roads, schools, and social services counties needed to provide. Such short-term thinking quickly became the defining characteristic of many Colorado mountain communities, leading to widespread criticism by antigrowth and environmental activists who often attacked county commissioners and boards for being too permissive in promoting growth as an economic solution. Ski resorts, like all recreational amenities, such critics argued, acted as magnets in causing growth by attracting thousands, or even millions, of tourists to rural communities, many of whom liked what they saw so much that they decided to stay. Such newcomers often then supplanted longtime residents, creating a paradox where those who first embraced tourism as an economic solution quickly saw their towns transformed in unintended ways that included rising costs of living, exurban growth, and political shifts.[26]

Such was the case with the town of Vail. Within a decade of its establishment, the resort town sprawled far down valley. Such growth left longtime locals feeling left out as newcomers changed the valley's culture and sense of place. John Donovan, a supervisor at Vail's Ski School, bar owner, and member of the Town of Vail Board of Trustees, best explained the problem in a *New York Times Magazine* article: "When I first got here it was a Brigadoon. This was the most prolific deer country. Now," he said, "development and people have pushed all the game off. It's the same with fishing—just too many people. The older people lean toward slow growth, but fresh money keeps showing up. I think we've been overwhelmed. The growth was faster than our thinking."[27] The issue of Vail's growth had arisen several times during 1972, Donovan explained, as the town's board of trustees debated specific taxing and zoning proposals that effectively placed a moratorium on further construction. But such NIMBY sentiments ran counter to Vail Associates' fiscal health, since the company's long-term plans required relatively consistent annual real estate sales and almost all of Vail Associates' property sat within the town of Vail. Such pressures to increase profits often overran local efforts to slow development. Or, as in the case of Beaver Creek, the pressure divided locals into two separate camps over desires to increase revenues and preserve open space.

A year after the defeat of the Olympics, Vail Associates submitted its application for a special-use permit to the Forest Service to begin the development of Beaver Creek. The Forest Service quickly began conducting an EIS on the proposed resort and its surrounding region, which the agency had labeled the Meadow Mountain Planning Unit—a triangle-shaped section of national forest that stretched between the Beaver Creek drainage west to Grouse Mountain, south to the foot of the Mount of the Holy Cross. Within a year, the agency released its draft EIS to the public, with Eagle County officials signing off on the project soon afterward. The news media made little mention of the EIS's release or the county's approval until late September of that year, when thirteen different state agencies, including the Colorado Department of Wildlife and Colorado Department of Health, published a scathing assessment of the Forest Service's work on the impact statement. State officials charged that the Forest Service had violated NEPA in preparing its EIS by ignoring the proposed ski resort's impact on local wildlife and water resources, and that it failed to address what many within state government believed to be the inevitable urbanization of the Upper Eagle Creek Valley that would be caused by Beaver Creek's development. The state's primary criticism of the Beaver Creek EIS was its failure to address the impacts of the new ski resort on the area's wildlife, notably its sizable elk herd. In the state's assessment of the EIS, Director of Colorado Division of Wildlife Jack Grieb noted that the development of Beaver Creek "will all but eliminate the elk herd which winters here, contrary to one of the original objectives of the plan."[28] Beyond elk, other species would undergo losses in habitat as well, Grieb contended. According to a survey conducted by the state's Department of Wildlife, completed in the months just prior to the Forest Service's release of the final EIS, state biologists counted 209 bird species and 51 species of mammals, all of which would suffer a significant reduction in numbers with the development of the ski resort and the thousands of houses planned for the area.[29]

Following the Department of Wildlife's negative assessment of the Forest Service's EIS, the Colorado Department of Planning also asserted that the Forest Service had failed to account for the inevitable higher levels of air and water pollution produced with Beaver Creek's development, arguing that urban runoff and sewage from the resort would contaminate the Eagle Valley, stating, "regardless of where or how many plants may be required, an exceedingly high level of treatment will be required."[30] Traffic was yet another concern. As early as 1973, Glenn Fritts, a planning and research engineer for the Colorado State Department of Highways, wrote Governor John Vanderhoof's environmental affairs expert, John Bermingham, that according to the department's initial analysis, the increase in traffic caused by the development of Beaver Creek would quickly exceed the carrying capacity of any road constructed from the forthcoming interstate to the new ski resort. Such increases in traffic would then have long-term negative impacts on the valley's air quality.[31]

In the face of such mounting criticisms, and with an eye on the upcoming gubernatorial elections, Governor John Vanderhoof wrote Forest Supervisor Evans requesting the postponement of the Forest Service's decision to designate the Meadow Mountain Unit a winter sports site, allowing for the construction of a ski area in the narrow Beaver Creek valley. In the letter Vanderhoof argued, "The detrimental effects of the proposed designation appear to outweigh the benefits so clearly that I must request you to postpone the proposed decision."[32] It was a bold move by the pro-growth governor. By betting his political future on delaying the Forest Service's designation, Vanderhoof hoped to negate use of the issue by whomever the Democrats nominated to run against him in the upcoming election. But the governor's political gamble failed when a little more than a month later, Evans denied Vanderhoof's request by announcing his decision to recommend the designation of Beaver Creek as a winter sports site. Assigning this designation to Meadow Mountain Unit was the first step in the process of Vail Associates securing the right to build and then operate a ski resort on the national forest. In order to approve the permit to begin construction, the Forest Service had to first determine if the area was suitable for development as a ski area. While sounding rather innocuous, such a designation was, in effect, the Forest Service's approval of the development of Beaver Creek. Evans defended his decision by arguing that any further delay in the process would hinder the timely development of a needed ski resort in the state, and that his staff had more than addressed the state's criticisms in the EIS. Furthermore, concerns over the future growth of the Upper Eagle Valley fell under the purview of the state and local government and not the U.S. Forest Service—the very same argument made by the White River office in defending its earlier decision to grant Marble Ski Area its permit.

Furious over Evans's decision, Vanderhoof ordered the Colorado LUC to hold hearings on the designation in the hopes of producing recommendations on how Colorado should best proceed in halting the development of Beaver Creek. As the lead witness in the hearings, Evans reiterated his argument that the Forest Service was not responsible for regulating growth outside the national forest. Like Marble Ski Area, Beaver Creek's opponents questioned such reasoning, arguing that the Forest Service's approval of Beaver Creek contained a tacit understanding of the larger impacts the development of a new ski resort would have on the valley. In her testimony before the committee, Marilyn Stokes of the Colorado Environmental Coalition underlined such concerns by pointing out that well-intended "good-projects" often precipitated additional poor developments. "We take the present urbanization of the lower Eagle Valley as an example. While the town of Vail was developed with good planning, the adjacent building was uncontrolled. I know that Vail Associates is the first to recognize this; but our question must be whether or not there are sufficient controls and fortitude to carry out these controls within the state and the county?"[33] State laws, she contended, were full of loopholes and gaps. Members of the commission agreed. The governor's environmental affairs director, John Bermingham, sharply criticized the Forest Service's assertion that state law could regulate the increased pollution and the continued expansion of rural communities by pointing out that many of the laws cited by the federal agency in its seventeen-page rebuttal against state concerns had either been repealed or did not apply.[34] Evans adamantly rejected such arguments, insisting that the Forest Service had been more than willing to work with state officials in mitigating the impacts of secondary growth caused by the development of Beaver Creek, an endeavor not reciprocated by state agencies. "I repeat my year-old comment," Evans told the commission in a rare public display of frustration, "we still need to get this state participation at the front-end of the planning process. Identifying matters of state interest through the 1041 process will help get the State's interest considered more timely."[35]

Similarly, ski industry proponents countered that such doom-and-gloom statements, made by groups like the Colorado Environmental Coalition, were worst-case scenarios and that existing laws and solid planning by Vail Associates and the Forest Service would mitigate most of the state commission's concerns. Vail Associates chairman Pete Seibert argued that Beaver Creek would be the most environmentally sensitive ski resort ever built in the Rocky Mountain West and warned that "if Beaver Creek cannot receive approval by the state, then no new recreational development of any kind is possible for the foreseeable future."[36] In many ways, Seibert was right. By the end of 1974, Beaver Creek had cost Vail Associates $6 million with its loan from the United Bank of Denver accruing $425,000 in interest every year. Combined with the additional costs of $420,000 in annual taxes and wages, the corporation was eager to open the resort as quickly as possible. Evans had all but cited Vail Associates' mounting debts as one of the reasons for his recommendation to designate Beaver Creek as a winter sports site in his testimony before the commission. "To further delay our process at this time," he wrote, "imposes an inequitable burden on private enterprise which has cooperated responsibly in the on- and off-site environmental planning of a public recreation area."[37]

Antigrowth advocates pointed to such statements as proof that the federal agency was complicit in promoting the development of the public's lands for private gain. An article in the *Rocky Mountain News* best summed up such anti–Forest Service sentiments, stating, "We're getting another ski area and we're getting it with the blessing of Colorado's biggest and most ruthless land developer, the U.S. Forest Service."[38] But Evans and others within the agency believed that the continued demand for skiing required them to open more areas to development and continued to argue that it was the responsibility of state and local governments to regulate any growth caused by the development of new ski resorts. As an ardent proponent of the need for the development of new and larger ski resorts, responding to a question of whether Colorado needed more ski resorts with an emphatic yes, Forest Service Regional Forester William Lucas went as far as to advocate the idea that the Forest Service should act as a "Consumer Advocate" in promoting the development of ski resorts in order to provide affordable skiing to as many Americans as possible. In remarks on criticisms that the Forest Service was culpable in promoting ancillary growth near such new resorts, Evans noted that if the Forest Service allowed prices to dampen demands so that fewer people could afford skiing, thus lessening competition and reducing the need for new ski resorts, it would not meet the larger public good. "Thus," he concluded, "you can probably see why I feel new areas, such as Beaver Creek, must be developed."[39] Other foresters within the Forest Service's Rocky Mountain Regional Office also held such opinions, including the White River National Forest's two skiing experts Paul Hauk and Erik Martin. During testimony before the Colorado LUC concerning the public review of the Meadow Mountain Proposal, Evans angrily responded to questions on the Forest Service's failure to listen to concerns over growth and its cooperation with state officials by stating, "It is deceptively easy for any of us to say 'We are going to cooperate.' To some of us that means a give-and-take process, to others it means doing things my way or not at all, or doing business as usual."[40] What Evans misread was the sea change occurring within Colorado politics from a blind embrace of pro-growth policies to the broader public's questioning of the benefits of growth, especially the Forest Service's role in the development of ski resorts. The struggle over the development of Beaver Creek once again came down to competing views of who held jurisdiction in regulating the externalities created by the development of new ski resorts.

In November, Governor Vanderhoof lost his bid for reelection to Richard Lamm. Riding a wave of popularity for his part in the defeat of the Olympic Games two years earlier, Lamm had continued to attack what he saw as Colorado's rampant growth, specifically Beaver Creek, throughout his campaign for the state's top job. Following his election, the governor-elect announced his plan to ask the Forest Service for a one-year moratorium in designating Beaver Creek as a winter sports area and requested that the agency withhold any action on it until the LUC made a formal recommendation to the governor's office. The Forest Service remained adamant that its decision was final and believed that such public statements were more about state politics than Forest Service policy. Finally, just days prior to Lamm's taking office, the LUC submitted its recommendations to Governor Vanderhoof. In a seven-to-two decision, the commission recommended the governor approve Beaver Creek's development, and hours before leaving office, Vanderhoof gave the Forest Service the state's consent to move forward with the designation.[41]

Vanderhoof and the LUC's endorsement of Beaver Creek enraged Colorado voters; many cried foul over what they saw as an insider deal made at the eleventh hour. Within days of taking office, Lamm set out to reverse the commission's action, first by replacing two pro-growth members on the LUC with antigrowth advocates, one of whom was J. E. DeVilbiss, who led the opposition to the development of Marble Mountain Ski Resort. Lamm also sent a telegram to Forest Service Regional Forester Lucas asking for a ten-day delay in announcing their decision designating the area as winter sports site and a one-year moratorium on the development of any new ski resort within the state. Lucas ignored the governor's request and on January 24, named Beaver Creek a winter sports site, further souring the already tense relationship between the Forest Service and the new governor. Jim Monaghan, a Lamm aide, accused Lucas of "welching" on an agreement with the governor's office to not make any announcement until he received a final copy of Lamm's position paper. "We had the rug pulled from under us," Monaghan told reporters after hearing the news of the Lucas's decision. For his part, Lucas contended he had made his decision after carefully balancing the facts against the allegations in the case. In a note to Governor Lamm, he explained, "I also reasoned that if I allowed on my part the opportunity for maneuvering to continue by failure to make a timely decision this could result in a decision by proponents of projects not to make environmental studies of the NEPA process as part of the decision-making process, but instead seek to use the political processes first in decision-making."[42]

Within days, Colorado's newly elected U.S. senator Gary Hart asked Forest Service Chief John McGuire for an immediate review of Lucas's decision. McGuire agreed to conduct a full administrative review of the decision and met with Lamm regarding the governor's concerns with the Forest Service's designation. Negotiations ensued over the next several months between the state, the Forest Service, Vail Associates, and Eagle County. At the same time, the Sierra Club appealed Lucas's decision in court, arguing that he had violated the Forest Service manual's provisions, which were inventoried under the Roadless Area Review (RARE) process, by not considering 9,000 acres of national forest land near Beaver Creek as potential wilderness. After looking over the evidence, McGuire agreed with the Sierra Club and postponed the designation of Beaver Creek for another twenty days, citing that at the time the decision was being made, the roadless policy was in its formative stages, and unbeknownst to Lucas, Supervisor Evans had placed the Grouse Creek Management Area Unit for consideration in the proposed Holy Cross Wilderness Roadless Area.[43]

The Sierra Club's victory in halting the designation of Beaver Creek as a winter sports area proved short-lived; later that following summer McGuire announced that the sports site designation would stand, but only after a one-year delay in the development of Beaver Creek, a concession he agreed to in light of Lucas's failure to address matters such as air and water pollution and wildlife habitat in the original EIS. McGuire also ordered a second, more comprehensive EIS of the proposed ski resort.[44] With the state's objections apparently addressed, all parties announced victory. Yet, the controversy over Beaver Creek continued. Soon after McGuire's announcement, Vail Associates said that a second EIS was not necessary and that the company would instead conduct an environmental analysis report (EAR).[45] State officials remained skeptical that the much more truncated EAR would satisfy the legal requirements under NEPA, but relented after striking a number of compromises with Vail Associates and the Forest Service over the construction of the new resort.[46] Lamm finally withdrew the state's objection to the development, giving Beaver Creek the go ahead by announcing, "Never before has the state been able to participate in an environmental assessment to the degree we have worked on this document."[47]

In exchange for the state rescinding its objections, Vail Associates agreed to lower the development's density to 1,900 housing units from 4,000, to use mass transit to transport skiers from the interstate to the resort base in order to reduce air pollution, and to install a pumping system that would guarantee minimum stream flows, enabling water to be taken from the lower part of Eagle Creek rather than farther upstream. A month after the compromise between the state and the resort developer, the Forest Service issued the requisite special-use permit to Vail Associates for the development of 2,775 acres of national forest. The controversy was temporarily overshadowed by a tragic derailment of Vail's gondola in late March, in which two gondola cabins fell 125 feet, killing four people. But by the end of the winter season, the deal over Beaver Creek returned to the front page of Denver's two newspapers when impending lawsuits and associated costs in replacing both the Vail Village Gondola and repair of the Lionshead Gondola forced Vail Associates' board to look for suitors to buy the corporation, which eventually led to the purchase of both Vail and Beaver Creek by Texas oilman Harry Bass and the subsequent firing of Pete Seibert a year later.[48]

Two last-ditch efforts to halt construction of Beaver Creek by local environmental organizations soon failed, and finally on July 28, 1977, groundbreaking ceremonies took place on Colorado's latest ski resort.[49] While widely celebrated, the opening was overshadowed by the drought that gripped much of the American West throughout the winter of 1976–1977, causing the region's annual snowpack to fall well below normal. The lack of snow translated into plummeting skier numbers for Colorado's ski resorts, along with tremendous losses in revenues. Only Keystone, located near the growing community of Frisco, experienced any measurable growth in visitor numbers during the season, and that was marginal when compared to previous winter seasons. Neighboring Winter Park Ski Resort survived the winter with just a minimal decline in visitor numbers due mainly to its fortuitous million-dollar investment in snowmaking equipment the prior summer and the opening of its Mary Jane expansion. Nevertheless, Winter Park still experienced an 8 percent drop in visitor numbers during the season. Two of the state's smaller ski areas, Purgatory, near Durango, and Geneva Basin, near Leadville, experienced a 90 percent drop in visitation, pushing both areas to the brink of bankruptcy. As the University of Colorado's Business Research Division's annual report on the state's ski resorts noted, "All in all, the 1976–77 ski season was not a very good year for most Colorado ski areas, as the lack of snow was a factor they could not control." In total, Colorado ski resorts experienced a 38 percent decrease in skier visits from the season before, the first decline in overall visits since 1962 when numbers dipped a paltry 1.2 percent.[50] Winter Park's success in weathering the drought inspired other ski resorts to follow its lead over the next five seasons to add snow-making machines as insurance against unpredictable winters. Yet, while snow making appeared to be a solution to inconsistent snow, and thus inconsistent profits, it came with an environmental cost. Snow making required enormous amounts of energy and enormous amounts of water.[51] Over the next several decades, environmentalists would target snow making as both incredibly wasteful and damaging to local watersheds.[52]

But as the drought wreaked financial havoc on the state's ski industry at large, Colorado's largest resorts, mostly located in the White River National Forest (WRNF), exploited the disaster by leveraging the Forest Service into lifting the long-established price regulations on lift ticket prices. Linked to the Front Range metropolitan area by the nascent Interstate 70, by the late 1970s, the WRNF's half dozen ski resorts constituted roughly 67 percent of the state's skier market and acted as the geographic center of Colorado's ski country. Yet, despite their economic success, the ski resorts in the WRNF chafed under what they saw as overly restrictive Forest Service regulation and "obstructionist" environmental activists. With the drought acting as the backdrop, Aspen Skiing Company's president and chairman of the National Ski Areas Association's (NSAA) Forest Service Committee D. R. C. Brown argued that ski resorts were losing out due to the undue influence of environmental activists on the Forest Service, as well as the miles of red tape ski resorts faced in meeting environmental regulations. Telling an audience in 1977 that Aspen had left $250,000 worth of ski lifts "lying in the parking lot," thanks in large part to government regulation and environmentalist obstruction, Brown demanded that a "quicker and simpler" process be put into place by the Forest Service to allow resort owners to seek government approval. Otherwise, he warned, the slopes "will get more and more crowded and the lift lines longer and longer."[53] Besides inconveniencing customers, Brown

asserted that cumbersome Forest Service regulations and meddling environmental groups threatened the ski resorts' ability to secure loans and investors. With the costs of operating and improving ski resorts growing almost
as fast as skier numbers, many resorts, such as Aspen, struggled in securing
funding. Without secure sources of funding, Brown and other ski industry
executives argued, many resorts would struggle simply to remain open.

Often, the single largest stumbling block that both proposed and existing ski resorts faced in securing enough operating capital was navigating
the Forest Service's cumbersome permit policy. Throughout the early 1970s,
the agency continued to require ski resorts to hold two permits in order to
operate—a special-use, one-year permit for the land on which the ski lodge
and other commercial facilities rested, and a term permit, which lasted thirty
years, for the hundreds of acres of national forest on which to develop ski
trails.[54] The limited nature of such special-use permits led many banks to
question the long-term economic and legal sustainability of ski resorts; if a
resort was unable to secure a special-use permit it would be unable to remain
open, placing any loan into serious jeopardy. Such a situation never occurred,
as the Forest Service had a vested interest in keeping established resorts open.
Nonetheless, the byzantine nature of the agency's permit structure often became a point of contention between ski resort operators and the Forest Service. Beyond the problem of permitting, bankers and other investors disliked
the uncertainty federal regulations created concerning ski resorts. "I feel almost certain we would not be able to provide bank funding for a new ski area
unless a particular area had a very strong guarantee—and I guarantee that it
would have to be very strong," said Tom Swanson, vice president of United
Bank of Denver. When asked why he thought potential ski resorts no longer
could provide those guarantees, Swanson pointed squarely at the increasing
regulatory behavior of the federal government, dictated by legislation such as
NEPA. "I am here to say that anytime government gets near an industry, we
bankers get nervous," said Swanson. The solution to the long-term economic
stability of ski resorts, he and others argued, lay in the reduction—if not outright removal—of federal oversight.[55]

Yet, the profitability of ski resorts was not the Forest Service's highest
priority. Rather, agency officials believed it was their job to ensure both affordable public access to national forests and long-term environmental
sustainability by closely overseeing how ski resorts operated. This belief
came from a strong culture of ownership within the agency. "We controlled

everything. They were our ski areas," recalled Erik Martin, former WRNF winter sports resorts program manager, on his experience during the 1970s. Hired by the Forest Service in 1971 to help organize the 1976 Denver Winter Olympic Games, Martin succeeded Hauk in 1977 as the WRNF's resident skiing expert, remaining with the Forest Service until the Salt Lake City Winter Olympics in 2002. Throughout the 1970s, both Martin and Hauk enjoyed immense power over ski resort operations within the WRNF. Every ski resort operator within the national forest had to gain the two men's approval on a myriad of management matters, from the construction of new ski trails to the raising of lift ticket prices. "These guys would come in with their hat in their hand, literally, and be as polite as possible and say, 'Can we raise our ticket price fifty cents or a dollar,'" recalled Martin on the extraordinary authority he shared with Hauk over the management of ski resorts within the forest.[56] Such control seemed only natural to WRNF officials, who saw themselves as stewards of the public trust and had long believed their mandate allowed them to retain some level of control over the resorts. In contrast, resort operators had long opposed the WRNF's administration, claiming that such oversight hurt their ability to meet public demand and turn a profit, and they demanded a lessening of both economic and environmental regulation. Such arguments were far from unique to the WRNF, though. Across the West, resort operators complained about the increasing difficulties created by federal regulations and Forest Service management.[57] Complaints often focused on the securing of annual permits, the completion of an EIS, or mitigating impacts on wildlife. But by the end of the decade, the fight over Forest Service management had taken on a surprising twist in the WRNF.

While most ski industry insiders blamed environmental laws and activists as the primary culprits for the industry's economic woes, criticism in the WRNF focused not on the Forest Service's bureaucratic permitting process or "obstructionist" environmental legislation but rather on, of all things, the control of lift ticket prices. Resort operators within the WRNF had long complained that the Forest Service's control over lift ticket prices was too restrictive. In 1969, D. R. C. Brown had warned that, in its zeal to see consumers pay fair and reasonable ski lift ticket prices, the Forest Service "could care less whether or not the area operated at a profit."[58] White River officials found Brown's criticisms absurd at the time, countering that close regulation of lift ticket prices was necessary in order to balance public need with resort profits—a policy consistent with larger Forest Service practices that closely regulated timber and grazing fees in order to guarantee long-term sustainability. While real estate made up a large share of most resorts profits, lift tickets remained an important, and, in some cases, primary source of revenue for ski areas throughout the WRNF. The problem, however, was that the ski industry, much like the timber and grazing industries, often defined sustainability in ways that were diametrically opposed to the Forest Service's version.[59] Most ski resorts within the forest, for example, believed that they needed to demonstrate to investors their long-term profitability in order to prove they could meet growing public demand. To do so meant being able to charge what they considered adequate prices for lift tickets. Still, the fight over the Forest Service's regulation of ticket costs was over more than simple economics; it was, in addition, a fight over the WRNF's role in the ski industry's larger economic growth. So while resorts could do little to lower the costs incurred by environmental laws, they could nonetheless secure the ability to pass some of those costs on to consumers through higher lift ticket prices—but only if they could eliminate the WRNF's regulatory power.

The ski industry's demands for a reduction in government price regulation reflected a growing call for deregulation across the American economy throughout the 1970s. As the nation slipped into what President Jimmy Carter infamously termed "a crisis of confidence," a growing number of economists, such as presidential advisor Alfred Kahn, argued for the deregulation of markets as the solution to rekindle the nation's stalled economy. Kahn and other proponents believed that opening industries, such as the airlines, to the free market would both increase competition and encourage innovation, which would in turn bolster profits.[60] Such arguments became increasingly popular in the latter half of the decade as the nation suffered its second bout of high inflation combined with high unemployment in less than ten years. After assuming office in 1977, President Carter moved to deregulate a number of industries, including the airline, trucking, banking, and communication industries, convinced that obsolete federal and state regulation stemming from New Deal and Great Society policies lay at the heart of the nation's economic turmoil.[61]

Like many industries, the ski industry found deregulation appealing, particularly larger ski resorts whose executives adamantly believed that federal regulations, both environmental and economic, were increasing their costs and hurting their competitiveness. Resort operators within the WRNF resented what they believed to be the Forest Service's meddling in their ability to maximize their profit margins, arguing that by keeping ski resort revenues in check the Forest Service was restricting their ability to maintain and even expand their resorts, both of which negatively impacted the public's enjoyment of their public lands. The timeliness of the 1977 drought worked in the industry's favor, causing what appeared to be a significant economic downturn for most resorts across the country. After two decades of remarkable growth, flattening skier numbers and resort revenues signified the beginning of a potential downturn within the industry. Colorado ski resorts looked to exploit fears caused by the drought to significantly reduce federal oversight. Within the WRNF, lift ticket prices were the most visible form of income and so they became the primary target for deregulation proponents.

Interestingly, rather than openly oppose the deregulation of lift tickets, which would lessen its control over ski resorts, the WRNF sought ways to embrace such a policy. In 1976, the forest contracted the accounting firm Laventhol and Horwath and regional consulting firm Ted Farwell and Associates to conduct a study on the economic implications of deregulation. The firms concluded that the WRNF's limits on lift ticket prices failed to reflect the actual costs of resort operation, and that by opening the lift ticket prices to the whims of the market, the public's interest would balance "the highest quality skiing with the lowest possible prices for the largest number of skiers, while reasonably assuring the continuation of the supply and, under warranted conditions, the expansion of capacity."[62] But what exactly constituted a reasonable price, and who decided that? The report's authors answered both questions by writing, "where the price to ski equates with the skiers' concept of value received, and the rewards to the ski area adequately compensate for the risks and motivate rational expansion."[63] The market then, would define what was reasonable based upon how much customers were willing to pay. On the surface, such a supply-and-demand model appeared reasonable; to remain both competitive and solvent, ski resorts needed to maximize profits, an ability WRNF officials were impeding by tightly controlling prices, the report argued. So, by removing the Forest Service's control over lift ticket prices, resorts could charge a fair market value, which would increase their ability to raise capital and secure additional financing to further meet public demands for terrain and improved facilities. On reviewing the report, the Forest Service appeared amenable to allowing the market to decide ticket prices, letting the agency focus instead on larger and more pressing issues such as wilderness, environmental impact statements, and grazing policy.[64]

But the issue of ticket prices quickly turned ugly when, in April 1977, U.S. Senator Floyd Haskell attacked the Forest Service's contract with Laventhol and Horwath, worth $90,000, as a backroom deal designed to benefit large ski resorts. One of the several Colorado Democrats who had ridden the state's anti-Olympic momentum into office, Haskell had made a modest name for himself during his single term as a U.S. Senator by promoting tax reforms and environmental issues. Concerned that the Forest Service's decision would soon price downhill skiing out of the reach of most middle-class Coloradoans, Haskell called the lifting of price controls a "travesty," and little more than a subsidy for "fat-cat ski resorts." What he found particularly galling about the report was the fact that just the previous year, when asked if they would like to be included in a bill providing federal disaster relief for the drought, most ski resorts in the WRNF declined; instead, many resorts had opposed the bill. "They said the situation was not all that bad. So after working to deny help to small business which needed and continue to need it, they come in this spring and get their own disaster relief in the form of a permanent subsidy paid for by consumers," the irate Haskell told reporters.[65]

Haskell was right. Ski resorts had long sought the removal of lift ticket price controls in order to increase profits. By seizing upon the public's fears over the economic impact of the drought on the West Slope, ski resort owners touted deregulation as an easy solution to the industry's economic woes. The Forest Service agreed and ceded its control over lift ticket prices starting with the 1977–1978 season. Ticket prices immediately skyrocketed as resorts raised prices by as much as 25 percent. Initially, resort consumers didn't seem to mind, though. The 1977–1978 ski season saw record-setting profits for the resorts within the WRNF due in large part to the combination of higher lift ticket prices, increased skier numbers, and heavy snows. If the 1976–1977 season had been a bust for many resorts, the 1977–1978 season was a bonanza. In its annual report the National Ski Areas Association noted, "For the first time in the ten years of this annual economic study, profits were at a level that can be judged adequate to compensate for the risks."[66] The lifting of ticket price controls within the WRNF created a ripple effect throughout the Western ski industry. With large resorts like Aspen, Breckenridge, and Vail now able to charge what they wished, other resorts, both in Colorado as well as throughout the rest of the West, quickly followed suit. Lift ticket prices and ski resort profits exploded across the region. As ski resorts celebrated above-average profits, consumers protested the massive jump in lift ticket prices. In response to the public's outcry the Carter Administration quickly stepped in, limiting increases within the WRNF for the following season to a mere 9.5 percent, still a significant amount for many skiers.[67] Over the next decade, lift ticket prices continued to rise, helping in part to cause skier numbers across the country to stagnate and further reinforcing skiing's affluent white image by slowly pricing out working-class and minority families.[68]

The deregulation of lift tickets within the WRNF underlined the problematic issue of private development in national forests, which continued to define the relationship between ski resorts and the Forest Service. Resort owners had long pressed for unfettered growth in order to maximize profits, increasingly at the expense of both the environment and the very public whom the Forest Service was mandated to serve. Yet, the deregulation of lift tickets within the WRNF was not unique to the Forest Service. In fact, such issues had long shaped the contested nature of public land management, from the construction of concessions on the southern rim of the Grand Canyon during the 1910s to battles over logging in the Pacific Northwest.[69] However, the WRNF's deregulation of lift tickets also displayed the collision between the decade's free market ideology and increasing environmental awareness— two forces that continued to affect the relationship between the Forest Service and the ski industry as the era of widespread development of ski resorts came to a close. Deregulation did in part solve resorts' growing needs to meet costs, but it also had the unintended consequence of pricing many out of the sport. Such consequences were small in comparison to free market idealism's profound effects on competition within the industry over the next two decades, causing, as we will see, a period of broad consolidation within the industry and increasing economic pressures to expand ski resorts on national forests not solely to meet public demand but rather to bolster profits.

As ski resorts in the WRNF secured the deregulation of lift tickets, another controversy of great concern to all western ski resorts unfolded in the California Sierras with Disney's proposed development of a ski area in the Mineral King Valley. Located just south of Sequoia National Park, the Mineral King Valley first gained the Forest Service's attention as a potential site for a ski area in 1946. But few investors showed interest in building a resort in the isolated valley until 1965, when the Disney Corporation purchased two parcels of land within the valley and began planning the development of its own ski resort complete with a European-style base village; a year later, the entertainment giant signed a three-year development contract with the Forest Service.

Opposition to the proposed ski resort immediately arose, led in large part by the Sierra Club. The environmental organization's protest against the development of Mineral King came with a bitter irony, however; in the late 1940s, the Sierra Club had tacitly approved the development of a ski area in Mineral King. But in the intervening two decades, both the club and the ski industry had drastically changed. Ski resorts were no longer small operations, and the Sierra Club had become one of the nation's foremost environmental organizations—leading the fight against the damming of Echo Park Canyon and passage of the Wilderness Act of 1964. Mineral King quickly gained national attention, pitting Mickey Mouse against the Sierra Club. In 1969, the environmental group sued to halt Disney's $35 million resort complex as well as the state of California's attempts to build a four-lane highway into the Mineral King Valley.

The suit slowly progressed through the federal court system, until 1972 when the U.S. Supreme Court rejected the Sierra Club's case in a three to four vote on the grounds that the group had not established that it was suffering direct harm from the Forest Service's actions in allowing the development of Mineral King. The Court's decision had long-ranging effects on future lawsuits concerning environmental standing. By rejecting the suit, the Supreme Court set the precedent that only individuals had standing in matters involving environmental law. This meant that as an organization, the Sierra Club could not sue to halt Mineral King. However, within the Court's decision lay the seed that would forever change the use of the legal system by the Sierra Club and other environmental organizations. In his minority opinion, Justice Potter Stewart noted that the Court's decision did not prohibit the club from filing a suit on the behalf of individual members, a strategy the organization soon seized upon, adding nine plaintiffs who visited the valley to the suit against Disney Corp. two months later. Seeing the writing on the wall, Disney withdrew its permit application, ending any chance of developing a ski resort in the Mineral King Valley. Finally in 1978, the federal government annexed the Mineral King Valley into Sequoia National Park, bringing an end to the controversy.[70]

The storm over Mineral King cast a further pall over the nation's ski industry. With Jimmy Carter in the White House and strong public opposition to the development of seemingly all proposed ski resorts, the decades-long boom in resort development was coming to an end. Writing in the *New York Times*, Rocky Mountain Bureau correspondent Grace Lichtenstein observed

Aerial photograph of proposed Beaver Creek Ski Resort. Photograph courtesy Denver Public Library, Western History Collection, Paul Hauk Collection, WH-1304.

in 1976, "The Western ski resort boom, which saw fourteen new ski areas open in the Rocky Mountain States from 1964 to 1974, is just about over."[71] By the end of the decade, Lichtenstein's prediction appeared to come to fruition. Federal legislation such as NEPA added years to the process of developing ski resorts on national forests, opening new resorts to legal challenges and making their development too costly and too risky for many investors.

After three years of construction, Beaver Creek opened to much fanfare on December 15, 1980. Skiers parked far below the resort, loading onto shuttle busses at the entrance of the valley for a short ride past what would become a private eighteen-hole golf course and club to a base village modeled after the European resorts of St. Moritz and Cortina. There, they disembarked and made their way to one of five chairlifts that would carry them to the top of the 11,400-foot mountain. Islands of trees sat in the middle of many of the trails mitigating the visual impacts of such clear cuts. Unlike Vail, Beaver Creek offered decidedly more advanced terrain, which frightened off many intermediate-level skiers and gave the mountain a much less crowded feel even on the busiest of holiday weekends. Colorado governor and long-time opponent of the resort Richard Lamm claimed credit for the environmentally sensitive manner in which Vail Associates had built Colorado's latest ski resort; he proudly declared that Beaver Creek was to be the "Cadillac of ski areas" in the nation.[72] Despite Lamm's rather tortured use of metaphor, Beaver Creek's opening was indeed a significant moment in the long-standing fight between antigrowth advocates and the state's ski industry with its ally, the U.S. Forest Service. The struggle culminated in the referendum that rejected Denver's hosting of the 1976 Winter Olympics. Beaver Creek, which played an important role in that controversy, was also the last major ski resort to open along Colorado's I-70 corridor and marked an end to a nearly four-decade long boom in resort development not only within the state, but throughout much of the Mountain West. Beaver Creek quickly earned the reputation of being the exclusive resort within Colorado, rivaling Aspen and Vail. Within the next decade, the town of Avon flourished below, and houses dotted the hillsides of Bachelor Gulch above the ski resort as wealthy second-home owners, including former President Gerald Ford, built lavish residences near the ski resort, visually adding to the sprawl below.[73]

The costs of developing Beaver Creek were tremendous. By the resort's opening, Vail Associates had spent more than $300 million on the new resort, more than six times the cost of Vail. Once again, the corporation pointed to increased state and federal environmental regulations as the main reasons for the skyrocketing costs, as well as the enormous amounts of capital investment now needed to simply open a new resort, making it more difficult to attract investors. Increased environmental protections obligated resort developers to mitigate impacts on wildlife, account for erosion, and plan for future growth, all increasing costs and making the construction of new resorts such as Beaver Creek difficult if not impossible. The political struggle over Beaver Creek also further strained the Forest Service's relationship with Colorado's government; several departments within the state government continued to attack the agency for its failure to adequately address a number of environmental and economic concerns. Yet despite the broader political backlash against the development of ski resorts and the battle over deregulating tickets, skier numbers continued to increase. By the 1980–1981 winter season Colorado resorts hosted more than 7 million skier days, an increase of more than 5 million skier visits over the previous decade. Still, the combined pressures of growing demand and increased regulation eventually forced ski resorts, and the Forest Service, to change the way they did business, setting the stage for the industry's next transformation.[74]

5

By the middle of the 1980s, it seemed every ski resort in the country was either planning or in the process of building a base village complete with condominiums, restaurants, and retail space in order to bolster profits. Such developments stemmed from increased operational and maintenance costs, beginning earlier in the decade, when, in order to remain competitive, many mid-sized resorts began pouring millions into on-mountain improvements such as newer high-speed detachable chairlifts, expanded snow-making operations, larger and more lavish on-mountain lodges, and added terrain. Resorts quickly saw real estate development as a way to raise enough revenue to pay for the upgrade of facilities and terrain expansions needed to attract an increasing share of a stagnant market. But the real estate solution proved to be a "devil's bargain," producing increased revenues but unleashing market forces that would bring about the collapse of smaller market ski areas and the consolidation of the ski industry under the control of a handful of corporate giants. At the beginning of the decade, the number of ski resorts in the United States began a steady decline from 735 to 509 by century's end, leading many industry critics to argue that there was no longer any need for the development of more ski resorts.[1] However, a closer look at the industry showed that Midwest and southeastern ski areas were experiencing the majority of the industry's losses due to inconsistent winter snows and rapidly increasing overhead costs, while resorts in the Rocky Mountain region, especially those in Colorado, were experiencing a nearly 15 percent increase in total visits. But rather than demonstrating skiing's stagnation, as environmental groups asserted, the numbers underlined the industry's uneven national growth and consolidation. In the White River National Forest (WRNF) alone, home to 63 percent of Colorado's skier visits, skier numbers rose from 9 million to 11 million skier days, causing ski resorts such as Vail and Breckenridge to seek to add nearly 8,000 acres in terrain.[2]

Undeterred by claims of the need for increased capacity given by western ski resorts, environmental groups argued that such development far exceeded public need and that therefore the Forest Service's continued approval of ski resorts' expansions not only was unsound public policy, but fueled a cycle of development and growth that negatively affected both national forest ecosystems and the mountain resort communities reliant on tourist dollars. Skiing was no longer an end unto itself, industry critics argued, but rather had become a marketing amenity used to sell real estate.[3] It was difficult to argue with such assessments, as a growing number of ski resorts embarked upon massive real estate developments beginning in the 1980s in order to remain competitive in what appeared to be an ever-tightening market. This widespread embrace of real estate and on-mountain development led to an all-out arms race among western ski resorts and the industry's consolidation by the century's end. In Colorado, three major corporations emerged to control the majority of the state's rather large skier market, beginning with the purchase of Vail and Beaver Creek by what would become Vail Resorts, Inc. in 1991. Within years, the corporate giant acquired three more Colorado resorts, starting a wave of consolidations that radically transformed the ski industry's economic landscape. By the end of the decade, Canadian-owned Intrawest, the American Ski Company, and Vail Resorts, Inc., controlled roughly 80 percent of Colorado's ski market, the largest market in the nation. The consolidation of the ski industry, not only in Colorado, but also throughout North America, furthered the drive for real estate development and resort expansions. Yet, the need for further expansion of Colorado resorts remained questionable. Despite the state's overall growth in skier numbers, the total capacity of Colorado resorts far exceeded the public's need.[4] All of this set the stage for a major showdown in the mid-1990s between environmentalists and Vail Resorts over Vail's planned Category III expansion. Once again, the Forest Service found itself caught in the middle of a heated battle pitting antigrowth environmentalists against profit-seeking developers over the expansion of the nation's largest ski resort.

The roots of the Category III expansion controversy lay in the purchase of Vail Associates by television mogul George Gillette in 1985. Gillette had initially sought to purchase Vail Associates in 1983 but was rebuffed by the corporation's board. The offer set off a bidding war for the ski giant, with no less than three serious bidders, including the corporation's majority stockholder, Goliad Oil. None satisfied Vail Associates' investors until 1985, when the stockholders accepted Gillette's offer, and Vail Associates became the sole property of Gillette Holdings. Both Vail and Beaver Creek blossomed under Gillette. In 1988, Vail celebrated its twenty-fifth anniversary with the opening of The Back Bowls, which included the newly constructed 33,000-square-foot Two Elks Lodge. The new terrain nearly doubled Vail's skiable acreage, making it the largest ski resort in the United States. The following winter, the ski resort hosted the World Alpine Ski Championships—the first time the event had been held in Colorado since 1950. The most popular destination for both out-of-state and in-state skiers, Vail topped 1.4 million skier days—nearly 15 percent of the state's total skier days, during the 1988–1989 ski season.[5] The popular ski resort was on a roll. Even Vail's cofounder and former CEO, Pete Seibert, returned to work for the resort.[6] Gillette reveled in Vail Associates' and the ski industry's success, raving to reporters during a 1988 press conference in Manhattan, "Five years ago this industry was in big trouble. But if you were to say it was in trouble today, you'd be wrong."[7]

In truth, Gillette was only partially right in his assessment. Skier numbers in Colorado had indeed risen from 7.8 million skier days during the 1980–1981 ski season to 9.8 million during the 1990–1991 season. But of the state's thirty ski resorts in 1990, seven comprised more than 70 percent of the market.[8] These larger, more popular resorts all offered more terrain, faster ski lifts with greater capacity, grander on-mountain facilities, and most importantly, real estate. Vail continued to be among the most popular ski resorts for both destination and day-use visitors, winning the Ski Magazine readers' top North American resort award three years in a row—1989, 1990, and 1991.[9] The disparity between the haves and the have nots was striking. In 1990, Vail hosted nearly 1.5 million skiers, more than a full third of Colorado's remaining ski areas combined. Smaller ski areas, unable to offer the same level of amenities, struggled to remain in the black as their numbers either flattened or dropped, while overhead costs continued to rise. Over the next decade, smaller ski areas continued to see their profits dwindle as larger ski resorts attracted greater numbers of customers with cheaper prices and more amenities.

The year following Gillette's taking ownership of Vail Associates, the WRNF released its new Master Development Plan for Vail. Under the Ski Area Permit Act of 1986, ski areas operating under a Term Special Use Permit from the U.S. Forest Service were required to write a Master Development Plan as a condition for the renewal of their permit. Intended merely as a planning tool, Master Development Plans were not meant to be decision-making documents, as were environmental impact statements (EIS) or environmental assessments (EA) as required under NEPA. Rather, they were meant to allow the Forest Service to evaluate the impacts of a ski resort on the national forest as a whole and provide comprehensive guidelines for the future management of the national forest lands ski areas leased. Site-specific proposals outlined under the Master Plan, such as chairlifts, restaurants, and even trails, were still required to undergo an EIS or EA as outlined by NEPA prior to any approval by the Forest Service. So, while Master Plans outlined larger environmental concerns over potential development by ski resorts, any individual developments had to meet NEPA requirements in order to gain approval. In recent years, environmental groups such as the Ski Area Citizens Coalition have pointed to Master Plans as indicators of a resort's potential environmental impacts arguing that such plans indicate future plans for further expansion into undisturbed terrain. Such causal arguments are misleading, as Master Plans are not decision documents, and so do not grant resorts approval for any future expansion. Many, if not most, master plans will never be followed through for various reasons, such economics, skier demand, and practicality. The Forest Service struggles to keep this differentiation between potential and actual future development clear, as it often leads to misinformation and mistrust between environmental groups and the agency.[10]

The 1986 Master Development Plan for Vail Ski Resort identified three major phases, or categories, for Vail Resort's development. Category I included the existing 2,000 acres within the resort's administrative boundary. Category II added an additional 2,000 acres of terrain on the southern side of Vail Mountain, including the China Bowl, Teacup chairlift, a Nordic center and trail system in Benchmark and Mushroom Bowls, and the possibility of a new ski lift in the Cascade Village area. Finally, Category III was a development scenario for the south side of the Two Elks Roadless Area, a 1,000-acre section of national forest land of which roughly 60 percent lay within the existing ski area boundary. The Forest Service approved the development of Category II in 1986, but required more comprehensive planning for Category III. Vail immediately set to work developing Category II, placing Category III onto the back burner until the mid-1990s for economic reasons.[11]

Despite the success of its Back Bowls and Two Elks Lodge, Vail's good times came to a crashing halt in 1991, when Gillette was forced to declare bankruptcy and sell Vail Associates to the investment firm Apollo Management L.P.[12] Apollo quickly moved to take Vail Associates public, offering $75 million in stock on the New York Stock Exchange in order to pay off Vail Associate's remaining debts and to provide enough capital to purchase other Colorado ski resorts. Renamed Vail Resorts, Inc., the new corporation sought to expand its market share of the Colorado ski industry by merging with St. Louis-based Ralcorp Holdings Inc., owners of Breckenridge, Keystone, and Arapahoe Basin ski resorts. The deal made Vail Resorts the largest ski resort owner in Colorado, controlling nearly 38 percent of the Colorado skier market, and setting off a series of mergers throughout North America as resorts sought to remain afloat in a tightening market: Canadian resort giant Intrawest took the reins at Vail's competitors Copper Mountain and Winter Park; the American Ski Company, owners of several ski resorts in New England, purchased Steamboat Ski Resort in Colorado and California's Heavenly near Lake Tahoe.

Concerns over the consolidation of North America's ski industry, stemming from fears that the creation of such mega-resorts would soon squeeze out smaller-market resorts, grew. Operators of smaller ski areas such as Silver Creek, outside the town of Granby, and Eldora Mountain, located thirty miles west of Boulder, believed that the merger would threaten their ability to remain competitive. Silver Creek's CEO, Steve Bromberg, feared that if Vail absorbed all three Ralcorp resorts and then sold a five-mountain ticket season pass at a reduced rate, there would be no way for him to remain both solvent and competitive. Silver Creek's clientele was a mixture of destination skiers looking for a smaller mountain and Front Range families looking to escape the high prices and high volumes of larger ski resorts. Arguably, such a niche market would remain if Vail Resorts and Ralcorp were allowed to merge, but the new conglomerate would have the luxury of dramatically undercutting the prices of Silver Creek and other smaller resorts in order to steal their customers. Larger resorts, including Silver Creek's neighbor Winter

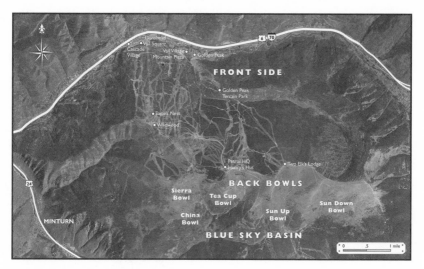

Vail Ski Resort. Map by Gerry Krieg.

Park, agreed that the consolidation of more than one-third of the state's skier market under a single owner would radically change the industry's economic landscape and possibly cause the collapse of several ski areas throughout the state along with further worries over the potential economic collapse of rural counties reliant on those tourist dollars and the abandonment of ski resorts on the public's lands.

In response to such concerns, the U.S. Justice Department and Colorado State Attorney General's office began a several-month-long investigation into the merger, paying critical attention to the market share issue. Fearing the Justice Department's rejection of the deal, Vail Resorts offered to donate Arapahoe Basin to the state. Justice officials refused the deal, stating it would set the bad precedent of allowing companies to give large holdings as charity to the state and then write them off as a tax-exempt gift.[13] Furthermore, both the Justice Department and the state were coming to object to the merger itself, believing that it violated antitrust laws. With the possible merger in doubt, Vail Resorts scrambled to find a buyer for Arapahoe Basin in order to make the deal more palatable for Justice Department lawyers. The diminutive ski area quickly became the center of a contentious battle over the future of the Colorado ski industry as opposing sides of the merger argued over its potential effect on not only the ski industry but on the state's tourist industry.

Events began to come to a head when, after reviewing the specifics of the deal, the Justice Department signed off on the merger, but only if Vail Resorts divested itself of Arapahoe Basin by June. This satisfied the federal government's concerns that consumers would have adequate options when choosing where to ski, while at the same time allowing the market to determine costs. Critics blasted the decision. Operators of small ski areas reliant on Front Range skiers continued to argue that the merger threatened their very survival. Others within the industry, including American Ski Company CEO Les Otten, who had recently lost a battle with the Justice Department over his own company's attempt to acquire four ski resorts in New England, argued that the federal government had no role in regulating the ski industry at all. "I believe it's wrong for our government to spend taxpayer money trying to regulate industries that are totally discretionary and deal with recreation that can be replaced with other recreation," Otten told reporters following the announcement of the Vail Resorts–Ralcorp merger.[14]

Conversely, City of Denver officials immediately decried the decision as antiregulatory. As the owner of Winter Park Ski Resort, the city had a vested interest in maintaining Winter Park's competitiveness within the state's ski industry. "These people must be smoking something," city attorney Daniel Muse told reporters. "They're suggesting that A-Basin is competitive, in terms of the type of skiing and amenities—with Beaver Creek, Vail, Breckenridge and Keystone. Arapahoe Basin is a spartan, macho skiing environment, the access is terrible and it has no amenities."[15] Muse had a point. Located on Loveland Pass, Arapahoe Basin was the smallest of the three Ralcorp holdings and had few amenities beyond a small ski lodge and a handful of ski lifts. Its slopes appealed largely to expert skiers and snowboarders and failed to attract novice and intermediate skiers in any significant numbers. On the other hand, Keystone and Breckenridge lay near the towns of Frisco and Dillon, respectively, and carried the significant potential for real estate development at their base. In fact, Vail Resorts had already made a deal with ski giant Intrawest to build a resort village at the base of Keystone. Once again, real estate, not skier numbers, appeared to be the true heart of the deal.

The merger also stirred a blizzard of questions from Front Range skiers who wanted to know what it would mean for their wallet. Vail president Andy Daily allayed skier and snowboarders' fears over any price increases by announcing that the company would offer a discount card that provided a discount for day lift tickets to all five of the company's mountains. Daily also assured customers that Vail would continue its popular Summit Pass season ticket, which allowed holders to ski at the four resorts in Summit County. Such a plan was nothing new. For years, ski resorts along the Interstate 70 corridor had used price discounts to attract Front Range skiers, who historically made up 30 percent of the state's ski market, with resorts in Summit and Grand counties enjoying a much larger percentage of Front Range business than those further away from the Denver Metropolitan Area. An internal marketing survey in 1986 reported that more than half of all Winter Park's visitors lived in Colorado, the majority from along the Front Range.[16] Still, while Front Range skiers made up a significant portion of the market in terms of ticket sales, the industry was primarily targeting destination visitors who spent more money on lodging, food, rentals, and entertainment. With great name recognition, and now with more capital, Vail Resorts looked to further add to its destination market while maintaining its day-use customers.

Worried that the merger would negatively affect the city's budget, the City and County of Denver, owner of Winter Park Ski Resort, filed a thirteen-page opposition letter with the U.S. Department of Justice. City officials requested the Justice Department nullify the merger, citing that the deal between Vail Resorts and Ralcorp would cost Denver roughly $2 million in annual payments from the nonprofit Winter Park Recreation Association (WPRA) that managed Winter Park Ski Resort for Denver. In 1994, Denver Mayor Wellington Webb sought to solve a shortfall within the city's budget by brokering a deal with the WPRA in which Winter Park operators would make annual payments of roughly $2 million to the city based on a formula of skier days, overall sales, and capital improvements.[17] The money was then used to fund the city's parks and recreation programs. City officials argued that the merger would threaten the WPRA's ability to make the annual payment. Formed in 1950 when Denver city officials realized that they could no longer operate the fast growing ski resort, the WPRA operated Winter Park like any other ski resort, except rather than turning its profits over to investors, the WPRA plowed any money made during the year back into the operation and maintenance of the ski resort.

Such an arrangement had worked well for both the city and the resort until the mid-1990s when the WPRA and Webb administration struck its deal, but left Grand County, home to Denver's ski resort, holding the bag when it came to paying for local services. As a nonprofit, the WPRA was not liable to pay county taxes. But as one of the county's largest tourist attractions, second only to Rocky Mountain National Park, and the largest employer in the area, the resort created significant financial strains for the rural county, particularly when it came to providing emergency services for the resort, road maintenance costs, and funding the local schools, which educated many of the children whose parents had moved to the county in order to work at the resort. When pressed on the issue of taxes and paying an equitable share of the costs of running the county's schools and other services, the resort often replied that it more than made up for such losses by bringing in tourists who in turn spent their money in the local restaurants, retail stores, and lodges. While certainly true, county and local government officials debated whether such spending offset the millions in lost potential tax revenues.

Hoping to gain $90,000 in the annual taxes it estimated the ski resort did not pay due to its status as a Denver city park, in 1985, Grand County brought the issue to the Colorado Board of Assessment Appeals. County officials argued that the ski resort had drifted so far from the city of Denver that it could no longer be considered a part of the city, especially after its announcement of its $60 million expansion, and thus should no longer enjoy its tax-exempt status. After hearing testimony from both the county and resort, the board sided with Grand County, ordering the WPRA to pay $50,000 in property taxes. While not the $90,000 they had hoped for, county officials were ecstatic. "Everybody that has testified has said the city and County of Denver has no control," Grand County's lawyer Jack DiCola said following the decision, "They conduct a commercial operation out there. We're not talking a museum here."[18] The decision set off another two years of appeals, finally reaching the U.S. District Court. The court disagreed with the county's argument, and reversed the lower court's decision, a crushing blow to the county's school district.[19] Meanwhile, Winter Park continued to grow in the decade following the court's ruling, adding 1,700 acres, a new on-mountain lodge, and six new chair lifts. Plans emerged on the future development of a base village. Both the expansions and the planned base development looked to further attract destination visitors rather than Winter Park's mainstay day-use clientele. But while Winter Park expanded, events along the Front Range would once again thrust the city-owned ski resort back into the political limelight, this time due to an unexpected challenge brought on by the construction of Denver's new airport.

Over budget, and already a year delayed, by 1994 Denver's new international airport had become a political boondoggle that threatened to end the political career of Denver's newly elected mayor Wellington Webb. Begun under former Denver Mayor Federico Peña, who would become Secretary of the Department of Transportation under President Bill Clinton, Denver International Airport was meant to be the most modern airport in the world, complete with three terminals connected via an underground train, expansive runways that would allow larger international aircrafts, and a revolutionary automated baggage handling system. But by 1991, construction cost overruns had ballooned to more than $5.3 billion, and the baggage system faced countless technical issues, causing Webb's office to temporarily reopen Denver's older Stapleton International Airport after all the furniture had been moved to the new airport.[20] In looking for solutions to shore up the city's budget in light of the soaring costs caused by the airport's delays, the mayor's office targeted its ski resort as a potential revenue source for the city. Under a 1979 agreement between Denver and the WPRA, the ski resort made annual payments of $7,000 to the city over a ninety-nine year lease period, despite the fact that the resort was making millions in profits. Webb argued that the city should be receiving a greater return and formed a small citizen's advisory committee to explore the best way to allow Winter Park to remain competitive and increase Denver's share of the profits.

After months of meetings, the advisory committee presented two options to the mayor for pulling more money out of Winter Park. The first was to simply sell the resort to a private buyer. A handful of the committee members argued that the city had no business running a resort sixty miles away, and, practically speaking, the city had no say in the operation of the resort. In a memo to the rest of the committee, member Medill Barnes underlined this fact, writing, "For all intents and purposes, Winter Park is operated as a private facility." Barnes pointed out the fact that the city had little oversight as to how the resort was operated, having no say in who sat on the WPRA board and no power to even audit the resort's books.[21] Besides this political hurdle, any potential sale of Winter Park would have to involve the deal with the Alberg Club, which still owned a large property between the Mary Jane and Winter Park base areas, in effect making any sale a "shotgun wedding from hell."[22] But following the public debacle over Denver International Airport, Webb stated that he did not want to be remembered as the mayor who sold Winter Park. Instead, the city and WPRA agreed on a second solution. The resort would pay the city roughly $2 million a year, with the caveat that during years of poor snow or economic hardship the WPRA would not be liable for the payment. In exchange, Winter Park would remain under the auspices of the City and County of Denver. The agreement tied Denver's city parks budget to Winter Park's profits, making the city acutely interested in the potential impacts of Vail and Ralcorp's merger.

In response to Denver's failure to stop the merger, and looking to bolster its profits, Winter Park drastically cut its season pass prices to $200 for the coming winter season, starting a price war among Colorado's ski resorts. To many, even the most infrequent of skiers, the deal was too good to pass up. Season pass sales skyrocketed, soaring 68 percent over the prior winter season. The timing of the heavily discounted season passes could not have been better for the industry's image, which had been taking a beating over its perceived lack of affordability: lift ticket prices had risen from an average of $32.78 per day throughout the Rocky Mountain region in 1994 to $47.89 in 1998—a 46 percent increase in just four years.[23] While consumers grumbled about the price hike, ski industry insiders pointed out that actual profits dropped a net 10 percent during the same period, and that it was misleading to judge expenses primarily upon lift ticket prices.[24] But such arguments failed to convince consumers that they were getting as good a deal as in the past. Instead, the growing costs of lift tickets only reinforced the perception that downhill skiing was an overly expensive sport. As the authors of the 1999 National Ski Areas Association's End of Season Survey explained, "The ski industry has a reputation for being expensive based in large part on advertised ticket prices, yet actual prices paid by the consumer are considerably lower than retail window prices."[25] Despite the reality that few paid full price, the dramatic increase in ticket costs did take a larger bite out of customers' wallets, causing many to ski less or quit the sport altogether. Other costs such as meals, rentals, lodging, and transportation also skyrocketed. Three-dollar Cokes and seven-dollar hamburgers quickly became the standard in many ski resort cafeterias. Ski rentals for a family of four for a week could be as expensive as five hundred dollars. The industry attributed these price increases to the resorts' mounting operational costs, as they spent millions on capital improvements to compete in an increasingly tight market where every dollar counted in maximizing shareholders' profits.[26]

Even with increased revenues from improved season pass sales, Winter Park and other resorts struggled to compete with larger resorts, which attracted greater numbers of destination skiers. By 1999, it was apparent to all involved that Winter Park would not be able to remain competitive with mega-resort conglomerates such as Vail Resorts whose revenues included much more than ticket sales. After months of public hearings and closed-door meetings, an agreement was reached between the WPRA and the City to develop a village at the base of the resort. By that point, two massive lodges had already been constructed at the resort's base area, but Denver residents were in no political mood to foot the bill for further development at the resort. Winter Park did not garner any further good will with the public when it failed to meet its yearly payment to the city for a second time. Faced with the reality that their ski resort was no longer competitive, Denver city officials began looking for a new partner to manage it. After a yearlong search, the City announced its merger with Canadian-owned Intrawest to develop a base village and manage the city's ski resort.[27]

The deal between the City of Denver and Intrawest was one of the many acquisitions made by the Canadian corporation during the 1980s and 1990s. Begun as a real estate development firm in 1976, Intrawest purchased British Columbia's Blackcomb Ski Resort in 1984. By 1993, Intrawest was the largest ski resort owner in Canada, having purchased the Tremblant Ski Resort in Quebec and Panorama Mountain in British Columbia. The resort giant soon began looking outside of Canada, purchasing Copper Mountain in Colorado in 1996. The same year, Intrawest merged Blackcomb with neighboring Whistler Ski Resort, creating the largest ski resort in North America—spanning 8,100 acres across two mountains. Along with Vail Resorts, Inc., and the New England–based American Ski Company, Intrawest emerged as one of the "Big Three" ski resort conglomerates in North America. The three corporations enjoyed huge market shares in an increasingly competitive North American ski industry, providing large pools of capital from which to further develop and expand their resorts and making it difficult for small regional ski areas to compete.

Like Vail and Breckenridge during the 1960s, growing numbers of North American ski resorts began developing multimillion-dollar base villages by the 1990s. With hundreds of condominiums, ski and snowboard rental shops, bars, and restaurants all within walking distance of ski lifts, these postmodern alpine villages offered everything a visitor could want and more. While weekend condo and ski rentals provided millions in revenue, real estate sales produced astounding profits for resorts. Buyers spent as much as $579,000 for an 878-square-foot, two-bedroom slope side condominium in Winter Park's new village.[28] Resorts quickly realized that selling slope side condos for $500,000 was much more lucrative than selling lift tickets, even at $48 to $100 apiece. By 2000, it was difficult to find any ski resort that did not already have, or was not in the process of developing, a base village complete with lodging, coffee shops, boutique restaurants, bars, spas, and ski rental shops. While such development promised to increase ski resorts' revenues, it was still skiing and snowboarding that drew customers to the mountain. In order to attract more business, ski resorts needed to offer visitors more on-mountain facilities, especially more terrain.

In February 1994, Vail Ski Resort submitted a request to the Forest Service for approval to develop the Two Elks Roadless Area as originally outlined in its 1986 Master Plan. Lying south of Vail's China Bowl, the rolling Two Elks area included mellow north-facing slopes covered in lodgepole pine and aspen trees, making it ideal for intermediate-level skiing. Much of the area had been included in the ski resort's original 1962 permit, with the rest added after the 1986 environmental review of the Vail Master Plan. Vail's 1994 request began a two-and-a-half-year study by the Forest Service that resulted in the release of a Draft Environmental Impact Study (DEIS). Contained in two volumes, the Vail Category III Development DEIS was an exhaustive assessment of the potential environmental, economic, and social impacts of the proposed Category III development. The study proposed four options, labeled Alternatives A, B, C, and D. Alternative A proposed not developing the Two Elks area at all. Alternative B offered the development of only the Center Ridge section of the area in order to protect wildlife habitat. The Forest Service's preferred choice, known as Alternative C, was the development of all 885 acres of skiable terrain, 63 percent of which would be left "naturally open." Only one road would be allowed into the area to provide maintenance access for the top terminal of a high-speed ski lift. Alternative C also included the construction of two picnic decks, and two warming huts, three bridges crossing the Two Elks Creek, and a fourth over a tributary. Lastly, Alternative D proposed the full development of the area as outlined in the 1986 Master Development Plan.[29]

Released for public comment in November 1995, the DEIS immediately came under attack. The Forest Service held three public meetings pertaining to the draft statement and extended the comment period an extra thirty days to accommodate the hundreds of interested parties who wanted to voice their opinion on the proposed expansion. The vast majority of comments submitted to the Forest Service came from individuals rather than environmental organizations or government agencies. And of these, the majority opposed the expansion, attacking its perceived environmental impacts and the Forest Service's failure to account for the socio-economic costs the expansion would cause in the surrounding communities. One such commenter wrote, "Where are the impacts from decreased quality of life? Where are the impacts to communities other than Vail that must increase law enforcement and fire protection, and increase costs to communities due to turnover from the high cost of living?"[30] Such concerns were legitimate since any growth in the Vail Valley would have a ripple effect on surrounding communities—even as far as Leadville, some forty miles and two mountain passes away. But, in the words of WRNF Supervisor Martha Ketelle, such comments often failed to provide specific and practical concerns that fell within the scope of the DEIS, writing in the Category III Record of Decision, "This is unfortunate, because the comments that were the most useful were those which raise substantive concerns or questions about the contents of the Draft Supplement," which concerned these externalities.[31]

Public comments are an often-misunderstood component of the EIS process. Many who voice their opinion on the management of their public lands expect that if popular opinion opposes a proposed action by the government, it will be abandoned or at least modified to meet the majority's concerns. This is not the case. Rather, environmental impact statements merely ensure compliance with the law. Because of the way the environmental review process works, federal agencies such as the Forest Service are not required to alter or cancel proposals based on the majority view. Under the law, any agency conducting an EIS or EA simply has to gather comments on a draft version and respond only to those comments that it deems substantive to the decision at hand. What makes a comment substantive is often relative to the agency conducting the study, the confines of the alternatives within each EIS or EA, and, of course, politics. For most agencies, comments by fellow state and federal agencies, environmental organizations, and other experts on specific points of fact are deemed substantive, while comments voicing general support for or opposition to a proposed action are not. This reliance on expert comment is meant to ensure the best possible environmental outcome for any proposed federal project, but often infuriates the public who believe their voices are not being heard, further feeding the belief that federal agencies are conspiring with industry to develop public lands.

While disappointing to many, there are good reasons for not allowing public sentiment to determine land management. Public comments are meant to help ensure that no point of fact is overlooked in the decision-making process. If decided by popular will public lands may be over-exploited or over-restricted. Striking a balance between public need and environmental protection requires the federal government to sometimes ignore popular opinion. However, many environmentalists argue that it only makes sense to include all public input on decisions pertaining to the management of the public lands, regardless of where individuals live or how much they know about the specific technical and scientific issues at stake. Land management agencies agree that although allowing popular sentiment to decide land policy would be democratic, it is unrealistic and would cause what is already a cumbersome and highly contested process to become even more mired in political fighting. "That is why we go to court so much," stated Sierra Club legal director Pat Gallagher. In fact, the courts offer the only true means by which individuals and organizations can oppose, and even stop, proposed federal projects. While public comments often reflect the divergent views on public land management, they are not meant to empower citizens to affect policy. Instead, they are gathered simply to keep in compliance with federal law. Such was the case with the Forest Service's decision on Category III.

While the Forest Service viewed most comments as outside the scope of the Cat III study, the agency did give weight to input from the Colorado Department of Wildlife (CDOW), much of which also denounced the proposed expansion. The state agency attacked the Forest Service's scientific evidence, arguing that the Category III expansion would have wide-ranging negative environmental impacts, particularly on the elusive Canada lynx. In its forty-page review of the DEIS, CDOW biologists blasted the Forest Service, stating the draft lacked "citation of technical literature and supporting documentation for contentions relating to impacts." They also contended that the preparers of the document "not only failed to obtain past and ongoing studies but failed to contact wildlife professionals that have years of field work" in the area.[32] CDOW officials argued that the DEIS contained conclusions that ignored years of observation and wildlife studies and that the conclusions in the DEIS could not be accepted unless these were re-addressed in a scientifically credible manner. Among these conclusions was the impact of human development on wildlife habitat, specifically those of the area's lynx and elk populations.

Relations between the Forest Service and CDOW had long been strained over development of ski resorts. The Forest Service had failed to include

CDOW in making the 1986 Master Development Plan for Vail Ski Resort and the subsequent mitigation agreement with the ski resort regarding future expansion projects. Prior the 1991 sale of Vail Associates, the two agencies signed a memorandum of understanding in which they agreed to include each other in decisions of mutual concern. Yet, CDOW officials argued that the Forest Service ignored the memorandum when, before the release of the Category III DEIS, the federal agency informed the CDOW that no such study would be completed.[33] The Forest Service responded that the DEIS provided "an adequate foundation upon which to make an informed decision regarding the Cat III proposal."[34] But CDOW biologists had grave concerns over the status of the lynx. Roughly twice the size of a housecat, with large paws and a heavy coat, making them well suited for cold, mountainous climates, the Canada lynx became the symbol of the fight over the Vail expansion. Historically, the lynx's range stretched throughout much of North America, dipping as far south as the southern Colorado Rockies. That was until 1973, when hunters trapped the last known lynx in Colorado near Vail. "This puts the lynx as considerably more rare than, say, UFOs," wrote *Denver Post* columnist Al Knight in a December 1997 op-ed on the resort expansion.[35] CDOW district managers reported finding lynx tracks in the area in 1989, but no confirmed sightings of the enigmatic predator had occurred in more than three decades since the Forest Service signed off on the Category III expansion.[36]

The DEIS severely rankled many within CDOW, which had already listed the lynx as an endangered species within the state. The Forest Service and CDOW differed on whether the cat qualified as an endangered species as outlined by the Endangered Species Act. The U.S. Fish and Wildlife Service (FWS) initially declined to place the lynx on the endangered species list in 1994, due to a lack of sufficient information on the animal. In 1997, CDOW reintroduced several lynx in the southwest corner of the state with the hope that the lynx would eventually be placed on the endangered species list. Indeed, that year, the FWS reversed its decision and listed the lynx as a Species of Concern.[37] While not the status many Category III opponents had hoped for, the FWS's decision gave environmentalists hope that the Forest Service would change its mind on allowing the Category III to proceed. It did not. Arguing that few lynx existed in Colorado, Forest Service officials declared that the area was a questionable habitat for the cat and that the ski resort's development would cause no significant impact.[38] The decision enraged environmental groups, which sued the agency over its decision. Although the courts sided with the environmentalists and placed the lynx on the endangered species list in 1997, the listing was not enough to stop Vail's planned expansion due to the uncertainty of the animal's continued presence and the Forest Service's efforts in mitigating the expansion's impact on any lynx that might range in the area.[39]

Lynx were not the only wildlife impacted by the expansion. In 1995, wildlife biologists James Morrison, William de Vergie, William Alldredge, Eugene Byrne, and William Andree released the findings of their seven-year study of two elk herds on the Vail and Beaver Creek ski resorts. Beginning in 1988, Vail undertook the largest ski resort expansion to date with the development of its back bowls. Adding 1,902 acres of skiable terrain, the Tea Cup, China, and Siberia bowls more than doubled the resort's size. At the same time, Beaver Creek built the Trapper's Cabin lodge and a picnic area overlooking Mud Springs. The study compared the number of elk on both resorts before and after each development. Elk activity overall decreased 70 percent on Vail following the development of the back bowls. China Bowl, the most heavily impacted area, saw elk use decrease 96 percent. And while elk use had rebounded to 76 percent of predevelopment numbers by 1992, it recovered by only 44 percent in the China Bowl. "Although our data indicate a linear increase in use after development," warned the authors, "this increase in elk use may level off and never approach pre-development conditions."[40]

Elk migration out of the back bowls began a ripple effect. Unable to compete with the larger elk for food, deer moved farther down the mountains into the valleys, which were being developed into condominiums, strip malls, and second homes. Both deer and elk lost in this conflict between wildlife and development, often leading herds to stand starving alongside the interstate during the long winter months due to a lack of adequate habitat. Making matters worse, Interstate 70 bisected the Eagle River Valley, essentially corralling wildlife on one side or the other of the high-speed four-lane highway. Deer and elk attempting to cross the highway created immense dangers for both themselves and drivers. Biologists for the U.S. Department of Transportation estimated that in 1991, a heavy snow year, more than seven thousand deer were killed on Colorado highways. That number has only increased as more automobiles traveled on the nation's rural highways and interstates. Correspondingly, a study conducted by Montana State University for the Federal Highway Administration showed that accidents between automobiles and wildlife doubled between 1990 and 2004. Costs in vehicle damage, injury (of both human and animal), and property exceeded $15 million per year. The

Canada Lynx. Photograph courtesy Colorado Division of Wildlife.

majority of fatal accidents in Colorado involved deer and elk. To mitigate this problem, the Colorado Department of Transportation announced plans in 2008 to construct a wildlife bridge, that when completed will allow elk, deer, moose, mountain lion, and lynx to cross Interstate 70 safely.[41] As of 2012, the bridge remained uncompleted as wilderness advocates worked with the Colorado Department of Transportation, Federal Highway Administration, Colorado Division of Parks and Wildlife, the U.S. Fish and Wildlife Service, and the Forest Service in finding ideal locations over the interstate.

The segmentation of elk and deer habitat by highways and other development created another major dilemma. With less land to migrate through and forage on, both species of ungulates experienced significant decreases in population. This issue of population reduction became a major point of contention between the Forest Service and CDOW over the federal agency's interpretation of the Morrison report, which examined the potential impact of Vail's Category III expansion on the area's elk population. Citing the Morrison report, the Forest Service stated that "elk use returned to 76 percent of its pre-development means within the four years following implementation of the China Bowl development," and thus elk activity in the Category III area "should not be extrapolated to expect full recovery."[42] In their comments on the draft EIS, CDOW biologists strongly disagreed with the Forest Service's conclusion, pointing out that the elk population in China Bowl returned to only 44 percent of predevelopment levels. "We believe that the elk studies completed on-site in the last ten years show that elk use has remained less than 50 percent of pre-disturbance levels since short-term human precedence that included habitat alternation." The Forest Service responded that it had incorporated the Morrison report into its final EIS and believed that certain design modifications to the plan would minimize impacts on elk activity in the area.[43] The two agencies continued to differ in opinion on the impact of the development on the local elk herds, finding no resolution over the matter.

Prior to the Forest Service's final decision, an article in the November 1996 issue of *Denver Westword News* drew attention to the difficulties between the two agencies over the Category III expansion. When asked about the length of the state agency's exhaustive forty-page critique of the DEIS, Bill Andree, Vail district wildlife manager for CDOW, dryly answered, "That would indicate that we had some problems with it." The magazine cited internal Division of Wildlife e-mails, which questioned the science within the Forest Service's draft. In one particular case, CDOW wildlife management supervisor Rick Kahn wrote that the state agency believed that the Forest Service was "using some 'contrived logic' in their biological evaluation."[44] CDOW submitted two alternative plans that differed significantly from the Forest Service's Proposed Action by drastically lowering the level of development through changing the alignment of trails, reducing or eliminating development along both sides of Two Elks Creek, and reducing the size of the ski area permit boundary to fit the only developed area.[45] The state agency and Forest Service's public wrestling match over Cat III's impact on the local wildlife further fueled the divisive rhetoric over the expansion, increasing mistrust on all sides of the debate. Unfortunately, such debates had become typical concerning both the development of ski resorts and public land management throughout the West. However, the stakes had never been this high before; the frustration over the Vail development finally reached a head one early morning in the fall of 1998.

That hunting season would prove unforgettable for Dave and Ken Alt, Steven and David Gaal, and Neil Sebo. Having driven up the backside of Vail Ski Resort on the afternoon of October 18, the five men set up camp near the resort's Two Elks Lodge. Early the next morning, as flames quickly engulfed the lodge, turning the massive wood building into an inferno and lighting up the mountaintop, Dave Alt awoke to the sound of what he later described to journalist Daniel Glick as the sound of flapping plastic on an unfinished building.[46] Abruptly realizing that the sound was a fire and remembering that Sebo had decided to sleep in one of the resort's heated bathroom structures further up the mountain, Alt quickly roused the others. Hastily throwing on clothes and boots, the four men quickly set off up the mountain toward the glow of an enormous fire, where they found Sebo standing on the bathroom's deck in his long underwear staring in shock at the Two Elks Lodge now in flames. With their friend safe, the hunting party quickly dialed 911, setting off a flurry of activity in the Vail Valley below.

Alarms soon sounded in Vail's firehouse, but it being elk season most of the company was out hunting, leaving only a captain and two rookies on duty. The three men loaded the company fire engine and raced up the mountain toward the blaze. Meanwhile, throughout the Vail and Eagle Valley, phone calls were waking up those first responders either not on duty or off hunting. Among them was Vail firefighter Mark Mobley, who noticed the flames on top of the resort while making his way to the station after receiving the call. "There was a glow in the sky, and I thought that there must be one hell of a wild land fire." Thoughts of wild fire quickly evaporated when he entered the town of Vail and clearly saw structures ablaze all over the mountain. Arriving at the fire station, Mobley and two fellow firefighters loaded up the department's four-wheel drive pickup, and raced to the base of the resort. The three quickly overtook the engine truck at the lower operator's shack of the High Noon chairlift, which was now also burning. Unable to go any further up the mountain due to the heavy snows from the night before, the several-ton fire engine remained at the operator's shack, while Mobley and the others headed to the top of the resort in the four-wheel drive to scout the fire at the Two Elks Lodge. Once at the summit, they found the lodge completely engulfed in flames. "It was unreal," recalled Mobley, who took the only photograph of the blaze. When asked why he was the only one to take a picture of the inferno, he jokingly recalled, "I was the only one smart enough to bring a camera."[47] With no water and the engine stuck miles down the mountain, nothing could be done, so the three stood and watched as the lodge burned. And within an hour the Two Elks Lodge, along with four other buildings, laid in a smoldering ruin atop the resort's ridgeline.[48]

Hours later, The Vail Trail, Vail's local newspaper and the regional National Public Radio affiliate KUNC each received an e-mail purportedly sent by members of the extremist group the Earth Liberation Front (ELF) claiming responsibility for the fires. Citing the Forest Service's approval of Vail's Category III (Cat III) expansion, which environmentalists had long maintained would disturb the habitat of the endangered Canada lynx and an important migration route for elk in the region, the brief e-mail proclaimed "Putting profits ahead of Colorado's wildlife will not be tolerated," and advised skiers to choose other ski destinations "until Vail cancels its inexcusable plans for expansion."[49] The e-mail quickly set off its own firestorm as the media scrambled to identify the shadowy ELF and its motivations in causing nearly $12 million in damages and making Vail the most notorious victim of "eco-terrorism" in American history.

Meanwhile, the arsonists William Rodgers and Chelsea Dawn Gerlach had made their escape to Denver from the Vail Valley while the search for them was unfolding, stopping to e-mail their communiqué to local media outlets and twenty-eight-year-old Portland environmental and animal rights activist Craig Rosebraugh. Two days after the fire, Rosebraugh opened his e-mail inbox, scanned down the list of new messages, and immediately noticed one from an unofficial spokesman of the ELF. Rosebraugh was used to receiving unsigned notes in his mailbox claiming responsibility for the release of test animals from a lab, the vandalism of a McDonalds restaurant, or the arson of a government horse corral. But such actions were often local, and arguably limited, in scope. This e-mail claimed something much bigger. "When I opened it, my jaw dropped," wrote Rosebraugh. He had heard about the fires a few days earlier, but never thought that they were in any way connected with the ELF, until receiving the e-mail. "Without any further hesitation I began writing a press release and prepared to send out the message across the United States."[50] News quickly spread that a shadowy group of environmental extremists were claiming responsibility for the arsons, and with no

Two Elks Lodge ablaze on the morning of October 18, 1998. Photograph courtesy Mark W. Mobley, Vail Fire.

one to address questions to about the fires, ELF, or their agenda, Rosebraugh became, in the words of *New York Times Magazine*, the face of eco-terrorism.[51]

The Vail arsons quickly catapulted the radical fringe group into the national spotlight. Prior to the arsons, few Americans had even heard of the Earth Liberation Front. ELF was founded in 1992 in Brighton, England, by militant members of Earth First! who had become increasingly frustrated by what they perceived as the organization's move toward mainstream activism and who launched a campaign of violent sabotage across the English countryside, causing what they claimed to be £2 million in damages in a single year. Such an escalation in violence and property destruction marked a growing ideological and generational divide within the radical environmental movement at the beginning of the 1990s. No longer primarily concerned with the preservation of wilderness or shaping public policy, younger members of groups such as Earth First! focused on the impacts of globalization and capitalism on the world's environment. They also began questioning the effectiveness of civil disobedience and what many within the radical movement termed "ecotage" in stopping the development of natural areas and drawing attention to environmental issues, such as air and water pollution, logging of old growth forests, and the destruction of ecosystems. Their answer, as demonstrated in Great Britain, was to significantly escalate the use of violence and property damage in order to stop the corrosive effects of global free-market capitalism on the planet's ecosystem. "There's a philosophical jump between seeing violence as the last step to what we see should be the first. It is the only option, the first option," explained one anonymous ELF member in the 1993 autumn edition of *Earth First! The Radical Environmental Journal*.[52]

Earth First! and the ELF were not the first groups to shun the legal process and embrace vandalism and sabotage to further their environmental agenda. Beginning in the late 1960s, individuals such as Jim Phillips, more commonly known by his alias, The Fox, plugged sewers, capped smokestacks, dumped rotten fish in corporate offices, and vandalized countless corporate facilities in order to draw wider attention to the polluting of the Fox River as it flowed through Wisconsin and Illinois. In 1971, the group Environmental Action published the *Earth Tool Kit*, which argued that serious environmentalists must use civil disobedience and direct-action tactics that break laws in order to further needed political and social change. During the same period, the mysterious Arizona Phantom waged a two-year campaign of sabotage against the Peabody Coal Mining Company in northeast Arizona, which climaxed with the attempted blowing up of a slurry line, inspiring Edward Abbey's 1975 novel, *The Monkey Wrench Gang*, which introduced the term "monkey wrenching," or the use of sabotage to stop development, into the popular vernacular.[53] By the end of the decade, acts of sabotage against bulldozers, billboards, survey stakes, and logging operations became increasingly common throughout the United States. While individuals took these actions mostly because they were angry over the development of their backyard, larger international organizations such as Greenpeace emerged during the decade, promoting the use of direct action in halting global environmental destruction.[54]

But such groups remained outliers within the broader environmental movement as quality-of-life concerns continued to shape most Americans' views on the environment, swelling the ranks and the coffers of the country's largest environmental organizations. Known collectively as the Group of Ten, each became more professional and well funded, opening offices in Washington, D.C., and hiring large staffs to lobby federal legislators and agencies on issues such as wilderness, air pollution, and wildlife.[55] Leadership shifted away from longtime firebrands to more media-savvy political lobbyists who were more willing to compromise with federal agencies than fight against continued environmental degradation. The shift away from the movement's grass roots outraged longtime environmental activists, who grew increasingly frustrated with their inability to influence politics. At the same time, many industries and politicians continued to label the larger groups as extremist. None more so than Earth First!.

Within a decade of its formation in 1980, Earth First! chapters spread across the United States, Great Britain, Canada, and much of Europe, as well as Africa and Asia. The group's annual rendezvous attracted thousands of activists, concerned citizens, ranchers, and even federal employees. But its growing notoriety for its advocacy and use of direct action quickly gained the attention of the government, and federal law officials began targeting the group. In 1990, after a several-month FBI investigation codenamed THREM-CON, the federal law agency raided Earth First!'s leader David Foreman's Tucson, Arizona, home, arresting him for conspiring with four Earth First! members from Prescott to cut several support bolts off a ski lift tower at the Snowbowl Ski Area near Flagstaff and attempting to down a transmission tower that led from the Palo Verde Nuclear Generation Station.

The arrest of Foreman and the other members, along with the attempted murder of Earth First! members Judi Bari and Darryl Cherney via pipe bomb, chilled many within the organization. Older members began to question the effectiveness of monkey wrenching, creating a schism within the organization as younger members began calling for more aggressive tactics and a broader focus on not just wilderness but on capitalism and globalization. Arguments broke out over what constituted acts of violence versus acts of civil disobedience. Disgusted with the direction of the organization that he had helped create, Foreman cut his ties with the group and founded the Rewilding Institute, calling for the reintroduction of predators into the wild. Foreman's departure marked a generational shift within Earth First!. The organization remained committed to the use of direct action, but divisions over tactics remained as a small minority pushed for an escalation in the use of violence in order to bring real and measurable change.

Among the new generation of activists was fifteen-year-old Chelsea Gerlach. "When I saw that political and economic systems themselves were the problem, working within these systems began to feel not only ineffective but almost unethical," Gerlach explained on the reasons for her becoming a member of the ELF cell known as "The Family."[56] Raised in Oregon, she grew up reading her parents' Greenpeace and Earth First! journals. She attended her first Earth First! protest as a teenager, driving hundreds of miles to central Idaho to help stop the timber sale of one of the largest roadless areas in the United States. It was there that she met William Rodgers. More than a decade older than Gerlach, Rodgers had long been active as an environmental activist. His bookstore in Prescott, Arizona, had acted as a haunt for radical activists from throughout the West. The two quickly became fast friends, and Rodgers remained in touch with Gerlach as she headed off to Evergreen College in Olympia, Washington. Remaining active with the local Earth First! chapter, Gerlach grew discouraged with what she saw as the group's ineffectiveness. By the end of her freshman year, she wrote Rodgers of her frustrations and asked whether she should remain in school or seek another path. Rodgers wrote back, suggesting that she drop out of school and join him in a more radical type of activism. Gerlach did and joined Rodgers in forming the nucleus of "The Family," which also included Gerlach's boyfriend Stanislaus Meyerhoff, as well as activists Josephine Overaker and Rebecca Rubin.[57]

Just months prior to the arsons, she and Rodgers attempted to shoot out the lens of a naval telescope outside Flagstaff, but failed. Following the failed attempt at destroying the telescope, Gerlach returned to her small home outside Eugene, Oregon. In early October, Rodgers showed up at her door, asking Gerlach and Meyerhoff if they would be interested in taking on an ambitious project. Up until that point, Gerlach had only read a little about the controversial Vail ski resort expansion in Colorado and the failure of mainstream environmental groups to halt its construction. Rodgers convinced her and Meyerhoff that all legal and other options had been exhausted in stopping Vail from developing into the endangered lynx habitat. Fellow cell members Josephine Overaker and Rebecca Rubin soon joined, and the group began planning its attack on the Colorado ski resort. According to the FBI, the five then conspired in the Vail arson, with Meyerhoff and Rubin helping Rodgers and Gerlach purchase the materials and build the timers for the fire bombs used to set fire to eight buildings at Vail Ski Resort. The group split up before the arsons when Overaker and Rubin disagreed with Rodgers that the fires were possible. Meyerhoff lost his nerve the day before the operation when Gerlach's truck got stuck in the mud on the way to the top of the resort to scout out the area. The next morning Rodgers ignited the homemade incendiary bombs in the most infamous act of eco-terrorism in American history.

Eco-terrorism is a highly problematic term. Coined in the 1980s by Wise Use Movement leader Ron Arnold in order to portray all actions of environmental activists as subversive, by the late 1990s, the term took on a more sinister definition as the ELF and its sister organization, the Animal Liberation Front, began using arson as their primary means of protest. Prior to 2003, the FBI often categorized such actions as sabotage or the malicious destruction of property, linking only five acts of domestic terrorism to environmental activists. But in 2003, federal law enforcement retroactively identified twenty-one different acts by the ELF starting with the Vail arsons in 1998, making eco-terrorism the single largest domestic terrorist threat in the nation.[58] In his testimony before a congressional hearing committee in 2002, FBI Domestic Terrorism Chief James Jarboe defined environmental terrorism for the committee as "the use or threatened use of violence of a criminal nature against innocent victims or property by an environmentally-oriented, subnational group for environmental-political reasons, or aimed at an audience beyond the target, often of a symbolic nature."[59] Such a wide-ranging definition, classifying the destruction of property as terrorism, particularly in a post 9/11 world, is debatable at best, and extremely biased toward industry at worst.

Those accused of eco-terrorism have long refuted the labeling of their actions as "terrorism." Indicted in 2006 for several counts of vandalism, including the Vail arsons, Gerlach contended that labeling her actions as terrorism "is stretching the bounds of creditability."[60] In his 2004 book, A Burning Rage of a Dying Planet, Rosebraugh attacked the labeling of ELF actions as acts of terrorism by writing, "This label (terrorism) was not used within the environmental movement itself, but rather by mainstream media, law enforcement, and politicians, who were acting deliberately to reduce public support and increase public condemnation of such acts."[61] Preferring the term "economic sabotage," ELF proponents contended that their actions were justified and that both the ELF and ALF went to tremendous lengths to ensure that no lives were put into harm's way. Those within federal law enforcement defended their categorizing of such crimes as terrorism by arguing that actions taken against the federal government with the direct intent to overthrow the government are legally acts of terrorism, even if no one is injured or killed.

"Terrorism is terrorism, no matter what the motive," FBI director Robert Mueller stated in a 2006 press conference announcing the indictment of eleven people for conspiracy involving seventeen attacks, including the Vail arsons.[62]

Yet, labeling groups such as the ELF as terrorist organizations is wholly consistent with federal law enforcement efforts of the past half-century. In 1956, the FBI began targeting organizations the federal government considered politically, socially, and economically subversive. Codenamed COINTELPRO, the fifteen-year long FBI investigation examined groups as diverse as the Weather Underground, Ku Klux Klan, and the Southern Christian Leadership Conference. The federal operation continued until 1971, when documents related to the program were leaked to the public after their theft from an FBI office in Media, Pennsylvania, by a group calling itself the Commission to Investigate the FBI. Public outcry led to a congressional investigation of the agency and the closing down of the program. The specter of COINTELPRO arose again in the late 1980s when the FBI's two-year investigation of Earth First! led to the arrest of several members of the organization. Dave Foreman still contends that the government's investigation and his subsequent arrest were part of a massive suppression effort of environmental groups by a government allied with business interests that wished to continue to exploit the nation's natural resources at the cost of ecological diversity. Whether such conspiracies are true or not remains unanswered, due in part to the FBI and the federal government's reluctance to engage in such debates.[63]

After six years of searching, the FBI had made little headway on the Vail arson case. During that period, ELF members claimed responsibility for a string of arsons across the West. Frustrated by its inability to capture the culprits of these crimes, as well as the increasing brazenness of the arsons, in 2004 the FBI merged seven separate investigations into alleged actions by the ELF. Designated Operation Backfire, the wide-ranging investigation targeted "The Family." The FBI charged that members of the cell were responsible for $40 million in damages over a five-year span, including the Vail arsons. Among the first members of The Family arrested by FBI investigators was William Rodgers. Captured on December 16, 2005, Rodgers was found dead in his holding cell six days later, an apparent suicide. Along with Rodgers, the FBI indicted four other members of the ELF cell, including Gerlach, Meyerhoff, Overaker, and Rubin. After months of refusing to cooperate with authorities, Gerlach finally relented and agreed to a plea bargain; Meyerhoff was convicted in the conspiracy to set the Vail arsons and was sentenced to thirteen years in prison; Overaker and Rubin remain at large. The FBI believes both live somewhere outside the United States.[64]

Lost in the din of the arsons and their aftermath, the appeal of the Vail Category III decision slowly made its way to the U.S. 10th Circuit Court of Appeals. In August 1999, nearly a year after the arsons, the court rejected the appeal, ending any hopes environmentalists had of halting the expansion. A small band of protesters kept heavy equipment from entering the Two Elks Area for a few days, but even that failed to attract the level of attention environmentalists needed to stop Category III.[65] Resigned to Vail's victory, local Sierra Club representative Kevin Knapmiller told *Outside Magazine*, "I guess that I am a fundamentally legalistic kind of person who believes in the country and the laws it is based on. For whatever reason Vail won this one. They went through the process, jumped the hurdles, and won. That's that. You play the game, and if you lose, you have to accept it, I guess all we can do is hope that the skiing will be good."[66]

In the end, the arsons proved more harmful than helpful in halting the Cat III expansion; the sprawling ski resort transformed in the public's eye from greedy corporation to tragic victim overnight. Environmental organizations quickly tried to distance themselves from the ELF, but the damage was done. Interviewed immediately following the blazes, executive director of the Colorado Wildlife Federation Diane Gansauer predicted that the fires would "make it harder ultimately to protect endangered wildlife, because people begin to associate protecting wildlife with extremism."[67] Rocky Smith, the former staff ecologist for the Colorado Environmental Coalition, agreed, stating that the ELF's actions hurt the local environmental organizations' efforts by making the ski resort a victim rather than a culprit in the destruction of critical habitat.[68] By using violence, the ELF lost the moral high ground in the debate over the protection of the environment. But advocates of direct action continued to contend that moral arguments often failed to halt environmentally destructive behaviors and that the use of tactics such as arson is justified in stopping the destruction of the environment.

But as the majority of the media focused on the ELF, and the FBI's claims of terrorism, some shifted their attention toward the ski resort's proposed expansion into the Two Elks Roadless Area and the controversy surrounding it. While arguments over wildlife, watershed protection, and real estate framed the debate over Vail's expansion, many of the expansion's opponents questioned why the nation's largest ski resort needed to expand at all. Stretching over 5,000 acres, Vail remained the largest ski resort in the country, and second in North America only to British Columbia's Whistler Blackcomb. "It would take a week to ski all the runs on Vail now," Earthjustice lawyer Ted Zukoski told the *Wall Street Journal*, arguing that the resort was more than large enough to accommodate the thousands of skiers and snowboarders who hit its slopes every winter.[69] Vail remained among Colorado's most popular destination ski resorts, hosting on average 1.6 million skier visits a year, nearly a half-million more than its next-largest rival, Breckenridge. Adding the fact that Vail Resorts, owners of Vail, also owned and operated three other ski resorts in the state—Beaver Creek, Breckenridge, and Keystone, giving the corporate giant control of over 40 percent of the Colorado skier market—Cat III's opponents contended that the expansion was the continuation of a larger trend within the ski industry of excessive and unnecessary development meant not to meet increasing public demand, but rather to bolster ski resorts' earning sheets. Both the industry and the agency continued to deny such allegations.[70]

The arsons cost Vail more than $12 million in damages and $13 million in lost revenues over the next season. Even with such losses, in December 2000, Vail opened Pete's Express Lift, completing the construction of Blue Sky Basin and putting the years of controversy and protest to rest. The new lift opened access to Pete's Bowl, named after the resort's cofounder, Pete Seibert. Blue Sky Basin's trails, which meandered through glades of aspen and lodgepole pine, gave skiers and snowboarders the feeling of backcountry skiing without the inherent risk of skiing out of bounds, a popular concept in an industry looking to attract a growing number of skiers drawn to the less restrictive backcountry. A new Two Elks Lodge opened that same season, with an additional 5,000 square feet of space added to the original design. The same winter that Vail opened Pete's Bowl and the new Two Elks Lodge, *Ski Magazine*'s readers ranked Vail as the best ski resort in North America, a direct outcome of the opening of Blue Sky Basin. Vail Resorts, Inc. reported a $77.3 million increase in revenues, and Vail remained among the most popular ski resorts in North America, enjoying a 2.5 percent increase in ski visits during the 1999–2000 season.[71]

As for the Canada lynx, in 1999 State Division of Wildlife biologists released ninety-six cats into the state's southern San Juan Mountains in efforts to reintroduce the predator to the state. Funded in part by Vail Resorts, the

Back Bowls of Vail Ski Resort. Photograph by Jack Affleck/courtesy Vail Resorts, Inc.

reintroduction quickly received criticism when the majority of the animals died due to starvation. Attacked for rushing reintroduction and failing to research on whether the region contained enough prey, CDOW scrambled to fend off what quickly became a public relations nightmare. A year later, the state agency, along with the help of the Forest Service and U.S. Fish and Wildlife Service, changed its release practices and the number and health of lynx in the region quickly rose; by 2006 there were 255 Canada lynx reported in the state. The ski industry's support of the reintroduction stemmed in part from Vail resort's experiences and in part from fears that the federal government would list the lynx as endangered under the powerful Endangered Species Act, a move that would potentially halt further resort expansions throughout Colorado.[72]

That same year Vail Resorts' board of directors decided not to exercise its option on the 5,000-acre Gillman tract that lay adjacent to the proposed Cat III expansion, which the resort giant had sought to develop with condominiums in a bid to recoup some of its losses. Turkey Creek, LLC, Vail's partner in the prepossessed development of the land, filed suit claiming that Vail's failure to aggressively pursue the development was a breach of their 1992 contract. The court agreed, and, in 2003, found in favor of Turkey Creek, forcing Vail Resorts to forfeit its $4.5 million investment in the property. Two years later the Ginn Company, a golf resort and real estate development company, bought the land for $32.75 million and announced its plans to build up to 1,700 homes, a gondola connecting the area to the backside of Vail Resort, and a private ski area for residents. Several hurdles remained in the way of the Gillman tract's development, the most significant being the listing of 500 acres within the area on the Superfund National Priority List, a result of the millions of tons of mine tailings that remained on the property. In 2008, the town of Minturn annexed the property after reaching an agreement with the development company in which the town would receive $6 million in tax revenues as well as a new wastewater facility. Town residents will also be able to purchase a season's pass for the private ski area for a mere $50. It remains to be seen if the new resort, in combination with Blue Sky Basin, will lead to the development of the small rural community hidden among the sprawling I-70 corridor.[73]

EPILOGUE

Located just an hour's drive west of Colorado's booming Front Range, the White River National Forest (WRNF) has been the very model of a modern forest. Established in 1891 as the White Plateau Timber Reserve, the forest's 2.3 million acres stretch over nine different Colorado counties and include 800,000 acres of wilderness and one of the nation's largest elk herds. The WRNF is also among the most visited national forests in the country, hosting upwards of 9 million hunters, fishers, hikers, mountain bikers, backcountry skiers and snowboarders, snowmobilers, campers, and picnickers every year. Home to half of Colorado's two dozen ski resorts, the forest is also the geographic heart of Colorado's ski country. The thriving tourist economies of Summit, Eagle, and Pitkin counties, all three of which reside within the WRNF, rely heavily on skiing and ski resorts. Linked to the Front Range metropolitan area by the increasingly gridlocked Interstate 70, in 2002 winter tourism supported roughly 27 percent of all employment in these three counties, with second home construction and spending and other ski-related activities providing an additional 38 percent. In all, tourism and construction—both the economic outgrowths of Colorado's ski industry—produced $5.3 billion in revenues in the three mountain counties. Such numbers underline the reality that skiing, and the real estate sales it helps drive, are big business in the WRNF. It was for this simple reason that the release of the Draft White River National Forest Plan to the public in 1999 immediately fell into controversy.[1]

Meant to revise the WRNF's fifteen-year-old master plan, the Draft Plan offered six alternatives, varying from no action to a comprehensive overhaul of recreational and extractive use within the forest. Seeking to fulfill the Clinton Administration's desire to strike a greater balance between human use and the conservation of physical and biological resources, the White River's preferred plan, labeled Alternative D, emphasized wildlife habitat protection and conservation over both extraction and recreation by greatly limiting future recreational development throughout the forest.[2] Under Alternative D, White River officials hoped to reduce the impact of recreationalists within the national forest by constricting where and how far hikers, bikers, and snow-mobilers could venture into the forest's popular backcountry. Moreover, the favored plan sought to restrict the potential future expansion of all ski resorts within the forest to their already established permit boundaries. Environmental groups applauded the Forest Service's efforts to address recreation's negative impacts on the nation's public lands. Meanwhile, recreational groups, politicians, and ski resorts, dismayed over Alternative D's restrictive language, countered that the agency's preferred option ran counter to its multiple-use mandate and would cripple local economies.

In an interview on the PBS television news program *News Hour with Jim Lehrer*, WRNF Supervisor Martha Ketelle responded to such criticisms by stating,

> In 1984, we had five million visitor days on the forest. In 1999, we had twelve million visitor days. And when we look at that [in] 2020 and we look at the population increases projected in Colorado, our counties in the Front Range, we can project twenty million visitors. So the question we have to ask is: Can we accommodate twenty million visits in 2020, or do we need to find a way to limit the visits that are being made?[3]

Ketelle's rhetorical question once again struck at the heart of the decades-long struggle over the Forest Service's management of recreation, especially ski resorts, in national forests throughout not just Colorado but the larger American West, pitting the region's tourism-reliant economy, along with the growth of rural communities driven in large part by the development of ski resorts and recreational tourism, against an environmental ethos that questioned the impact of ski resorts, off-road vehicles, and even backcountry use on fragile mountain ecosystems.

The most vocal opposition to the WRNF's plan came from Vail Resorts, owners of four of the state's largest ski resorts. The corporate giant asserted that the Forest Service's plan was too restrictive and would lead to future financial difficulties for all ski resorts within the national forest. Under the existing management plan written in 1985, resorts retained the ability to expand far beyond their permit boundaries in order to meet any potential future demand. Now, the Forest Service was seeking to emphasize biodiversity over recreational use by revoking this ability and confining resorts to their current permit boundaries. The ski industry argued that such restrictions flew in the face of growing demand and the possible future need for ski resorts to increase capacity. Vail Resorts' spokesman Paul Witt summed up the company's criticisms of the proposed restrictions best by stating, "It's puzzling. You know, the Forest Service acknowledges that there is going to be growth in the use of the forest. There'll be growth in the number of skiers coming to use the forest, and yet with Alternative D, they're not going to be planning for that future growth," he argued. "They'll be to a great extent handcuffing us in ways that we'll be able to deal with that growth."[4] Without the flexibility to meet future demand, the ski industry argued, ski resorts would soon be overcrowded, pushing skiers—and their pocketbooks—toward other resorts. Conversely, environmental groups saw the shift in policy as a significant stride towards a more balanced management of the national forest. "It's a giant step forward. You've got to compliment the Forest Service. I didn't think they had it in them," said Jasper Carlton, executive director of the Biodiversity Legal Foundation.[5] Vera Smith, public lands director for the Colorado Mountain Club, agreed: "They're [The Forest Service] playing catch up. They're not doing anything radical. They're doing what they should have been doing all along."[6] Groups like the Colorado Mountain Club and Biodiversity Legal Foundation pointed to the increase in wilderness in each of the plan's four alternatives as a positive step and applauded the proposed restriction of recreational access for ATV users, mountain bikers, and even backcountry skiers in order to protect wildlife habitat.

Environmentalists particularly liked the Forest Service's attempts to limit future ski resort expansions. Such expansions, many conservationists argued, were more about real estate sales than skier days. "It's the real estate market for second homes that is really driving the ski industry," said Kevin Knapmiller, president of the Blue River chapter of the Sierra Club. "Why should the Forest Service be a partner in jacking up the price of adjacent private land?" he asked, echoing conservation groups' long-running complaint on the relationship between the Forest Service and the ski industry.[7]

Following the draft plan's release, the WRNF's administrative offices in Glenwood Springs were deluged with letters, the majority of which opposed the closure of their favorite playgrounds. Recreational advocacy organizations such as the International Mountain Biking Association, the BlueRibbon Coalition, and the Colorado Snowmobile Association attacked the agency's proposed restrictions to recreational access as being excessive and without any scientific backing. In an interview on the controversy surrounding the management plan, Jerry Abboud, executive director of the Colorado Off-Highway Vehicle Coalition, told High Country News, "We believe that the plan is overly restrictive, is based upon inadequate site-specific analysis, and potentially is going to have a severe economic impact on not only the White River itself, but statewide." Colorado's third district congressional representative and chair of the House Subcommittee on Forests and Forest Health Scott McInnis contended that the Forest Service's plan would turn the WRNF into "a tree museum without visitors."[8] Calling for a compromise, McInnis released his own plan, which sought to relax the restrictions on future ski resort expansions. Ketelle replied that the WRNF was open to compromise, but maintained that curbing recreation's impact on the environment was crucial.

In the end, no one was completely satisfied with the final version of the plan. As environmental groups had feared, many of the restrictions on ski resort growth were removed from the final draft. Rather than restrict ski resort growth, WRNF officials chose a "blended alternative" that permitted much of the recreational development Alternative D had sought to restrict.[9] The new plan did, however, add an additional 62,000 acres of wilderness, but it also increased summer motorized and winter nonmotorized access; opened 400,000 of the 600,000 roadless acres within the forest to logging; and eliminated a measure to assure minimum stream flows in 10 percent of the WRNF streams and rivers. Perhaps most galling to supporters of the now dead Alternative D, the new plan allowed ski resorts in Summit and Eagle Counties to expand beyond their permit boundaries.[10] Environmentalists criticized the Forest Service's yielding to corporate interests, while ski resorts complained that the plan failed to provide the flexibility they needed in meeting future demand. "The fact that nobody thinks they got everything they wanted usually says we struck a good balance," concluded Ketelle on the release of the plan.[11] Neither side of the debate agreed with her assessment, each claiming that the Forest Service had once again caved to political pressures.

As the fight over the WRNF Master Plan demonstrated, the future of the Colorado ski industry will very likely mirror its past. For anyone stuck in weekend traffic along Interstate 70 during the winter months, it is apparent that the state's resorts remain as popular as ever, if not more so. Weekend traffic along Interstate 70 often gridlocks, with skiers taking three to four hours on the weekends to drive from the Front Range to resorts such as Keystone, Breckenridge, Copper, and Vail. While solutions ranging from the construction of a monorail to charging tolls have been suggested as ways to solve the congestion along the state's most important mountain corridor, none have found significant political backing. Realizing that the majority of their customers are concerned about the environment, most resorts have taken on campaigns to become more environmentally sensitive. Yet, controversies over resort expansions and real estate development remain as prevalent today as at any time in the past century. Proposed resort expansions at Breckenridge and Crested Butte have drawn the public's attention and environmentalists' ire, as each resort looks to further add to their bottom line by attracting more skiers and snowboarders. Expansion opponents continue to point out that such developments are unnecessary, that current resort capacity more than meets the public's demand. Such arguments are difficult to make, as Western destination ski resorts, most owned by corporate giants, continue to grow in popularity at the expense of smaller independently operated ski areas in the Midwest and Southeast.

However, while the majority of Colorado's ski resorts remain under the ownership of corporate giants, a handful of new, smaller ski areas opened in the first decade of the twenty-first century seeking to find a niche within the market. Outside the former mining town of Silverton, a single-lift-access ski area opened in 2002, offering guided skiing to some of the state's most rugged mountains. Owners Jen and Owen Brill's idea is to offer backcountry skiing to experts, an idea that seems to have struck a cord with many experienced skiers and snowboarders. On the opposite side of the spectrum, Echo Park, near the town of Evergreen, looks to attract Front Range skiers and snowboarders by offering cheap lift tickets, manmade snow, and night skiing all within thirty-five miles of downtown Denver. Built on the former site of Squaw Pass Ski Area, which closed in 1975, Echo Park offers limited terrain, but has become popular among Front Range families unwilling to face weekend traffic along I-70 and the ever-increasing expense of skiing for the entire family. Both ski areas hearken back to the sport's earlier days in Colorado, and so, perhaps, offer just a small glimpse into skiing's future. But despite the success of these smaller operations, Colorado's larger corporate-owned ski resorts remain the dominant economic and political force within the state's, if not the nation's, ski industry.

In response to growing criticisms over the ski industry's failure to confront mounting environmental concerns, the National Ski Areas Association (NSAA), to which the majority of Colorado resorts belonged, launched its Sustainable Slopes Program (SSP) in 2000. "As an industry, we need to apply the same vision and pioneering spirit of our founders," wrote NSAA president Michael Barry in the SSP Charter. "It is not enough to simply provide opportunities for fun and recreation; we must also be a part of the solution."[12] A voluntary program, the SSP set out to change the industry's increasingly tarnished environmental image by creating a framework of environmental principles, including sustainable planning, optimal water use, and reduction of greenhouse gases. Environmental advocates attacked the program as little more than "green washing," pointing to the SSP's voluntary basis and failure to address issues such as continued resort expansion, growth, and habitat fragmentation. Dissatisfied with the SSP, a coalition of western environmental organizations, including Colorado Wild, the Colorado Environmental Coalition, and the Utah-based Save Our Canyons, formed the Ski Area Citizens' Coalition (SACC) to draw greater attention to the environmental issues surrounding the ski industry they believed important. The coalition began releasing an annual environmental report card, grading ski resorts in eleven western states and Canada on criteria such as real estate development and snow making. Vail Resorts often receives a score of 50 percent, or a C grade under the coalition's rubric, while fellow WRNF resort Aspen Mountain scores well into the 90th percentile.[13]

In 2004, George Washington University professor Jorge Rivera and University of Denver professor Peter deLeon investigated the effectiveness of the SSP. Publishing their results in The Policy Studies Journal, the two concluded the voluntary nature of the SSP proved problematic, as there were no consequences for ski resorts if they failed to meet the standards set by the program. In addition, those ski areas involved in the SSP were more likely to have lower third-party environmental performance ratings.[14] The NSAA attacked criticisms of its SSP by both the SACC and the Rivera and deLeon study as flawed and unwarranted. By Rivera and deLeon's own admittance, the original study of the SSP held three flaws—it was preliminary in nature, it lacked clear causality between hypothesis and conclusion, and it used a subjective method for measuring the environmental performance of ski resorts. It was to this last point that the NSAA most forcefully objected. The Rivera and deLeon study relied upon the SACC's report card, which measured a much different set of parameters than promoted by the SSP. "As an example, the SACC Scorecard barely accounts for energy efficiency programs, a cornerstone of the Sustainable Slopes Program," wrote Judy Dorset, founder and principal of the environment consulting firm The Brendle Group, in defense of the SSP in the NSAA's trade journal.[15] The "green washing" debate, argued Dorset, distracted from the importance of the SSP's actual goals of raising the collective environmental performance of the ski industry.

Two years after publishing their initial appraisal of the SSP, Rivera and deLeon, along with PhD student Charles Koerber, repeated their study and reached much the same conclusions as two years prior. Writing that, "Facing SSP's weak institutional mechanisms for preventing opportunistic behavior, it appears that once enrolled, ski areas may predominantly adopt natural resources conservation practices that are known to be easier and more visible for their customers (such as recycling) or those that offer immediate short-term benefits with relatively small investment such as energy and water conservation."[16] Such conclusions reinforced environmentalists' arguments that the SSP was little more than a marketing gambit to attract customers concerned over the environmental impacts of their activities. Other extractive industries have used similar tactics, including the natural gas and coal industries, in attempting to sell their industry to an American populace increasingly concerned about environmental issues. For ski resorts, appearing environmentally friendly was of particular importance in maintaining, and ideally increasing, skier and snowboarder numbers.

But by the 1999–2000 winter season, skier/snowboarder numbers nationwide flattened to an average of 52.4 million skier days per season nationally, leading many critics to once again argue that the expansion of ski resorts like Vail, Breckenridge, and Winter Park were unnecessary and ecologically irresponsible.[17] The number of skiers hitting the slopes began to flatten in the late 1970s, leading in part to the consolidation of the ski industry during the 1990s, when the overall number of ski resorts shrunk by one-third. However, snowboarding's arrival in the mid-1980s helped many resorts boost their ticket sales. The sport's rebellious image initially kept many resorts from allowing snowboarders on their mountains, but the promises of increased revenues along with the sport's mainstream appeal led to the majority of ski resorts allowing snowboarders onto the slopes by the early 1990s.[18]

Snowboarding's acceptance also demonstrates the industry's changing demographics. With the aging of the Baby Boomers, the very generation that helped turn the sport into a multibillion-dollar industry, skiing is slowly turning grey. By 2000, the average age of both skiers and snowboarders hitting the slopes was 34.8 years old, an increase of nearly three years in age since 1997. While the sport remains largely composed of 18- to 45-year-olds, the percentage of participants over the age of 45 increased by nearly 6 percent between the 1997–1998 season and the 1999–2000 winter season. Additionally, men generally outnumbered women by a three-to-two margin, and while such numbers seem to indicate a relative equality between the genders, women comprise the majority of first-time skiers and snowboarders, roughly 56 percent, but are only 24 percent of expert skiers.[19]

Perhaps more importantly than age, race remains a significant concern of many within the ski industry. In its annual national demographic study for 2000, the National Ski Areas Association pointed out the fact that 88 percent of skiers surveyed during the 2004–2005 ski season were white, a number that has remained rather static since the organization began keeping track of race in 1997.[20] According to the Outdoor Industry Foundation in 2004, only 15 percent of Hispanics nationwide either skied or snowboarded, this despite the fact that Hispanics are the single largest minority group within the West.[21] Similarly, both the U.S. Forest Service and the National Park Service have conducted several studies showing that up to 95 percent of visitors to both national forests and national parks are white.[22] What accounts for this disparity in use? As historian Annie Gilbert Coleman has pointed out, skiing has long been the province of mainly affluent white consumers, because of the "financial costs involved in taking a ski vacation, and the extent to which skiers are bombarded with images of whiteness."[23] But arguably, economic, cultural, and geographic factors play a far more important role in determining minority participation in skiing than practiced exclusion by the industry's selling skiing as a "white" sport. Skiing's northern European roots, along with the historic limited economic access to leisure time and travel by racial minorities better explains why the sport has remained largely a white pursuit throughout the twentieth century. Still, race remains a concern throughout the ski and outdoor recreation industries, both as a potential new market, and as a growing cultural and economic influence on the management of public lands.[24]

The issues of sustainability, race, gender, and age are all contributing factors to the debate over skier numbers and the industry's justification for further development. Environmental groups point to skiing's overall flattening of numbers as evidence that further ski resort development is unneeded: "In light of these events and the demographics of skiing, why do we hear the constant pleading for, and announcements of, new terrain expansions, new

luxurious amenities and new real estate developments? The industry is using our environment, our public lands and our communities to milk every
last drop out of the shrinking skiing public."[25] The result, organizations like
the SACC argue, will be the further destruction of fragile ecosystems and the
collapse of local economies. Others, such as University of Colorado business
professor and ski industry expert Charles Goeldner, disagree with such predictions. In 1991, he presented a paper at the Mountain Resort Development
conference in Vail in which he argued that while not experiencing the astro-
nomical growth numbers of the 1970s—numbers that reached 15 percent annually—the North American ski industry saw a healthy annual growth rate
of 4.3 percent. "I would argue that this was a fantastic performance. To get a
4.3 percent increase on 9.5 million skier visits means a numerical increase of
406,914. A number that far exceeds the 229,000 skier days recorded in Colorado during the 1958–1959 season," Goeldner argued.[26] In the two decades
following the 1980s, skier days increased from 11 million to 12.5 million skier
days per season in Colorado alone. So, while skier numbers have flattened
nationwide, they have grown tremendously at western destination resorts.[27]

However, the largest potential threat to the ski industry may not be stag-
nating numbers of skiers and snowboarders or decreasing real estate values,
but global climate change. In 2001, the United Nation's Intergovernmental
Panel on Climate Change (IPCC) released its third report on climate change.
The work of over one hundred scientists from around the world, the report
concluded that "human activities have increased the atmospheric concen-
trations of greenhouse gases and aerosols since the pre-industrial era." The
report also noted that the global average surface temperature had risen by
0.6 degrees centigrade during the twentieth century, and that the 1990s were
very likely the warmest decade in the instrumental record.[28] If continued unchecked, the report's authors warned of dire consequences for the planet's
climate and ecosystems and called for a significant reduction in greenhouse
emissions. But, like most of the environmental controversies during the late
twentieth century, global climate change has quickly become embroiled in political gamesmanship. Global warming critics such as Fred Singer, an emeri-
tus professor of environmental sciences at the University of Virginia who has
spent most of his career countering the scientific consensus on topics as diverse as secondhand smoke to acid rain, immediately called into question the
science behind the IPCC's conclusions, arguing that the group's report was

"a political statement" based on theoretical models that did not conform to existing scientific data. Despite scientific consensus that climate change is occurring and that it is being caused by human activities, such attacks have gained traction with a considerable segment of the American public uncertain about the issues, helping to create the impression that a "debate" exists over the reality of climate change. However, the real debate over global climate change is not scientific, but rather economic and thus political. Climate change opponents fear that any regulation seeking to slow or reduce global warming will hinder economic growth. Solutions such as cap-and-trade, a market-based approach to controlling carbon emissions, have attempted to balance the continued need to produce these emissions with the need to reduce them with little success, and the debate over climate change remains gridlocked at the beginning of the twenty-first century.[29]

Rather than opposing further regulations that seek to slow, or even lower, greenhouse emissions, the ski industry has embraced a proactive stance on climate change. In 2005, several ski resorts voiced their support of the Lieberman-McCain Climate Stewardship Act, which looked to cap greenhouse emissions of certain industrial sectors at 2000 levels. In its letter of support for the bill, the NSAA noted, "Scientific models suggest that as warming continues, we could experience decreasing snowpack, warmer nights, wetter shoulder seasons, and reduced weather predictability."[30] Each of these conditions would negatively impact ski resorts' bottom line. While the bill was defeated, its support by the ski industry demonstrated the industry's worries about the long-term implications of declining snowpack on its profitability. Furthermore, the NSAA's Sustainable Slopes Program touts the embrace of wind and solar power by some member resorts as a significant sign of the industry's commitment to environmental sustainability. Such concerns may sound self-serving to industry critics, but the ski industry's embrace of green technologies appeals to its customers, many of whom share the same environmental and social concerns. Whether these programs are a method to rebrand ski resorts as "green" or an honest attempt by the industry to reconcile its impacts on the environment, climate change has added a new, and important, wrinkle to the broader debate over the resort industry—one that promises to further complicate the management of ski resorts and the national forests on which they sit.

In a 1994 Pastoral Letter to his parishioners across Colorado's Western Slope, Archbishop of Denver J. Francis Stafford wrote,

Growth must be prudent, varied and sustainable. It is unfair and unrealistic to "lock up" so much of nature as to prevent the spread of economic activity. But all growth must be calibrated to remain in balance with nature. Human beings must act as stewards of the earth, rather than conquerors and extractors; we must develop a fraternal relationship with the environment . . . Reverence for creation, founded on self-restraint, stands in direct contrast to the past boom-and-bust cycles of Colorado's economy.[31]

Writing four years before the Vail arsons, Stafford identified the problematic relationship between preservation and exploitation of the Western Slope's natural resources, whether through mining or through the development of ever larger resorts, as the foremost challenge not only facing Colorado's Western Slope but also the greater American West. From the creation of the Denver Mountain Parks in the 1910s, to the state's boom in population and growth in the decades following World War II, the transformation of public lands—and the communities that depend upon them—has driven the region's remarkable growth throughout the latter half of the twentieth century. But as Stafford pointed out, such growth comes with both social and environmental costs. From the rejection of the 1976 Denver Winter Olympic Games and the decade-long battle over the development of Beaver Creek to the Vail arsons in 1998, the debate over those costs not only shaped Colorado's history during the latter half of the twentieth century, but also that of the American West as a whole. Throughout the region, downhill skiing, and more broadly outdoor recreation, remains one of the Forest Service's most difficult management challenges. The American public's love for skiing shows no signs of slowing down, and that in turn will continue to drive ski resorts to grow and expand, no doubt leading to future controversies over the environmental costs of developing private enterprises on public lands. And, of course, the Forest Service is positioned to once again be at the center of those controversies as the agency struggles to accommodate the ever-growing—and evolving—demands that come with managing our national forests.

NOTES

INTRODUCTION

1. McKenzie Funk, "Firestarter," *Outside*, September 2007, 105.

2. ELF communiqué, October 19, 1998, in Leslie James Pickering, *The Earth Liberation Front*, 1997–2002, 2nd ed. (Portland: Arissa Media Group, 2007), 13.

3. Al Knight, "Missing Lynx: Vail Plan Eases Way for Species," *Denver Post*, December 14, 1997; Dustin Solberg, "Locals Protest Vail Expansion," *High Country News*, March 30, 1998; Tony Perez-Giese, "The Missing Lynx," *Denver Westword News*, November 6, 1999.

4. While true nationally, skier numbers rose significantly in Colorado due to the ski industry's consolidation throughout the 1990s. See: National Ski Areas Association and RRC Associates, Inc., "Kottke National End of the Season Survey 1999/00 Final Report" (Lakewood, CO: National Ski Areas Association, August 2000).

5. Daniel Glick, *Powder Burn: Arson, Money, and Mystery on Vail Mountain* (New York: PublicAffairs, 2001), 35–46.

6. "Security Beefed Up at Ski Resort," *CBS News*, http://www.cbsnews.com/stories/1998/10/22/national/main20785.shtml.

7. James Brooke, "Suspicious Fires Shed a Light on Dark Grumblings in Vail," *New York Times*, October 21, 1998, A18.

8. Rocky Smith, former staff ecologist for the Colorado Environmental Coalition, interview by author, April 14, 2008.

9. Allen Best, "Vail Fires Outrage Community," *High Country News*, November 7, 1998.

10. Daniel Bell, *The Coming of the Post-Industrial Society: A Venture in Social Forecasting*, Special Anniversary Edition (New York: Basic Books, 1999), 14.

11. Hal K. Rothman, *Devil's Bargains: Tourism in the Twentieth-Century American West* (Lawrence: University Press of Kansas, 1998), 17; Thomas Michael Power, *Lost Landscapes and Failed Economies: The Search for a Value of Place* (Washington, DC: Island Press, 1996); William Wyckoff, "Postindustrial Butte," *Geographical Review* 85 (October, 1995): 478–96.

12. Charles Wilkinson, "Paradise Revised," in William E. Riebsame et al., eds., *Atlas of the New American West: Portrait of a Changing Region* (New York: W. W. Norton, 1997), 17.

13. Nationally, Colorado and California ski resorts rank one and two in skier numbers, followed by Utah, then Pennsylvania, Michigan, and Washington. "Kottke National End of the Season Survey," 5.

14. Chris Walsh, "State Ski Industry a Peak Producer," *Rocky Mountain News* (April 1, 2004).

15. Hal Clifford, *Downhill Slide: Why the Corporate Ski Industry Is Bad for Skiing, Ski Towns, and the Environment* (San Francisco: Sierra Club Books, 2002), 8.

16. Rothman, *Devil's Bargains*, 10; John Fry, *The Story of Modern Skiing* (Hanover, NH: University Press of New England, 2006), 303–6.

17. Charles Goeldner et al., *The Colorado Ski Industry: Highlights of the 1998–1999 Season* (Boulder: University of Colorado Graduate School of Business Administration, Business Research Division, 1999), 5; Charles Goeldner, "Skiing Trends in North America," in *Mountain Resort Development: Proceedings of the Vail Conference, April 18–21, 1991* (Burnaby, British Columbia: Simon Fraser University Centre for Tourism Policy and Research, 1991), 7–20.

1. A GATEWAY INTO THE MOUNTAINS

1. *Eagle Valley Enterprise*, "Making Denver City Beautiful," February 25, 1909. On Robert Speer and his role in the creation of Denver's mountain parks, see Lyle Dorsett, *The Queen City: A History of Denver* (Boulder, CO: Pruett Publishing, 1977), 121–86; William Wilson, *The City Beautiful Movement* (Baltimore: Johns Hopkins University Press, 1989), 234–53.

2. Warwick M. Downing, "How Denver Acquired Her Celebrated Mountain Parks: A Condensed History of the Building of America's Most Unique Park System," *Municipal Facts* (March–April 1931), 14.

3. See Denver Parks and Recreation Department Records, Boxes 27–30, Western History and Genealogy Department, Denver Public Library, Denver, Colorado.

4. "Travel in Mountain Parks Increased Heavily," *Denver Municipal Facts* (November 1918), 5.

5. On the Olmsted brothers, particularly Frederick Law Olmsted Jr., see Ethan Carr, *Wilderness by Design: Landscape Architecture and the National Park Service* (Lincoln: University of Nebraska Press, 1998), 68–69, 184; Charles Birnham and Robin Karson, *Pioneers of American Landscape Design* (New York: McGraw Hill, 2000), 13, 272.

6. Park Commission, Denver Colorado Mountain Parks, Report on Land Recommended for Acquirement to Accompany Plan Number 58, Olmsted Brothers, Brookline, MA, January 20, 1914, Denver Parks and Recreation Department Papers, Box 1, FF2, Western History and Genealogy Department, Denver Public Library, Denver, Colorado.

7. Henry Graves, "A Crisis in National Recreation," *American Forestry* (July 1920): 391–97.

8. Ibid., 391.

9. "Colorado Has Right Combination of Sun and Snow, Ski Tournaments Already Pave Way for Others," Colorado Arlberg Club Papers, Colorado Skiing: newspaper clippings, 1921, Box 12, FF28, Western History and Genealogy Collection, Denver Public Library, Denver, Colorado; Genesee Park Mountain Skii [*sic*] Club—construction of ski course, tournament: correspondence, Denver Parks and Recreation Department Records, Box 28, FF26, Western History and Genealogy Collection, Denver Public Library, Denver, Colorado.

10. Thanks to Seth Masia for explaining the difference between the Lilienfeld and Arlberg techniques. For more, see E. John B. Allen, "Mathias Zdarsky: The Father of Alpine Skiing," *Skiing Heritage*, http://www.skiinghistory.org/index.php/2011/09/mathias-zdarsky-father-of-alpine-skiing/.

11. Jack A. Benson, "Before Skiing Was Fun," *Western Historical Quarterly* (October 1977): 431–41; James Whiteside, *Colorado: A Sports History* (Boulder: University Press of Colorado, 1999), 91–99; Abbott Fay, *A History of Skiing in Colorado* (Montrose, CO: Western Reflections, 2003), 21–31; Annie Gilbert Coleman, *Ski Style: Sport and Culture in the Rockies* (Lawrence: University Press of Kansas, 2004), 13–40.

12. Joseph Arave, "The Forest Service Takes to the Slopes: The Birth of Utah's Ski Industry and the Role of the Forest Service," *Utah Historical Quarterly* (Fall 2002): 34–55.

13. Earl Pomeroy, *In Search of the Golden West: The Tourist in Western America* (Lincoln: University of Nebraska Press, 1957); John Sears, *Sacred Places: American Tourist Attractions in the Nineteenth Century* (Amherst: University of Massachusetts Press, 1999); Marguerite Shaffer, *See America First: Tourism and National Identity, 1880–1940* (Washington, DC: Smithsonian Institution Press, 2001); Cindy Aron, *Working at Play: A History of Vacations in the United States* (New York: Oxford University Press, 2001).

14. U.S. Congress, Transfer Act of 1905, 58th Cong. 3rd sess., 1905.

15. Samuel Hays, *Conservation and the Gospel of Efficiency: The Progressive Conservation Movement* (1959; repr., Pittsburgh: University of Pittsburgh Press, 1999), 71–73; Hal K. Rothman, "'A Regular Ding-Dong Fight': Agency Culture and Evolution in the

NPS-USFS Dispute, 1916–1937," *Western Historical Quarterly* 20 (May, 1989): 143–45; Robert Wolf, "National Forest Timber Sales and the Legacy of Gifford Pinchot: Managing a Forest and Making It Pay," in *American Forests: Nature, Culture, and Politics*, Char Miller, ed. (Lawrence: University Press of Kansas, 1997), 87–108; Harold Steen, *The U.S. Forest Service: A History* (Seattle: University of Washington Press, 2005), 76–78.

16. Frank Waugh, *Recreation Use on the National Forests* (Washington, DC: 1918), 26–27.

17. "National Forest Recreation Use, 1924–1996," U.S. Forest Service History http://www.foresthistory.org/ASPNET/policy/Recreation/RecreationVisitors.aspx; Graves, "A Crisis of National Recreation," 391–400; John Wilkinson and H. Michael Anderson, *Land Resource Planning in the National Forests* (Washington, DC: Island Press, 1987), 312–17; Steen, *U.S. Forest Service*, 113–22.

18. Mark Daniel Barringer, *Selling Yellowstone: Capitalism and the Construction of Nature* (Lawrence: University Press of Kansas, 2002).

19. Tom Quinn, *Public Lands and Private Recreation Enterprise: Policy Issues from a Historical Perspective* (Portland, OR: U.S. Department of Agriculture, Forest Service: Pacific Northwest Research Station, September 2002), 12; Paul Sutter, *Driven Wild: How the Fight against Automobiles Launched the Modern Wilderness Movement* (Seattle: University of Washington Press, 2002), 60–62; Carr, *Wilderness by Design*, 100–104.

20. E. A. Sherman, "The Forest Service and the Preservation of Natural Beauty," *Landscape Architecture* 6 (April, 1916): 115–19; E. A. Sherman, "Use of the National Forests of the West for Public Recreation," *Proceedings of the Society of the American Foresters* 11 (July 1916): 293–96; Rothman, "'Regular Ding-Dong Fight,'" 143–46; Sutter, *Driven Wild*, 60–64.

21. Tom Wolf, *Arthur Carhart: Wilderness Prophet* (Boulder: University of Colorado Press, 2008), 39–42; Andrew Kirk, *Collecting Nature: The American Environmental Movement and the Conservation Library* (Lawrence: University Press of Kansas, 2001), 25–27; Steen, *U.S. Forest Service*, 154–58.

22. Arthur Carhart, Recreational Engineer, "Preliminary Report Recreation Plan Mount Evans Area," 1919, Arthur H. Carhart Papers, Box 22, FF55, Western History and Genealogy Collection, Denver Public Library, Denver, Colorado.

23. Arthur Carhart, "Memorandum for Record, March 22, 1967," Arthur H. Carhart Papers, Box 22, FF55, Western History and Genealogy Collection, Denver Public Library, Denver, Colorado.

24. Carhart, "Preliminary Report Recreation Plan Mount Evans Area."

25. Arthur Carhart, "Memorandum: Uses, White River," February 1, 1920, Arthur

H. Carhart Papers, Box 22, FF9, Western History and Genealogy Collection, Denver Public Library, Denver, Colorado.

26. Sutter, *Driven Wild*, 59–60.

27. "Memorandum for Mr. Leopold," District 3, December 10, 1919, Arthur H. Carhart Papers, Box 8, FF9, Western History and Genealogy Collection, Denver Public Library, Denver, Colorado.

28. Aldo Leopold, "Wilderness and Its Place in Forest Recreational Policy," *Journal of Forest Policy* (November 1921): 718–21.

29. Leopold remained critical of recreation's impact on the environment, writing in 1938, "Barring love and war few enterprises are undertaken with such abandon, or by such diverse individuals, or with so paradoxical a mixture of appetite and altruism as that group of advocates known as outdoor recreation." Aldo Leopold, "Conservation Ethnic," in *A Sand County Almanac and Sketches Here and There*, 2nd ed. (London: Oxford University Press, 1968), 165.

30. Arthur Carhart, "Recreational Plan, San Isabel National Forest, 1920," Arthur Carhart Papers, Box 22, FF54, Western History and Genealogy Collection, Denver Public Library, Denver, Colorado.

31. Ibid.

32. Arthur Carhart, "Preliminary Report, Recreation Reconnaissance, Superior National Forest, Minnesota, 1919," Carhart Papers, Box 7, FF27, Western History and Genealogy Collection, Denver Public Library, Denver, Colorado.

33. Interview with Arthur Carhart, quoted in Donald Baldwin, *The Quiet Revolution: Grass Roots of Today's Wilderness Preservation Movement* (Boulder, CO: Pruett Publishing, 1972), 25.

34. Arthur Carhart, "Recreational Plans Superior National Forest, 1921," Arthur Carhart Papers, Box 7, FF29, Western History and Genealogy Collection, Denver Public Library, Denver, Colorado.

35. Arthur Carhart, "Denver's Greatest Manufacturing Plant," *Municipal Facts Monthly*, (September–October, 1921), 3.

36. Carhart, "Denver's Greatest Manufacturing Plant," 3–7.

37. Carhart, "Recreational Plans Superior National Forest."

38. Baldwin, *Quiet Revolution*, 114–24.

39. Andrew Kirk argues that Carhart's transformation from hunter to librarian reflects larger transformations of the American environmental movement and the complex relationship between man and nature. Correspondingly, Tom Wolf stresses Carhart's moderate approach to environmental issues of his day. Both assert Carhart's

contributions place him among the leading environmentalists of the mid-twentieth century. Kirk, *Collecting Nature*, 34–47; Wolf, *Arthur Carhart*, 265–70.

40. C. W. Buccholtz, *Rocky Mountain National Park: A History* (Boulder, CO: Colorado Associated University Press, 1983), http://www.nps.gov/history/history/online _books/romo/buchholtz/chap5.htm.

41. Robert Black, *Island in the Rockies: The Pioneer Era of Grand County* (Granby, CO: County Printer, 1969), 357–59.

42. Ibid., 343–47; Carl Abbott, Stephen Leonard, and Thomas J. Noel, *Colorado: A History of the Centennial State*, 4th ed. (Boulder: University Press of Colorado, 2005), 269–71.

43. Black, *Island in the Rockies*, 386.

44. "Ski Mecca for Nation Is Started: First Shelters on Berthoud Pass Begun by US Forest Service," Colorado Arlberg Club Papers: newspaper clippings 1932, Western History and Genealogy Department, Denver Public Library, Denver, Colorado.

45. Ward White, "Denverites Awaken to Berthoud Resources," *Rocky Mountain News*, December 19, 1937.

46. Denver Ski Patrol Ninth Annual Accident Report, 1946–1947, Charles Minot Dole Papers, Box 2, FF25, Western History and Genealogy Department, Denver Public Library, Denver, Colorado.

47. Colorado Arlberg Club BOD Minutes, newspaper clippings, December 9, 1929–November 8, 1946, Arlberg Club Papers, Box 1, FF9, Western History and Genealogy Department, Denver Public Library, Denver, Colorado.

48. Graeme McGowan to H. G. Hodges, secretary of Colorado Arlberg Club, March 24, 1936, Arlberg Club Papers, Box 1, FF6, Western History and Genealogy Department, Denver Public Library, Denver, Colorado.

49. Ibid.

50. Colorado Arlberg Club: Portal Resorts, Inc.: Lease agreement (original), articles of incorporation, notice of dissolution, annual report (copies), Arlberg Club Papers, Box 1, FF1, Western History and Genealogy Department, Denver Public Library, Denver, Colorado.

51. Denver Parks and Recreation Department Records, Mountain Parks—Winter Park, Box 29, FF10, Denver Parks and Recreation Department Records, Western History and Genealogy Department, Denver Public Library, Denver, Colorado; Coleman, *Ski Style*, 92–93; Tom Weir et al., *Winter Park: Colorado's Favorite for Fifty Years, 1940–1990* (Denver: Winter Park Recreation Association, 1989), 24–25.

52. Hugh Russell Fraser, "George Cranmer Serves His Native Denver Well," *Cervi's Rocky Mountain Journal*, March 19, 1958, 4.

53. On George Cranmer and his role in the creation of Winter Park Ski Area, see Dorsett, *Queen City*, 208–9; Coleman, *Ski Style*, 92–93.

54. Allen Peck, Regional Forester, to George Cranmer, August 10, 1939, Denver Parks and Recreation Department Papers, Box 29, FF10, Western History and Genealogy Department, Denver Public Library, Denver, Colorado.

55. The Colorado Mountain Club, *Trail and Timberline*, December 1938, George E. Cranmer Papers, Box 1, FF41, Western History and Genealogy Department, Denver Public Library, Denver, Colorado.

56. Jack Carberry, quoted in *Cervi's Rocky Mountain Journal*, March 19, 1958; George E. Cranmer Papers, Box 1, FF41, Western History and Genealogy Department, Denver Public Library, Denver, Colorado.

57. Senators Alva Adams and Ed Johnson, and Representative Lawrence Lewis successfully lobbied Interior Secretary Harold Ickes for a $9,000 WPA grant to begin construction of Winter Park in 1939. Memorandum, George Cranmer, January 5, 1939, George E. Cranmer Papers, Box 1, FF13, Western History and Genealogy Department, Denver Public Library, Denver, Colorado.

58. Marshall Sprague, "Denver's $600,000 Investment," *New York Times*, February 8, 1959; W. M. Jeffers to George Cranmer, August 10, 1938, George E. Cranmer Papers, Box 1, FF13, Western History and Genealogy Department, Denver Public Library, Denver, Colorado; Ralph Budd to George Cranmer, February 14, 1938, George E. Cranmer Papers, Box 1, FF13, Western History and Genealogy Department, Denver Public Library, Denver, Colorado.

59. Glenn G. Saunders to F. E. Wilson, February 24, 1942, George E. Cranmer Papers, Box 1, FF13, Western History and Genealogy Department, Denver Public Library, Denver, Colorado.

60. Gerald Nash, *The American West Transformed: The Impact of the Second World War* (Lincoln: University of Nebraska Press, 1985), 222.

2. GO BUILD IT ON THE MOUNTAIN

1. Winter Park 1947–1948 Season, Memorandum, George E. Cranmer Papers, Box 1, FF22, Western History and Genealogy Department, Denver Public Library, Denver, Colorado.

2. John W. Spencer, Regional Forester, to George Cranmer, May 27, 1947, George E. Cranmer Papers, Western History and Genealogy Department, Denver Public Library, Denver, Colorado.

3. Steve Bradley interview, Winter Park Marketing Files, Winter Park Ski Resort, Colorado.

4. Tom Weir et al., *Winter Park: Colorado's Favorite for Fifty Years, 1940–1990* (Denver: Winter Park Recreation Association, 1989), 28–29; Bradley interview; Winter Park: Ticket Prices, Ski Tow Improvements, Agreements, Contracts, Correspondence, Product, and Equipment Brochures, Denver Parks and Recreation Department Records, Box 30, FF12, Denver Public Library Western History and Genealogy Department, Denver, Colorado.

5. C. R. Goeldner et al., *The Colorado Ski Industry: Highlights of the 1998–1999 Season* (Boulder: University of Colorado Business Research Division, Graduate School of Business Administration), 5.

6. According to the Forest Service, a recreational visitor day is a reporting unit consisting of twelve visitor hours. Beginning in 1965 the definition and units of recreation use were changed to reflect better estimates and the passage of the Wilderness Act and the Land and Conservation Fund Act. National Forest Recreational Use, 1924–1996, Forest History Society, http://www.foresthistory.org/ASPNET/policy/Recreation/RecreationVisitors.aspx.

7. In addressing the Society of American Foresters 1947 annual meeting in Minneapolis, Minnesota, Spencer asserted, "Recreation is no longer a seasonal activity covering merely the summer visitors to the forests . . . As a logical consequence the national forests are rapidly becoming an important part of the nation's winter sports playgrounds, and recreation is now a year-long activity." John W. Spencer, "The Place of Recreation in the Multiple-Use Management of the National Forests," *Proceedings: Society of American Foresters Meeting, December 17–20, 1947* (Washington, DC: Society of American Foresters, 1948), 179.

8. On the Forest Service's response to postwar challenges, see John Sticker, "Recreation on the National Forest," *Annals of the American Academy of Political and Social Science* (September, 1957): 129–31; Dennis C. Le Master, *Decade of Change: The Remaking of the Forest Service Statutory Authority during the 1970s* (Westport, CT: Greenwood Press, 1984), 1–15; Harold Steen, *The U.S. Forest Service: A History* (Seattle: University of Washington Press, 2005), 297–307; Paul Hirt, *A Conspiracy of Optimism: Management of the National Forests Since World War Two* (Lincoln: University of Nebraska Press, 1994), 63–68.

9. Philip Jackson and Robert Kuhlken, *A Rediscovered Frontier: Land Use and Resource Issues in the New West* (Boulder, CO: Rowman & Littlefield, 2006), 66–67.

10. Paul Hauk, "A-Basin Ski Area Chronology" (Washington, DC: U.S. Department of Agriculture, Forest Service, 1979), Paul Hauk Papers, Box 2, Denver Public Library Western History and Genealogy Department, Denver, Colorado.

11. Charles Minot Dole, NSPS Arapahoe Basin (at Loveland Pass) Report and

Prospectus, Box 1, FF13, Charles Minot Dole Papers, Western History and Genealogy Department, Denver Public Library, Denver, Colorado.

12. John Spencer to Max Dercum, May 9, 1946, Lawrence Jump Papers, Arapahoe Basin U.S. Forest Service 1946–1949, Western History and Genealogy Department, Denver Public Library, Denver, Colorado.

13. U.S. Department of Agriculture, *Forest Service News Bulletin*, Sunday, May 18, 1947.

14. Lawrence Jump to Forest Supervisor William Fay, Arapahoe National Forest, January 26, 1950, Lawrence Jump Papers, Box 3, FF1, Western History and Genealogy Department, Denver Public Library, Denver, Colorado; Lawrence Jump to Forester Supervisor William Fay, April 2, 1951, Lawrence Jump Papers, Box 3, FF1, Western History and Genealogy Department, Denver Public Library, Denver, Colorado.

15. Lawrence Jump to Edward Cliff, June 6, 1951, Lawrence Jump Papers, Box 3, FF9, Western History and Genealogy Department, Denver Public Library, Denver, Colorado.

16. Edward Cliff to Lawrence Jump, July 6, 1951, Lawrence Jump Papers, Box 3, FF9, Western History and Genealogy Department, Denver Public Library, Denver, Colorado.

17. Countless ski areas have failed and were abandoned in Colorado. In the mid-1990s a group of ski history enthusiasts went about identifying nearly 150 "lost resorts" within the state. See http://coloradoskihistory.com/lostresorts.html.

18. Peter W. Seibert, *Vail: Triumph of a Dream* (Boulder, CO: Mountain Sports Press, 2000), 32–33.

19. Fred Smith, "Six Square Miles of Powder," *Sports Illustrated* (November 23, 1964), 52–62.

20. Perhaps the most famous of Vail's newest residents was President Gerald Ford, who first visited the resort in 1968. Quickly falling in love with both the majestic beauty of the surrounding mountains and the skiing, the former president spent several months of every year skiing and playing golf in the Vail area until his death.

21. Paul Hauk, "Chronology of Vail" (Washington, DC: U.S. Department of Agriculture, Forest Service, 1979), 4, Paul Hauk Papers, Box 2, Denver Public Library Western History and Genealogy Department, Denver, Colorado.

22. It is difficult to overstate the impacts of the 10th Mountain Division on the ski industry in America. In Colorado alone, three of the state's most popular ski resorts were opened by veterans of the famed division: Aspen, Arapahoe Basin, and Vail. Because of the division's impact much has been written on its history. See H. Benjamin Duke, Jr., "Skiing Soldiers to Skiing Entrepreneurs: Development of the Colorado Ski

Industry," manuscript, Earl E. Clark Papers, Series 1, National Association of 10th Mountain Division, Box 1, FF45, Denver Public Library Western History and Genealogy Department, Denver, Colorado; Hal Burton, *The Ski Troops* (New York: Simon and Schuster, 1971); Peter Shelton, *Climb to Conquer: The Untold Story of World War II's 10th Mountain Division Ski Troops* (New York: Scribner, 2003); Mckay Jenkins, *The Last Ridge: The Epic Story of America's First Mountain Soldiers and the Assault on Hitler's Europe* (New York: Random House, 2004); Annie Gilbert Coleman, *Ski Style: Sport and Culture in the Rockies* (Lawrence: University Press of Kansas, 2004), 104–105; Norma Tadlock Johnson, *Soldiers of the Mountains: The Story of the 10th Mountain Division of World War II* (New York: PublishAmerica, 2005); Charles J. Sanders, *The Boys of Winter: Life and Death in the U.S. Ski Troops during the Second World War* (Boulder: University Press of Colorado, 2005).

23. Seibert, *Vail*, 46–49; E. John B. Allen, *From Skisport to Skiing: One Hundred Years of an American Sport, 1840–1940* (Amherst: University of Massachusetts Press, 1993), 109–14.

24. A key mineral used in nuclear fission and the source of the United States' newfound global military supremacy, uranium remained in short supply following World War II. The creation of the Atomic Energy Commission in 1947 transferred atomic energy from military to civilian production and the nation's growing need for what was once considered a waste rock prompted hundreds of prospectors like Eaton to scour the Intermountain West with Geiger counters in the hopes of striking it rich. Raye Ringholz, *Uranium Frenzy: Boom and Bust on the Colorado Plateau* (New York: W. W. Norton, 1989), 4; Michael A. Amundson, *Yellowcake Towns: Uranium Mining Communities in the American West* (Boulder: University Press of Colorado, 2002), 19–28.

25. Seibert, *Vail*, 31–32; Dick Hauserman, *The Inventors of Vail* (Edwards, CO: Golden Peak Publishing, 2003), 19–20.

26. Hauserman, *Inventors of Vail*, 26.

27. Ibid., 29; *The Vail Project: Real Estate Development, 1960*. Vail Associates Papers, Box 1, Western History and Genealogy Department, Denver Public Library, Denver, Colorado.

28. Paul Hauk, Memo Mill Creek, Two Elk Creek Ski Area Proposal, September 4, 1957, Paul Hauk Papers, Box 2, Western History and Genealogy Department, Denver Public Library, Denver, Colorado.

29. "Forest Draw Ski Boom Plan," *Denver Post*, October 4, 1959.

30. Glen Robinson, *The Forest Service: A Study in Public Land Management* (Baltimore: Johns Hopkins University Press, 1975), 127–28; James Briggs, "Ski Resorts and National Forests: Rethinking Forest Service Management Practices for Recreational Use," *Boston College Environmental Affairs Law Review* 28 (2000): 94–95.

31. In the Matter of the Application of Earl V. Eaton and Peter W. Seibert for a Special Use Permit for the Vail Project in the White River National Forest Statement under Regulation A-10, U.S. Department of Agriculture, U.S. Forest Service, White River National Forest, Paul Hauk Papers, Box 2, Western History and Genealogy Department, Denver Public Library, Denver, Colorado.

32. E. H. Mason to Earl Eaton and Peter Seibert, May 28, 1959, Vail Associates Papers, Box 2, Western History and Genealogy Department, Denver Public Library, Denver, Colorado.

33. The Vail Corporation: Plans and Estimate, March 12, 1960, Vail Associates Papers, Box 1, Western History and Genealogy Department, Denver Public Library, Denver, Colorado.

34. Minutes of a special meeting of the Board of Directors of Vail Associates, Inc., December 27, 1965, Vail Associates Papers, Box 2, Western History and Genealogy Department, Denver Public Library, Denver, Colorado.

35. Paul Hauk, "Breckenridge Ski Area Chronology" (Washington, DC: U.S. Department of Agriculture, Forest Service, 1979), 2, Paul Hauk Papers, Box 2, Western History and Genealogy Department, Denver Public Library, Denver, Colorado; Carl Abbott, Stephen J. Leonard, and Thomas J. Noel, *Colorado: A History of the Centennial State*, 4th ed. (Boulder: University Press of Colorado, 2005), 334.

36. Abbott Fay, *A History of Skiing in Colorado* (Montrose, CO: Western Reflections, 2003), 9.

37. Hauk, "Breckenridge Ski Area Chronology," 2.

38. Henry Harrison, Chief, Division RLAM, by Robert Cardner, Memo, January 10, 1961, Breckenridge Ski Area Chronology, Paul Hauk Papers, Box 2, Western History and Genealogy Department, Denver Public Library, Denver, Colorado.

39. Paul Hauk, "Special Use Permits—Breckenridge Winter Sports Area and the Vail Corporation," Memorandum, January 17, 1961, Breckenridge Ski Area Chronology, Paul Hauk Papers, Box 2, Western History and Genealogy Department, Denver Public Library, Denver, Colorado.

40. New permit applicants were required at the time to provide letters of reference from neighboring permit holders. While seemingly counterintuitive, the idea was to demonstrate the viability of any potential new resort.

41. John Tweedy to Henry Tiedemann, February 9, 1961, Breckenridge Ski Area Chronology, Paul Hauk Papers, Box 2, Western History and Genealogy Department, Denver Public Library, Denver, Colorado.

42. Hauk, "Breckenridge Ski Area Chronology," 8.

43. Henry Harrison, "Special Use Permits—Breckenridge Winter Sports Area,"

Memo, June 23, 1961, Breckenridge Ski Area Chronology, Paul Hauk Papers, Box 2, Western History and Genealogy Department, Denver Public Library, Denver, Colorado.

44. Attendance jumped nearly tenfold from 17,000 skier days during the 1961–1962 winter season to over 165,000 by 1970.

45. Hauk, "Breckenridge Ski Area Chronology," 7–8.

46. On the story of Colorado's lobbying for the extension of Interstate 70 through the Rocky Mountains, see Thomas A. Thomas, "Roads to a Troubled Future: Transportation and Transformation in Colorado's Interstate Highway Corridors in the Nineteenth and Twentieth Century" (PhD diss., University of Colorado, Boulder, 1996), 185–242; William Philpott, "Consuming Colorado: Landscapes, Leisure, and the Tourist Way of Life" (PhD diss., University of Wisconsin–Madison, 2002), 165–219.

47. Thomas, "Roads to a Troubled Future," 236–42; Philpott, "Consuming Colorado," 188–90.

48. "Summary of the Facts Concerning the Red Buffalo Route on I-70 in Colorado," Governor's Office, PUC Correspondence, Various Projects, 1970–1971, Governor John E. Love Papers, Box 66772, Colorado State Archives, Denver, Colorado.

49. Colorado Department of Highways, *Interstate Highway Location Study Dotsero to Empire Junction*, E. Lionel Pavlo Engineering Company, March 1960, 10–23.

50. "Summary of the Facts Concerning the Red Buffalo Route on I-70 in Colorado," Governor's Office, PUC Correspondence, Various Projects, 1970–1971, Governor John E. Love Papers, Box 66772, Colorado State Archives, Denver, Colorado.

51. "I-70 to By-Pass High Country," *Summit County Journal*, September 30, 1966, Governor's Office, PUC Correspondence, Various Projects, 1970–1971, Governor John E. Love Papers, Box 66772, Colorado State Archives, Denver, Colorado.

52. Edward Emrich to Charles Shumate, Chief Engineer, Colorado Department of Highways, October 18, 1966, Governor's Office, PUC Correspondence, Various Projects, 1970–1971, Governor John E. Love Papers, Box 66772, Colorado State Archives, Denver, Colorado.

53. Town of Vail to Governor John E. Love, July 24, 1967, Governor's Office, PUC Correspondence, Various Projects, 1970–1971, Box 66772, Colorado State Archives, Denver, Colorado.

54. Chas Shumate, Chief Engineer, to Hon. Peter Dominick, U.S. Senator, July 19, 1967, Governor's Office, PUC Correspondence, Various Projects, 1970–1971, Governor John E. Love Papers, Box 66772, Colorado State Archives, Denver, Colorado.

55. William Cronon, "The Trouble with Wilderness; Or, Getting Back to the Wrong Nature," in William Cronon, ed. *Uncommon Ground: Rethinking the Human Place in Nature*

(New York: W. W. Norton, 1995), 69. On the early history of the wilderness debate, see Donald Baldwin, *The Quiet Revolution: The Grass Roots of Today's Wilderness Preservation Movement* (Boulder, CO: Pruett Publishing, 1972), 183–96; Samuel Hays, *Beauty, Health, and Permanence: Environmental Politics in the United States, 1955–1985* (Cambridge: Cambridge University Press, 1987), 118–19; Mark Harvey, *Wilderness Forever: Howard Zahniser and the Path to the Wilderness Act* (Seattle: University of Washington Press, 2007); Michael Johnson, *Hunger for the Wild: America's Obsession with the Untamed West* (Lawrence: University Press of Kansas, 2007); Sara Dant, "Making Wilderness Work: Frank Church and the American Wilderness," *Pacific Historical Review* 77 (May 2008): 237–72.

56. I want to thank Ralph Swain, Sara Dant, and Mark Harvey for helping untangle the story on the Wilderness Act's setting special conditions on the designation of the Gore Range–Eagle's Nest Primitive Area as wilderness. Wilderness Act of 1964, Public Law 88–577, 88th Congress, 2nd sess. (September 3, 1964), 2.

57. Charles Wilkinson, "Paradise Revised," in *Atlas of the New American West*, William E. Riebsame et al., ed. (New York: W. W. Norton, 1997), 17.

58. Wilderness Act of 1964, Public Law 88–577, 88th Congress, 2nd sess. (September 3, 1964), 1.

59. On the definition of wilderness through recreation, see Richard White, "'Are You an Environmentalist, or Do You Work for a Living?' Work and Nature," in *Uncommon Ground*, ed. Cronon, 171–85; Roderick Frazier Nash, *Wilderness and the American Mind*, 4th ed. (New Haven, CT: Yale University Press, 2001); Mark Daniel Barringer, *Selling Yellowstone: Capitalism and the Construction of Nature* (Lawrence: University Press of Kansas, 2002); Liza Nicholas, Elaine M. Bapis, and Thomas J. Harvey, eds., *Imagining the Big Open: Nature, Identity, and Play in the New West* (Salt Lake City: University of Utah Press, 2003); Paul S. Sutter, *Driven Wild: How the Fight against Automobiles Launched the Modern Wilderness Movement* (Seattle: University of Washington Press, 2004); Hal K. Rothman, *The New Urban Park: Golden Gate National Recreation Area and Civic Environmentalism* (Lawrence: University Press of Kansas, 2004); David Louter, *Windshield Wilderness: Cars, Roads, and Nature in Washington's National Parks* (Seattle: University of Washington Press, 2006).

60. Andrew Kirk, *Collecting Nature: The American Environmental Movement and the Conservation Library* (Lawrence: University Press of Kansas, 2001), 105; "Colorado Open Space Council," Box 2, Edward Hilliard Jr. Papers, Western History and Genealogy Department, Denver Public Library, Denver, Colorado.

61. Colorado Open Space Coordinating Council, Statement in Opposition to the Red Buffalo Tunnel through the Gore Range–Eagle's Nest Primitive Area at a Public

Hearing of the Colorado State Highway Commission, October 20, 1966, Colorado Environmental Coalition Papers, Box 35, FF10, Western History and Genealogy Department, Denver Public Library, Denver, Colorado.

62. Ibid.

63. "Summary of the Facts Concerning the Red Buffalo Route on I-70 in Colorado," Governor's Office, PUC Correspondence, Various Projects, 1970–1971, Governor John E. Love Papers, Box 66772, Colorado State Archives, Denver, Colorado.

64. Statement by Orville L. Freeman, Secretary of Agriculture, "Decision on the Request by the Colorado Department of Highways to Route Interstate Highway 70 through the Gore Range–Eagle's Nest Primitive Area, Arapaho and White River National Forests," 1968, Forest History Society, http://www.foresthistory.org/Research/usfscoll/policy/Wilderness/1968_I-70.html.

65. Colorado Department of Transportation, "Eisenhower Tunnel Traffic Counts," http://www.coloradodot.info/travel/eisenhower-tunnel/eisenhower-tunnel-traffic-counts.html.

66. Abbott, Leonard, and Noel, *Colorado: A History of the Centennial State*, 373–91.

3. RICH MAN'S GAMES, POOR MAN'S TAXES

1. Richard Olson, Director of Vail Associates, replaced Coors on the committee a year later.

2. James Whiteside, *Colorado: A Sports History* (Boulder: University Press of Colorado, 1999), 147; Laura Lee Katz Olson, "Power, Public Policy, and the Environment: The Defeat of the 1976 Winter Olympics in Colorado" (PhD diss., University of Colorado, 1974), 90–95.

3. Norman Brown quoted in Mark Foster, "Little Lies: The Colorado 1976 Winter Olympics," *Colorado Heritage* (Winter 1998): 28.

4. In a scathing article on the failure of the Denver Olympic Games published a year after their defeat, Ted Farwell, the DOC's technical director responsible for the planning, design, and development of all of the competition sites for the 1976 Games, explained the DOC's secretive nature by writing, "The public relations attitude of the DOC was 'say nothing.' Because if you answer you just dig yourself in deeper." Ted Farwell, "The Olympic Bubble," *Colorful Colorado* (January/February 1973), 26; Whiteside, *Colorado*, 157.

5. Vail/Beaver Creek Site Report, 1971. William McNichols Papers, Box 101, FF14, Western History and Genealogy Department, Denver Public Library, Denver, Colorado.

6. Stewart Udall, *The Quiet Crisis* (New York: Holt, Rinehart and Winston, 1963), xvii.

7. Hal K. Rothman, *Saving the Planet: The American Response to the Environment in the Twentieth Century* (Chicago: Ivan R. Dee, 2000), 113; Ted Steinberg, *Down to Earth: Nature's Role in American History* (New York: Oxford University Press, 2002), 240.

8. Lisa McGirr, *Suburban Warriors: The Origins of the New American Right* (Princeton, NJ: Princeton University Press, 2001), 212–15; Becky Nicolaides, *My Blue Heaven: Life and Politics in the Working-Class Suburbs of Los Angeles, 1920–1965* (Chicago: University of Chicago Press, 2002), 322–27; Lizabeth Cohen, *A Consumers' Republic: The Politics of Mass Consumption in Postwar America* (New York: Vintage Books, 2003), 347–63; Matthew Lassiter, *The Silent Majority: Suburban Politics in the Sunbelt South* (Princeton, NJ: Princeton University Press, 2006), 1–21; Mark Hamilton Lytle, *America's Uncivil Wars: The Sixties from Elvis to the Fall of Richard Nixon* (New York: Oxford University Press, 2006), 330–32; Rick Perlstein, *Nixonland: The Rise of a President and the Fracturing of America* (New York: Scribner, 2008), 460–61.

9. For more on the politics to preserve open space in opposition to suburban sprawl during the 1960s, see Adam Rome, *Bulldozer in the Countryside: Suburban Sprawl and the Rise of American Environmentalism* (New York: Cambridge University Press, 2001), 119–52.

10. Steinberg, *Down to Earth*, 250–52; Hal K. Rothman, *The Greening of a Nation?: Environmentalism in the United States since 1945* (Orlando: Harcourt Brace, 1998), 105–21.

11. Scholars have long equated quality-of-life issues with liberal politics. While I agree with these assertions, I argue that such labels as liberal and conservative obfuscate much broader concerns over pollution, air quality, open space, consumer goods, and other quality-of-life issues. See Carl Abbott, *How Cities Won the West: Four Centuries of Urban Change in Western North America* (Albuquerque: University of New Mexico Press, 2008), 205; Elizabeth Carney, "Suburbanizing Nature and Naturalizing Suburbanites: Outdoor-Living Culture and Landscapes of Growth," *Western Historical Quarterly* (Winter 2007): 480–81; Amy Scott, "Remaking Urban in the American West: Urban Environmentalism, Lifestyle Politics, and Hip Capitalism in Boulder, Colorado," in Jeff Roche, ed., *The Political Culture of the New West* (Lawrence: University Press of Kansas, 2008), 253–55; Karl Boyd Brooks, *Before Earth Day: The Origins of American Environmental Law* (Lawrence: University Press of Kansas, 2009), 120–22.

12. "I-70 to By-Pass High Country," *Summit County Journal*, September 30, 1966, Governor's Office, PUC Correspondence, Various Projects, 1970–1971, Governor John E. Love Papers, Box 66772, Colorado State Archives, Denver, Colorado; William Philpott, "Consuming Colorado: Landscapes, Leisure, and the Tourist Way of Life" (PhD diss., University of Wisconsin–Madison, 2002), 212–14.

13. U.S. Census Bureau, Decadal Census Counts, http://www.census.gov/popula tion/censusdata/urpop0090.txt.

14. Tom Gaven, quoted in Rick Reese, "The Denver Winter Olympic Controversy," in Presentation by Rick Reese to Salt Lake Winter Olympics Feasibility Study Committee, November 16, 1984, Western History and Genealogy Department, Denver Public Library Central Branch, Denver, Colorado.

15. Gary McGraw, former vice president of operations for Winter Park Ski Resort, interview by author, December, 2008.

16. Whiteside, *Colorado*, 146.

17. Farwell, "Olympic Bubble," 20; John E. Findling and Kimberly D. Pelle, eds., *Encyclopedia of the Modern Olympic Movement* (Westport, CT: Greenwood Press, 2004), 351.

18. Denver's organizing body changed three different times during its short history. First organized as the Denver Olympic Committee (DOC) it later became the Denver Organizing Committee (DOC) before finally restructuring into the Denver Olympic Organizing Committee (DOOC). *Rocky Mountain News*, April 4, 1971.

19. *Denver Post*, December 13, 1969.

20. Citizens for Colorado's Future, Records 1971–1972, Papers, Western History and Genealogy Collection, Denver Public Library, Denver, Colorado.

21. Ted Farwell, former technical advisor to the Denver Olympic Committee and owner of Winterstar Evaluations, Inc., interview by author, June 2010.

22. Douglas Looney, "'Bah!' . . . Say a Lot of Colorado Folks When Talk Turns to the Olympics," *National Observer*, February 19, 1972, 6.

23. Mark Foster, "Colorado's Defeat of the 1976 Winter Olympics," *Colorado Magazine* 53 (Spring 1976): 163–86, 170.

24. *Denver Post*, August 8, 1970.

25. *Rocky Mountain News*, October 25, 1970.

26. Lola Wright to John Love, September 2, 1970, Governor John E. Love Papers, Colorado State Archives, 1976 Olympics, Box 66339.

27. Mrs. John Steidl to John Love, August 31, 1970, Governor John E. Love Papers, Colorado State Archives, 1976 Olympics, Box 66339.

28. Lance Dittman to Senator Harry Locke, January 1971, Protect Our Mountain Home Collection, Papers, Colorado Historical Society Library, Denver, Colorado; Mark Foster, "Colorado's Defeat of the 1976 Winter Olympics," *Colorado Magazine* (Spring 1976): 173–76.

29. Sport Site Relocation, XII Olympic Winter Games, Denver Organizing Committee for the 1976 Winter Olympics, Papers, Western History and Genealogy Department, Denver Public Library, Denver, Colorado.

30. For more on the "Sell Colorado" campaign, see Governor John Love, "Sell Colorado Campaign," Governor's Office, Governor John E. Love Papers, Colorado State Archives, Box 66948.

31. CCF, bumper stickers, Files of CCF, Folder 4, Western History and Genealogy Department, Denver Public Library, Denver, Colorado; Olson, "Power, Public Policy, and the Environment," 30. David Wrobel notes that such anti-California statements stemmed from anxieties over the development and destruction of pristine landscapes and the eradication of simple and affordable lifestyles as wealthy Californians and others, notably Texans, migrated into western states such as Oregon and Colorado. Such sentiments illustrate the larger problem of westerness and a thematic construct, argues Wrobel, by bringing into question differing understandings of what it means to be "western." In response, locals often drew on their primacy in identifying newcomers, whom Hal Rothman termed neonatives, as the culprits in the destruction of what made such places unique. Such tensions continued throughout the twentieth century and often sat at the center of debates over growth in ski resort communities. David Wrobel, *Promised Lands: Promotion, Memory, and the Creation of the American West* (Lawrence: University Press of Kansas, 2002), 189–91; Hal K. Rothman, *Devil's Bargains: Tourism in the Twentieth-Century American West* (Lawrence: University Press of Kansas, 1998), 26.

32. John Denver, "Rocky Mountain High," RCA, 1972.

33. For local reactions to newcomers throughout the American West during the late twentieth century, see Peggy Clifford and John M. Smith, *Aspen/Dreams and Dilemmas: Love Letter to a Small Town* (Chicago: Swallow Press, 1970); Rick Bass, *Winter: Notes from Montana* (Boston: Houghton Mifflin, 1991); George Sibley, *Dragons in Paradise: On the Edge between Civilization and Sanity* (Frisco, CO: Mountain Gazette Publishing, 2004); Jim Stiles, *Brave New West: Morphing at the Speed of Greed* (Tucson: University of Arizona Press, 2007).

34. Paul Hauk, *Chronology of Beaver Creek* (Glenwood Springs, CO: U.S. Department of Agriculture, U.S. Forest Service, 1979), 2–3, Paul Hauk Papers, Western History and Genealogy Department, Denver Public Library, Denver, Colorado; F. George Robinson to Paul Hauk, June 21, 1967, Paul Hauk Papers, Western History and Genealogy Department, Denver Public Library, Denver, Colorado.

35. Paul Hauk, Site Selection Meeting of March 14, 1967, and Site Selection Committee Meeting of February 20, 1967, Paul Hauk Papers, Western History and Genealogy Department, Denver Public Library, Denver, Colorado.

36. Paul Hauk, *Copper Mountain Ski Area Chronology* (Glenwood Springs, CO: U.S. Department of Agriculture, U.S. Forest Service, White River National Forest, 1979),

1, Paul Hauk Papers, Western History and Genealogy Department, Denver Public Library, Denver, Colorado.

37. Ibid., 6–9.

38. Hauk, *Chronology of Beaver Creek*, 3; Farwell, "Olympic Bubble," 5. Both Hauk and Farwell point to the decision as an example of the Denver Olympic Committee's early lack of organization and of the chaos surrounding the eventual selection of Beaver Creek as the venue.

39. "Olympic Alpine Site Conflict Brewing," *Rocky Mountain News*, April 7, 1971.

40. Olson, "Power, Public Policy, and the Environment," 149–53.

41. White River National Forest, Ski Administration, "'76 Olympic Games," Grouse Mountain Planning Team, Paul Hauk Papers, Box 2, Western History and Genealogy Department, Denver Public Library, Denver, Colorado; Erik Martin, former winter sports resorts program manager for the White River National Forest, interview by author, June 6, 2008.

42. Ibid.

43. Farwell, "Olympic Bubble," 34–35.

44. Memo from Carl DeTemple to Bob Pringle and F. G. Robinson, January 20, 1972, Denver Organizing Committee for the 1976 Winter Olympics, Denver Olympic Committee Papers, Western History and Genealogy Department, Denver Public Library, Denver, Colorado.

45. *Rocky Mountain News*, April 1971.

46. "The 1976 Winter Olympics Some Questions and Answers Dealing with Financial Aspects of the XII Winter Games," February, 1971, Denver Olympic Organizing Committee Records, Papers, Colorado Historical Society Library, Denver, Colorado.

47. John Parr, "Face to Face with the Olympic Gods," *The Capital Ledger* 1, no. 3 (March 1972): 8, Richard Lamm Collection, Papers, Clippings, Colorado Historical Society Archive, Denver, Colorado.

48. On Avery Brundage and the role of commercialism in the modern Olympic Games, see Allan Guttmann, *The Games Must Go On: Avery Brundage and the Olympic Movement* (New York: Columbia University Press, 1984); Robert Barney, Stephen Wenn, and Scott Martyn, *Selling the Five Rings: The International Olympic Committee and the Rise of Olympic Commercialism* (Salt Lake City: University of Utah Press, 2002); Vyv Simson, *The Lords of the Rings: Power, Money, and Drugs in the Modern Olympics* (London: Stoddart, 1991); John Gold and Margaret Gold, eds., *Olympic Cities: City Agendas, Planning, and the World's Games, 1896–2012* (New York: Routledge, 2007).

49. *Denver Post*, October 11, 1972.

50. Norman Upeviz, "Small but Artful Activist Group Wielding Rare Power," *Denver*

Post, October 11, 1972; Whiteside, *Colorado*, 168–69. On Richard Lamm's early environmental activism, see Richard Lamm Collection, Papers, Box 3A FF14, Conservation and Environment Business, 1965, Colorado Historical Society Archive, Denver, Colorado.

51. "A Presentation to the International Olympic Committee from the Citizens for Colorado's Future, Sapporo Japan, January 29–February 1, 1972," Richard Lamm Collection, Papers, Box 2, Colorado Historical Society Archive, Denver, Colorado; "Denver Suffers Sapporo Ordeal," *New York Times*, February 2, 1972; Whiteside, *Colorado*, 168–70.

52. Charles Carter, "Olympic Vote Proposed," *Denver Post*, March 3, 1972; "McNichols against New Olympics Vote," *Denver Post*, March 15, 1972.

53. *Denver Post*, July 6, 1972; Olson, "Power, Public Policy, and the Environment," 188–89; Whiteside, *Colorado*, 171.

54. Whiteside, *Colorado*, 172.

55. "'76 Olympics Cost $1.5 Million," *Denver Post*, March 27, 1972; *The Colorado Destiny: A Publication of Citizens for Colorado's Future*, September 2, 1972, Citizens for Colorado's Future Records, Papers, Western History and Genealogy Department, Denver Public Library, Denver, Colorado.

56. Norman Udevitz, "Cost of Olympic Games Debated," *Denver Post*, September 29, 1972.

57. "Look at Olympics as Challenge, Vote No on Both Propositions," *Denver Post*, October 22, 1972.

58. Rocky Mountain Chapter of the Sierra Club Press Release Concerning the Denver Winter Olympics, Richard Lamm Collection, Papers, Box 2, Colorado Historical Society Archive, Denver, Colorado.

59. *Colorado Destiny*.

60. Rothman, *Devil's Bargains*, 227–51; Rome, *Bulldozer in the Countryside*, 119–52.

61. Farwell, "Olympic Bubble," 34.

62. Peter Seibert to Robert Pringle, December 14, 1971, William McNichols Papers, Box 101, FF14, Western History and Genealogy Department, Denver Public Library, Denver, Colorado.

63. Farwell, interview by author.

64. June Simonton, *Vail: Story of a Colorado Mountain Valley* (Denver: Vail Chronicles, 1987), 112–17.

65. Hauk, *Chronology of Beaver Creek*, 4.

66. *The Ski Industry's Employees News Letter*, December 1971; quoted in Olson, "Power, Public Policy, and the Environment," 152.

67. Farwell, "Olympic Bubble," 35.

68. Governor John Love, speech before Colorado General Assembly, *Denver Post*, March 13, 1972.

69. Richard O'Reilly, "Olympic Site Mulled as Potential Wilderness," *Rocky Mountain News*, February 10, 1972.

70. W. J. Lucas, Regional Forester, White River National Forest, to Honorable Gordon Allott U.S. Senator, June 8, 1972, Vail Associates Papers, Box 3, Western History and Genealogy Department, Denver Public Library, Denver, Colorado.

71. Glen Robinson, *The Forest Service: A Study in Public Land Management* (Baltimore: Johns Hopkins Press, 1975), 126–28; David A. Clary, *Timber and the Forest Service* (Lawrence: University Press of Kansas, 1986); Dennis Le Master, *Decade of Change: The Remaking of Forest Service Statutory Authority during the 1970s* (Westport, CT: Greenwood Press, 1984); Paul Hirt, *Conspiracy of Optimism: Management of the National Forests since World War Two* (Lincoln: University of Nebraska Press, 1994).

72. "Olympics: Even in Rest No Peace," *Denver Post*, November 8, 1972.

73. Joanne Ditmer, "End of '76 Games Can Be Beginning," *Denver Post*, November 9, 1972.

74. "DOOC Dissolves, but Can't Say So," *Denver Post*, November 9, 1973; John Kennedy Jr., "Innsbruck," in *Encyclopedia of the Modern Olympic Movement*, John E. Findling and Kimberly D. Pelle, eds. (Westport, CT: Greenwood Press, 2004), 367–372, 368.

75. Richard Lamm, former governor of Colorado, interview by author, July 13, 2006.

76. It bears mentioning that despite Democratic gains in the state, the vast majority of Colorado voters voted for Richard Nixon for president over Democratic nominee George McGovern, reflecting national election results in which Nixon won his second term in a landslide victory. Steven Schulte, *Wayne Aspinall and the Shaping of the American West* (Boulder: University Press of Colorado, 2002), 278–79; Stephen Sturgeon, *The Politics of Western Water: The Congressional Career of Wayne Aspinall* (Tucson: University of Arizona Press, 2002), 128–43.

77. Jack Grieb to Dr. Wil Ulman, November 13, 1974, Colorado Environmental Coalition Papers, Box 20, Conservation Collection, Denver Public Library, Denver, Colorado.

78. *Denver Post*, December 2, 1988; Talmey Research and Strategy, Inc., "1988 Winter Olympics Survey of Colorado Voters," October 1988, 1.

79. William Schmidt, "Colorado Spurns Olympics No More," *New York Times*, April 19, 1988.

4. THE LAST RESORT

1. Grace Lichtenstein, "Ski Resort Boom Is Over Despite Crowds in Rockies," *New York Times*, February 21, 1976, 51.

2. Skier numbers in Colorado rose an astounding 161 percent between the 1969–1970 season and the 1978–1979 season.

3. Paul Hauk, *Beaver Creek Ski Area Chronology* (Glenwood Springs, CO: U.S. Department of Agriculture, U.S. Forest Service, White River National Forest, 1979); Paul Hauk, *Chronology of Beaver Creek* (Glenwood Springs, CO: U.S. Department of Agriculture, U.S. Forest Service, 1979), 2–3, Paul Hauk Papers, Western History and Genealogy Department, Denver Public Library, Denver, Colorado.

4. J. E. DeVilbiss to William Lucas, Regional Forester, March 26, 1973, Land Use Marble Ski Area: Correspondence, Environmental Impact Statement, 1973–1975, Colorado Environmental Coalition Papers, Box 20, FF32, Western History and Genealogy Department, Denver Public Library, Denver, Colorado.

5. "Rumors Rife on Ski Area at Marble," *Glenwood Sage*, December 5, 1963; "Rumors of Ski Area Near Marble Confirmed—Maybe," *Glenwood Sage*, December 12, 1963.

6. Guidebooks on Colorado published throughout the second half of the twentieth century list Marble as a ghost town. Most note the collapse in the cost of marble in the early 1940s as the death knell for the small community despite the fact that several dozen people remained in residence in the area. For examples see: Robert L. Brown, *Ghost Towns of the Colorado Rockies* (Caldwell, ID: The Caxton Printers, 1968), 217–22; Laurel Michele Wickersheim and Rawlene LeBaron, *The Lost Cities of Colorado* (Bowie, MD: Heritage Books, 2002), 136–37.

7. "Perry Park Adds Ranch," *Denver Post*, January 19, 1971.

8. Paul Hauk, *History of Marble Ski Area from 1963 to 1984 and the Changing Scene for Other Proposals Primarily on the White River National Forest*, April 1993, 3–4, Paul Hauk Papers, Western History and Genealogy Department, Denver Public Library, Denver, Colorado.

9. "Preliminary Analysis of Hotel and Condominium Markets in Vail, Colorado," Vail Associates Papers, Box 1, Western History and Genealogy Department, Denver Public Library, Denver, Colorado.

10. The Forest Service stressed that the development of trails on national forest land would have little to no impact on the region's elk, but the agency would restrict human use of ski areas during calving season and build a fenced corridor for migration if determined necessary. "Big Game Management in Upper Crystal River Valley in Relation to Developing Recreational Complex February 26, 1973," Land Use Marble

Ski Area: Correspondence, Reports, Maps 1970–1972, Colorado Environmental Coalition Papers, Box 20, FF31, Denver Public Library, Denver, Colorado.

11. J. E. DeVilbiss to William Lucas, March 26, 1973, Land Use Marble Ski Area: Correspondence, Reports, Maps 1970–1972, Colorado Environmental Coalition Papers, Box 20, FF32, Denver Public Library, Denver, Colorado.

12. On the growth of ski towns in Colorado during the era, see Hal K. Rothman, *Devil's Bargains: Tourism in the Twentieth-Century American West* (Lawrence: University Press of Kansas, 1998), 227–51; Annie Gilbert Coleman, *Ski Style: Sport and Culture in the Rockies* (Lawrence: University Press of Kansas, 2004), 182–214; Edward Duke Richey, "Living It Up in Aspen: Post-War America, Ski Town Culture, and the New Western Dream, 1945–1975" (PhD diss., University of Colorado, Boulder, 2006).

13. Thomas Evans, Forest Supervisor White River National Forest, to David Mc-Cargo Jr., November 20, 1973, Land Use Marble Ski Area: Correspondence, Reports, Maps 1970–1972, Colorado Environmental Coalition Papers, Box 20, FF31, Denver Public Library, Denver, Colorado.

14. Tom Evans, Disapproval Recommended for Proposed Ski Area Expansion, Forest Service, U.S. Department of Agriculture Press Release, October 31, 1975, Paul Hauk Papers, Western History and Genealogy Department, Denver Public Library, Denver, Colorado.

15. Richard Schneider, "U.S. Probes for Illegal Sales in Marble Ski Area," *Rocky Mountain News*, June 11, 1974; "Ex-Marble Area Broker Charged with Sales Fraud," *Glenwood Post*, February 19, 1976.

16. Denver land developer Michael Stover attempted to resuscitate the dead resort in 1984, but the expansion of the Maroon Bell Wilderness in 1981 ended whatever dream he or others had in building a world-class ski resort on the site. Rick Karlin, "Developer Eyes Defunct Marble Ski Area Site," *Glenwood Post*, March 2, 1984.

17. Andrew Gulliford, *Boomtown Blues: Colorado Oil Shale, 1885–1985* (Boulder: University Press of Colorado, 1989), 119–50 and 151–95. Published seven years after the collapse of the oil shale industry in western Colorado, Gulliford's study provides a recent account of Colorado's oil shale boom and bust, comparing it to previous oil shale booms and busts in the region's history.

18. Candida Harper, "Oil Shale vs. Tourism, Colorado Is Caught between the Rockies and a Hard Place," *Aspen: The Magazine*, 1977, 12–32, 13.

19. Richard Lamm and Michael McCarthy, *The Angry West: A Vulnerable Land and Its Future* (Boston: Houghton Mifflin, 1982), 35.

20. Lamm's remarks were made largely in response to Exxon Corporation's sudden exit from its multimillion-dollar Colony Project outside of the company town of

Parachute in May 1982. Christened "Black Sunday" by Garfield County locals, the corporation's closing of the massive project brought about the very economic ruin Lamm later wrote about in *The Angry West*. To the governor and other state politicians, Exxon's behavior demonstrated the inherent problems of relying on extractive industries for the state's long-term economic stability. Ibid., 50.

21. Richard White, *"It's Your Misfortune and None of My Own," A New History of the American West* (Norman: University of Oklahoma Press, 1991), 562–63; Patricia Nelson Limerick, *The Legacy of Conquest: The Unbroken Past of the American West* (New York: W. W. Norton, 1987), 142–52; Gulliford, *Boomtown Blues*, 2–4; William R. Travis, *New Geographies of the American West: Landscapes and the Changing Patterns of Place* (Washington, DC: Island Press, 2007), 20–22; Patricia Limerick, William R. Travis, and Tamar Scoggin, *Boom and Bust in the American West*, Report from the Center of the American West, no. 4 (Boulder: Center of the American West, University of Colorado at Boulder, 2002), 1–2.

22. Richard Lamm, former governor of Colorado, interview with author, July 13, 2006.

23. Steve Wynkoop, "Beaver Creek Objections Pushed by State Agencies," *Denver Post*, December 18, 1974.

24. House Bill 1034 section 1, chapter 106, Colorado revised statutes 1963, article 8, 1974.

25. House Bill 1041 section 1, chapter 106, Colorado revised statues 1963, article 7, 1974.

26. Rothman, *Devil's Bargains*, 26–28.

27. Christopher S. Wren, "Environmentalism, Colorado-Style: I've Got Mine Jack," *New York Times Magazine*, March 11, 1973, 34.

28. Jack Grieb, Director of Colorado Division of Wildlife to Dr. Wil Ulman, Land-Use Coordinator, Colorado Land Use Commission, November 13, 1974, Colorado Environmental Coalition Papers, Box 20, FF17, Western History and Genealogy Department, Denver Public Library, Denver, Colorado.

29. George T. O'Malley Jr., Director of Colorado Division of Park and Outdoor Recreation, to Dr. Wil Ulman, Land-Use Coordinator, Colorado Land Use Commission, November 26, 1974, Colorado Environmental Coalition Papers, Box 20, FF17, Western History and Genealogy Department, Denver Public Library, Denver, Colorado; Alex Cringan, P. H. Neil, and B. H. Hamilton, "Wildlife Impact Study of Avon–Beaver Creek, Colorado for Vail Associates, Inc. Conducted for the Rocky Mountain Center on Environment," June 1974, Colorado Environmental Coalition Papers, Box 20, FF17, Western History and Genealogy Department, Denver Public Library, Denver, Colorado.

30. Kenneth Webb, PE planning consultant to Dr. Wil Ulman, Land-use co-

ordinator, Colorado Land Use Commission, November 13, 1974, Colorado Environmental Coalition Papers, Box 20, FF17, Western History and Genealogy Department, Denver Public Library, Denver, Colorado.

31. Glenn Fritts, Planning and Research Engineer, Colorado State Department of Highways, to John Bermingham, Assistant to the Governor Environmental Affairs, November 27, 1973, Colorado Environmental Coalition Papers, Box 20, FF17, Western History and Genealogy Department, Denver Public Library, Denver, Colorado.

32. Governor John Vanderhoof to Mr. Thomas Evans, Forest Supervisor, September 19, 1974, Colorado Environmental Coalition Papers, Box 20, FF17, Western History and Genealogy Department, Denver Public Library, Denver, Colorado.

33. Marilyn Stokes, Statement to the Land Use Council, December 17, 1974, Colorado Environmental Coalition Papers, Box 20, FF17, Western History and Genealogy Department, Denver Public Library, Denver, Colorado.

34. Steve Wynkoop, "Opponents Pressing Beaver-Area Attack," *Denver Post*, December 18, 1974.

35. Opening statement by Thomas C. Evans at Colorado Land Use Commission Public Review of Meadow Mountain Proposal, December 16, 1974, F14.5, Recreation: Skiing—Beaver Creek, Forest History Society Archives, Durham, North Carolina.

36. "Vail Associates Defends Beaver Creek Ski Plan," *Denver Post*, January 8, 1975.

37. Steve Wynkoop, "Beaver Creek Area Sports Plan Pushed," *Denver Post*, December 15, 1974.

38. Hauk, *Beaver Creek Ski Area Chronology*, 5.

39. Remarks by W. J. Lucas, Regional Forester, Rocky Mountain Region, Forest Service, U.S. Department of Agriculture, January 15, 1975, F14.5, Recreation: Skiing—Beaver Creek, Forest History Society Archives, Durham, North Carolina.

40. Opening statement by Thomas C. Evans at Colorado Land Use Commission Public Review of Meadow Mountain Proposal, December 16, 1974, Forest History Society Archives, Durham, North Carolina.

41. "Land-Use Unit OKs Beaver Creek Resort," *Denver Post*, January 14, 1975; Governor John Vanderhoof to W. J. Lucas, Regional Forester, Rocky Mountain Region, January 14, 1975, F14.5, Recreation: Skiing—Beaver Creek, Forest History Society Archives, Durham, North Carolina.

42. Bob Juan, "Lamm Ousts 2 Who Supported Ski Area," *Denver Post*, January 17, 1975; Ted Carey, "Beaver Creek Area Named Sports Site," *Rocky Mountain News*, January 25, 1975; Sierra Club, Part IV Attachment to Responsive Statement of William J. Lucas, Regional Forester, Colorado Environmental Coalition Papers, Box 20, FF18, Western History and Genealogy Department, Denver Public Library, Denver, Colorado.

43. Before the Chief, United States Forest Service, Re: Winter Sports Site Designation for Beaver Creek, Meadow Mountain Planning Unit, White River National Forest. Sierra Club Appellant, Brief in Support of Appellant Sierra Club's Motion for Reconsideration and for Oral Presentation; John McGuire to S. Chandler Visher and H. Anthony Ruckel, Attorneys for the Sierra Club, October 9, 1975, Colorado Environmental Coalition Papers, Box 20, FF18, Western History and Genealogy Department, Denver Public Library, Denver, Colorado.

44. Sierra Club Legal Defense Fund, Inc., Beaver Creek Ski Area Review, press release, July 18, 1975, Colorado Environmental Coalition Papers, Box 20, FF18, Western History and Genealogy Department, Denver Public Library, Denver, Colorado.

45. In-house studies used by the Forest Service prior to the passage of NEPA, EARs determined the environmental impacts of an action on national forest lands. The passage of NEPA in 1970 replaced EARs with Environmental Assessments (EAs), each filling the same function in determining whether a project complied with federal law. The reason the White River National Forest undertook an EAR rather than an EA, despite the passage of NEPA in January 1970, appears to stem from the initial confusion over the of enactment of NEPA following its passage.

46. Jill Vig, "Beaver Creek 'Dam' Broken," *Vail Trail*, July 25, 1975.

47. Charlie Meyers, "Beaver Creek Gets Lamm Nod," *Denver Post*, February 20, 1976.

48. Forest Service, U.S. Department of Agriculture, "Accident Report Lionshead Gondola II, Vail Ski Area White River National Forest, Colorado March 26, 1976," May 1976; Paul Hauk Papers, Western History and Genealogy Department, Denver Public Library, Denver, Colorado; Seibert, *Vail*, 136–7.

49. Hauk, *Beaver Creek Ski Area Chronology*, 8.

50. Charles R. Goeldner and Sally Courtney, *Colorado Ski and Recreation Statistics*, 1977 (Boulder: University of Colorado Graduate School of Business Administration, Business Research Division, 1977), 24; Michael Strauss, "Colorado Turns More to Snow Makers," *New York Times*, November 28, 1976, 205.

51. It takes roughly 160,000 gallons of water to cover one acre of snow one foot deep. For most ski resorts this translates into million of gallons of water used per year, water that is taken from local streams, rivers, and reservoirs.

52. In recent years, snow making has becoming increasingly controversial. Legal suits over Colorado's Arapahoe Basin and Arizona's Snowbowl have focused on the environmental costs of the transporting, storing, and runoff of man-made snow. In the case of Snowbowl, treated wastewater has been proposed due to the area's lack of readily available water sources. Making the issue more complicated is sacredness of the San Francisco Peaks in local Native American cultures. In both cases the U.S.

Forest Service approved snow making despite widespread public disapproval and scientific studies suggesting snow making will have significant environmental impacts.

53. "Forest Service Blamed for Ski Lag," *Rocky Mountain News*, January 30, 1977.

54. Glen Robinson, *The Forest Service: A Study in Public Land Management* (Baltimore: Johns Hopkins University Press, 1975), 127–28.

55. Jack Phinney, "Forest Service Blamed for Ski Lag," *Denver Post*, January 30, 1977.

56. Erik Martin, former winter sports resorts program manager for the White River National Forest, interview by author, June 6, 2008.

57. Other conflicts include the proposed expansion and development of Snowbowl Ski Area outside of Flagstaff, Arizona. In Utah, controversy erupted over the expansion of Snowbird Ski Resort into neighboring White Pine Wilderness Area. But perhaps the most famous fight over the Forest Service's management of ski resort development was Disney Corp's planned development of Mineral King Valley in the California Sierra Nevada.

58. D. R. C. Brown, "National Ski Areas Association Forest Service Committee Report," December 12, 1969, Recreation: Skiing—Snow Skiing on National Forests, Papers, U.S. Forest History Collection, Durham, North Carolina.

59. David A. Clary, *Timber and the Forest Service* (Lawrence: University Press of Kansas, 1986), 94–125; Paul Hirt, *Conspiracy of Optimism: Management of the National Forests since World War Two* (Lincoln: University of Nebraska Press, 1994), 171–92.

60. Reflecting on the deregulation revolution, Kahn wrote, "something of a consensus was already emerging in the early 1970s among disinterested students that regulation had suppressed innovation, sheltered inefficiency, encouraged a wage/price spiral, promoted a severe misallocation of resources by throwing prices out of alignment with marginal costs, encouraged competition in wasteful, cost-inflating ways, and denied the public the variety of price and quality choices that a competitive market would have provided." Alfred Edward Kahn, *The Economics of Regulation: Principles and Institutions* (Boston: Massachusetts Institute of Technology, 1988), xvi.

61. Anthony Campagna, *Economic Policy in the Carter Administration* (Westport, CT: Greenwood Press, 1995), 190–98; Bruce J. Schulman, *The Seventies: The Greatest Shift in American Culture, Society, and Politics* (Cambridge, MA: Da Capo Press, 2001), 124–25; W. Carl Biven, *Jimmy Carter's Economy: Policy in an Age of Limits* (Chapel Hill: University of North Carolina Press, 2002), 127–134.

62. Laventhol and Horwath in Association with Ted Farwell and Associates, Inc., "Forest Service, U.S. Department of Agriculture Ski Area Price Evaluation Study," vol. 1 (April 1977), (U.S. Forest History Collection, Durham, North Carolina), 6.

63. Ibid., 8.

64. "Letting Go," SKIING (October, 1981), 21.

65. "Haskell Raps Ski Rate Hike Guidelines," Rocky Mountain News, April 23, 1977.

66. C. R. Goeldner and Ted Farwell, "National Ski Areas Association: Economic Analysis of North American Ski Areas," Boulder: University of Colorado Graduate School of Business Administration, Business Research Division, 1976, 45.

67. Dave Danforth, "Ski Areas Limited to 9.5 Percent Increase," Glenwood Post, April 10, 1979.

68. Annie Gilbert Coleman, "The Unbearable Whiteness of Skiing," Pacific Historical Review 65, no. 4 (November 1996): 583–614.

69. Hirt, Conspiracy of Optimism; Nancy Langston, Forest Dreams, Forest Nightmares: The Paradox of Old Growth in the Inland West (Seattle: University of Washington Press, 1995), 157–200; Paul S. Sutter, Driven Wild: How the Fight against Automobiles Launched the Modern Wilderness Movement (Seattle: University of Washington Press, 2002), 58–60.

70. Christopher D. Stone, "Should Trees Have Standing? Toward Legal Rights for Natural Objects," 45 Southern California Law Review 450 (1972): 3–55; Susan R. Schrepfer, "Establishing Administrative 'Standing': The Sierra Club and the Forest Service, 1897–1956," Pacific Historical Review 58, no. 1 (1989): 55–81; Lary Dilsaver and William Tweed, Challenge of the Big Trees: A Resource History of Sequoia and Kings Canyon National Parks (Three Rivers, CA: Sequoia Natural History Association, 1990), 278–82 and 298–301; Joseph L. Sax, Mountains without Handrails: Reflections on the National Parks (Ann Arbor: University of Michigan Press, 1980), 67–70.

71. Grace Lichtenstein, "Ski Resort Boom Is Over Despite Crowds in Rockies," New York Times, February 21, 1976, 51.

72. "Update on Beaver Creek," Skiing (November 1980), 60.

73. Linda Harbine, "Beaver Creek Aborning," Skiing (November 1981), 77–81, 202; Bill Pardue, "Fords to Buy Home Site at Beaver Creek Resort," Denver Post, September 26, 1979.

74. Martin, interview by author; C. R. Goeldner et al., "The Colorado Ski Industry: Highlights of the 1998–1999 Season" (Boulder: University of Colorado Graduate School of Business Administration, Business Research Division, 1999), 5.

5. FIRE ON THE MOUNTAIN

1. National Ski Areas Association and RRC Associates, Inc., "Kottke National End of the Season Survey 2005/06 Final Report" (Lakewood, CO: National Ski Areas Association, August 2006), 17.

2. Ski Area Citizen's Coalition, "How Are Ski Areas Graded?" http://www.skiarea citizens.com/index.php?nav=how_we_grade.

3. Hal Clifford, *Downhill Slide: Why the Corporate Ski Industry Is Bad for Skiing, Ski Towns, and the Environment* (San Francisco: Sierra Club Books, 2002), 8.

4. Using numbers provided by the National Ski Areas Association the total utilization of ski resorts in the Rocky Mountain Region had plummeted from 50 percent in mid-1980s to around 30 percent by the late 1990s. Despite such figures, ski resorts continued to argue for further expansion to meet demand.

5. C. R. Goeldner et al., "The Colorado Ski Industry: Highlights of the 1998–1999 Season" (Boulder: University of Colorado Graduate School of Business Administration, Business Research Division, 1999), 15.

6. Jon Bowermaster, "Who Skis?" *New York Times*, November 27, 1988.

7. Ibid.

8. The seven largest Colorado ski resorts in 1988 in order of percentage of skier days were: Vail (15.7 percent), Breckenridge (11.3 percent), Steamboat (10.6 percent), Keystone (9.5 percent), Winter Park (9 percent), Copper Mountain (8 percent), and Snowmass (6 percent).

9. Reade Bailey, "The Survey Says—SKI's Readers Tell Which North American Resorts Are Tops," Ski *Magazine*, October 1989, 94; Reade Bailey, "Top of the Charts—SKI's Readers Choices for America's Best Ski Resorts," Ski *Magazine*, October 1990, 56; Reade Bailey, "Chart Toppers—Readers' Picks of Top North American Resorts," Ski *Magazine*, October 1991, 44.

10. Don R. Dressler, e-mail to author, December 11, 2007. On the Ski Area Citizens Coalition's use of Master Plans in scoring ski resorts' environmental impact, see http://www.skiareacitizens.com/.

11. Vail Master Development Plan, September 1986, White River National Forest, Holy Cross River Ranger District, Rocky Mountain Region, U.S. Department of Agriculture, Forest Service; Record of Decision: Vail Category III Ski Area Development, August 1996, White River National Forest, Holy Cross River Ranger District, Rocky Mountain Region, U.S. Department of Agriculture, Forest Service.

12. In 1986, Gillette teamed up with junk bond king Michael Milken, borrowing more than $2 million from the infamous brokerage firm of Drexel Burnham & Lambert. Gillette used the loans to purchase twelve television stations. The dam began to crack for Gillette and others reliant on loans from firms dealing in high-risk bonds (more commonly known as junk bonds), with loan payments ballooning out of control and increased competition from cable stations causing a paradigm shift within the communications industry.

13. Penny Parker, "Vail Resorts Offered State A-Basin, Justice Department Nixed Proposal Deal," *Denver Post*, August 23, 1996.

14. Penny Parker, "Inside Vail's Merger: Market Share Fed's Concern," *Denver Post*, January 12, 1997.

15. Penny Parker, "Vail Deal Challenged Again: Denver Now Hopes to Convince Judge," *Denver Post*, July 26, 1997.

16. Colorado Ski Country USA, in conjunction with the Colorado Association of Ski Towns and Public Service Company of Colorado, *The Colorado Ski Industry, 1991* (Denver: Browne, Bortz and Coddington, 1991), 3; Winter Park Marketing Survey, 1985–1986, Winter Park Resort Marketing Department, Winter Park Resort, Colorado. Colorado Ski Country USA reported that of the 9.8 millions skier days during 1991, 30 percent were made by "day visitors," or local and regional skiers.

17. Chuck Green, "How Good Is the Winter Park Deal?" *Denver Post*, May 1, 1994.

18. Doug Freed, "Ski Area Told to Pay Property Taxes," *Winter Park Manifest*, June 27, 1985, 3.

19. "WP Not Taxable: County Appeal of District Court Decide Uncertain," *Winter Park Manifest*, January 29, 1987; "Winter Park Ski Area Estimated Actual Value," Grand County Assayer's Office. Thanks to Stu Findley for providing this number.

20. On the controversies surrounding Denver International Airport see: Paul Stephen Dempsey, Andrew Goetz, and Joseph Szyliowicz, *Denver International Airport: Lessons Learned* (New York: McGraw Hill, 1997).

21. Medill Barnes to Members of the Winter Park Advisory Committee, RE: Proposed sale of Winter Park, January 1, 1994, Winter Park Advisory Committee Memoranda, Winter Park Marketing Department Collection, Papers, Winter Park Ski Resort, Colorado.

22. Medill Barnes, to Bruce Alexander and Cathy Reynolds, co-chairs Winter Park Advisory Committee, 18 January 1994, transcript of memoranda in author's possession.

23. National Ski Areas Association and RRC Associates, Inc., "Kottke National End of Season Survey 1998/1999" (Lakewood, CO: National Ski Areas Association, 1999), 27; National Ski Areas Association and RRC Associates, Inc., "Kottke National End of Season Survey 1994/1995" (Lakewood, CO: National Ski Areas Association, 1995), 18. The National Ski Areas Association defines the Rocky Mountain region as the states of Montana, Idaho, Wyoming, Utah, Colorado, and New Mexico. The region included only 93 of the nation's 520 ski resorts but represents roughly 35 percent of the total number of ski days nationwide.

24. To measure profits ski resorts rely on a formula dividing total revenues by total skier visits to measure yield: the greater the yield, the greater the profit.

25. "Kottke National End of Season Survey 1998/1999," 31.

26. Food prices at ski resorts continue to rise. In the three years I took to research and write this book, prices increased at my favorite resort by more than $3 for a hamburger.

27. Jason Blevins, "Intrawest Gains Leverage at Denver Area Ski Resort," *Denver Post*, September 2, 2002; Kristi Arellano, "Denver Signs Deal for Intrawest to Operate Winter Park Ski Area," *Denver Post*, December 24, 2002.

28. "Zephyr Mountain Lodge Availability of Condominiums," sales pamphlet, Intrawest Playground Destinations Properties, Inc., December 11, 2006.

29. U.S. Forest Service, *Final Environmental Impact Statement: Vail Category III Ski Area Development, White River National Forest, Holy Cross Ranger District, Rocky Mountain Region*, vol. 1, U.S. Department of Agriculture, August 1996, 2-15–2-17.

30. Ibid.

31. Record of Decision: Vail Category III Ski Area Development, August 1997, White River National Forest, Holy Cross Ranger District, Rocky Mountain Region, U.S. Department of Agriculture, Forest Service, 12.

32. Colorado Department of Natural Resources, Colorado Division of Wildlife, Detailed Comments, Vail Category III Ski Area Development Draft EIS, January 26, 1996, 1. In U.S. Forest Service, *Final Environmental Impact Statement: Vail Category III Ski Area Development, White River National Forest, Holy Cross Ranger District, Rocky Mountain Region*, vol. 2, U.S. Department of Agriculture, August 1996, 3–11.

33. CDOW Response, Vail Category III Ski Area Expansion, Response to Comments on Draft Environmental Impact Statement, August 1996, White River National Forest, Holy Cross Ranger District, Rocky Mountain Region, U.S. Department of Agriculture, Forest Service, 2.

34. Record of Decision: Vail Category III Ski Area Development, August 1996, 10.

35. Al Knight, "Missing Lynx: Vail Plan Eases Way for Species," *Denver Post*, December 14, 1997.

36. *Colorado Environmental Coalition, et al. v. Dombeck*, 185 F.3d 1162, 1166 (10th Cir. 1999).

37. Robert Stewart, Regional Environmental Officer to Loren Kroenke, January 11, 1996. In U.S. Forest Service, *Final Environmental Impact Statement: Vail Category III Ski Area Development*, vol. 2.

38. Record of Decision: Vail Category III Ski Area Development, August 1996, 33.

39. Mark Derr, "Starvation Intrudes in a Bid to Save the Lynx," *New York Times*, April 27, 1997, F3; Keith Kloor, "Lynx and Biologists Try and Recover after Disastrous Start," *Science*, vol. 282, July 16, 1999, 320–21.

40. James Morrison et al., "The Effects of Ski Area Expansion on Elk," *Wildlife Society Bulletin* 23, no. 3 (Autumn 1995): 481–89, 487.

41. Laura A. Romin and John A. Bissonette, "Deer: Vehicle Collisions: Status of State Monitoring Activities and Mitigation Efforts," *Wildlife Society Bulletin* 24, no. 2 (Summer 1996): 276–83, 278; M. P. Huijser et al., "Wildlife-Vehicle Collision Reduction Study," Report to Congress, U.S. Department of Transportation, Federal Highway Administration, Washington, DC, August 2007; Howard Pankratz, "Helping Wildlife Cross Road: Plans for Under- and Overpasses Are Response to Surge in Animal-Vehicle Accidents," *Denver Post*, February 2, 2008.

42. U.S. Forest Service, *Final Environmental Impact Statement: Vail Category III Ski Area Development*, vol. 1, 4–73.

43. Ibid., 3–56.

44. Tony Perez-Giese, "The Missing Lynx," *Denver Westword News*, November 6, 1996.

45. U.S. Forest Service, *Final Environmental Impact Statement: Vail Category III Ski Area Development*, vol. 1, 3–11.

46. Daniel Glick, *Powder Burn: Arson, Money, and Mystery on Vail Mountain* (New York: PublicAffairs, 2001), 25–26.

47. Mark Mobley, Vail Valley Fire Department engineer, interview by author, June 1, 2010.

48. Steve Lipsher, "Remote Area Makes Fighting Fire Tough," *Denver Post*, October 20, 1998.

49. ELF communiqué, October 19, 1998, in Leslie James Pickering, *The Earth Liberation Front, 1997–2002*, 2nd ed. (Portland: Arissa Media Group, 2007), 13.

50. Craig Rosebraugh, *Burning Rage of a Dying Planet: Speaking for the Earth Liberation Front* (New York: Lantern Books, 2004), 60. Gerlach encoded the e-mail to be bounced through several different e-mail servers, explaining the two-day delay from the time she sent the e-mail to when Rosebraugh, the *Vail Trail*, and KUNC received it.

51. Robert Sullivan, "The Face of Eco-Terrorism," *New York Times Magazine*, December 20, 1998, 46–49.

52. "E.L.F. Earth Liberation Front Ignites Britain," *Earth First! The Radical Environmental Journal* (Mabon, 1993), 34.

53. Edward Abbey, *The Monkey Wrench Gang* (New York: J. B. Lippincott, 1975). Set in the American Southwest, the novel portrays a small band of saboteurs led by ex–special forces demolitions expert George Washington Hayduke who travel throughout the region wreaking havoc on billboards, coal trains, and bulldozers before their capture by Utah law enforcement.

54. Douglas Long, *Ecoterrorism* (New York: Facts on File, 2004), 5–9; Rik Scarce, *Eco-Warriors: Understanding the Radical Environmental Movement*, 2nd ed. (Walnut Creek, CA: Left Coast Press, 2002), 47.

55. The Group of Ten included Defenders of Wildlife, Environmental Defense Fund, Greenpeace, National Audubon Society, National Wildlife Federation, The Nature Conservancy, World Wildlife Fund, the Sierra Club, and the Wilderness Society.

56. McKenzie Funk, "Firestarter," *Outside Magazine*, August 2007, 104.

57. Sara Burnett, "Chelsea Gerlach: Life as a Radical," *Rocky Mountain News*, June 6, 2007.

58. Hal Bernton, "Is Ecosabotage Terrorism?" *Seattle Times*, May 7, 2006.

59. Testimony of James F. Jarboe, Domestic Terrorism Section Chief, Counterterrorism Division, FBI, before the House Resources Committee, Subcommittee on Forests and Forest Health, "The Threat of Eco-Terrorism," February 12, 2002.

60. Funk, "Firestarter," 104.

61. Rosebraugh, *Burning Rage*, 236.

62. Matt Rasmussen, "Green Rage," *Orion Magazine*, January/February http://www.orionmagazine.org/index.php/articles/articles/6/.

63. In researching this book I submitted several Freedom of Information requests to the FBI in the hopes of learning more on the investigation of the Vail arsons. In response, the FBI mailed several pages of an investigation into a trashcan fire in Vail during the same year as the arsons. On calling the FBI, I was told that there was no record of an investigation into the arson of twelve buildings on Vail Ski Resort in 1998. While such a story is easily explained by a difference in search terms, it underlines the obfuscation of history by federal government agencies and suggests how conspiracies concerning federal behavior are maintained.

64. Valerie Richardson, "Four Indicted in Vail Ecoterrorism," *Washington Times*, May 5, 2006; Federal Bureau of Investigation, "Four People Indicted by Federal Grand Jury in Denver for 1998 Vail Arson Fires," Press Release, May 19, 2006.

65. *Colorado Environmental Coalition, et al. v. Dombeck*; Allen Best, "Protests Proceed at Vail," *High Country News*, August 2, 1999.

66. Robert S. Boynton, "Powder Burn," *Outside Magazine*, January 1999.

67. Allen Best, "Vail Fire Outrages Community," *High Country News*, November 9, 1998.

68. Rocky Smith, former staff ecologist for the Colorado Environmental Coalition, interview by author, April 14, 2008.

69. Bon Ortega, "For Ski Resorts, Gold in Them Thar Hills Is Real Estate," *Wall Street Journal*, July 29, 1998, B1.

70. C. R. Goeldner et al., *The Colorado Ski Industry: Highlights of the 1998–1999 Season*

(Boulder: University of Colorado Graduate School of Business Administration, Business Research Division, 1999), 11.

71. Jason Blevins, "Revenues Up 16 Percent at Vail, Colo. Ski Resort," *Denver Post*, September 14, 2000; Jason Blevins, "Resort Gives Blue Sky Basin a Huge Lift," *Denver Post*, December 16, 2000.

72. Allen Best, "Lynx Reintroduction Links Unexpected Allies," *High Country News* (May 10, 1999).

73. Alex Markel, "From Superfund Town to Pristine Ski Resort," *New York Times*, http://travel.nytimes.com/2005/12/11/realestate/11nati.html; Environmental Protection Agency, Superfund Site Progress Profile: Eagle Mine, http://cfpub.epa.gov/supercpad/cursites/csitinfo.cfm?id=0800159#CleanupImpact; Steve Lyn, "Private Ski Resort Touts Benefits for Minturn," *Vail Daily*, January 18, 2008, http://www.vaildaily.com/article/20080118/NEWS/215412207.

Epilogue

1. Lloyd Levy Consulting, "Job Generation in the Colorado Mountain Resort Economy: Second Homes and Other Economic Drivers in Eagle, Grand, Pitkin and Summit Counties Executive Summary" (Denver: Levy, Hammer, Siler, George Associates, 2002), 14.

2. U.S. Department of Agriculture, Summary of the Final Environmental Impact Statement to Accompany the Land and Resource Management Plan—2002 Revision (U.S. Forest Service, Rocky Mountain Region, 2002), 3–4.

3. Online Newshour, "Managing the White River National Forest," http://www.pbs.org/newshour/bb/environment/jan-june00/white_river_4–18.html.

4. Bob Edwards, "Profile: White River National Forest in Colorado Considering Limiting Recreational Activities in Order to Protect Its Ecosystem and the Wildlife," *Morning Edition*, NPR, February 23, 2000.

5. Allen Best, "STOP—A National Forest Tries to Rein in Recreation," *High Country News* (January 17, 2000).

6. Ibid.

7. Ibid.

8. Allen Best, "In Their Own Words," *High Country News* (January 17, 2000).

9. U.S. Department of Agriculture, *Record of Decision for the Land and Resource Management Plan—2002 Revision* (U.S. Forest Service, Rocky Mountain Region, 2002), 13.

10. Ibid., 2–31.

11. Rebecca Clarren, "White River Forest Plan Friend to All—And to None," *High Country News* (July 8, 2002).

12. Michael Berry, "Introduction," in *Sustainable Slopes: The Environmental Charter for Ski Areas* (Lakewood, CO: National Ski Areas Association, 2000), 1.

13. Ben Doon, e-mail to author, January 19, 2007. For more on the Ski Area Environmental Report Card see: Ski Area Citizens' Coalition, http://www.skiareacitizens.com/index.php.

14. Jorge E. Rivera and Peter deLeon, "Is Greener Whiter? The Sustainable Slopes Program and the Voluntary Environmental Performance of Western Ski Areas," *Policy Studies Journal* 32, no. 3 (2004): 417–37.

15. Judy Dorset, "Debunking the SACC Scorecard," *NSAA Journal* (October/November 2004): 11.

16. Jorge E. Rivera, Peter deLeon, and Charles Koerber, "Is Greener Whiter Yet? The Sustainable Slopes Program after Five Years," *Policy Studies Journal* 34, no. 2 (2006): 216.

17. The 1990–1991 season proved to be an aberration due in large part to poor snow conditions across the country, particularly in the Rocky Mountain States. Dry years historically equate to much lower skier/snowboarder numbers. A drought in 1977 led to the widespread use of snow making during the late 1970s. Still, many resorts suffer significant losses during drier winters. National Ski Areas Association and RRC Associates, Inc., "Kottke National End of Season Survey 1999/00 Final Report" (August 2000), 4–6.

18. Susanna Howe, *Sick: A Cultural History of Snowboarding* (New York: St. Martin's Griffin, 1998), 38–41.

19. RRC Associates, *National Ski Areas Association: National Demographic Study* (Boulder, CO: RRC Associates, December 2000), 2.

20. Ibid., 8.

21. Outdoor Industry Foundation, *A Targeted Look at Participants with Potential* (July 2004), 28.

22. U.S. Census Bureau, "U.S. Hispanic Population Surpasses 45 Million, Now 15 Percent of Total" (Washington, DC: U.S. Department of Commerce, May 1, 2008).

23. Annie Gilbert Coleman, "The Unbearable Whiteness of Skiing," *Pacific Historical Review* 65, no. 4 (November, 1996): 583–614, 606.

24. On race and outdoor recreation see: Mark Spence, *Dispossessing the Wilderness: Indian Removal and the Making of the National Parks* (New York: Oxford University Press, 1999); Wendy Rex-Atzet, "Narratives of Place and Power: Laying Claim to Devil's Tower," in *Imagining the Big Open: Nature, Identity, and Play in the New West*, Liza Nicholas, Elaine Bapis, and Thomas J. Harvey, eds. (Salt Lake City: University of Utah Press, 2003), 73–91; Jason Bryne and Jennifer Wolch, "Nature Race, and Parks: Past

Research and Future Directions for Geographic Research," *Progress in Human Geography* 33 (March 2009): 743–65.

25. "National Ski Industry Demographics and Trends, 2008," prepared by Colorado Wild and the Ski Area Citizen's Coalition (September 2008).

26. Charles Goeldner, "Skiing Trends in North America," in *Mountain Resort Development: Proceedings of the Vail Conference, April 18–21, 1991*, Alison Gill and Rudi Hartman, eds. (Burnaby, British Columbia: Simon Fraser University Centre for Tourism Policy and Research, 1991), 7–20.

27. Colorado Ski Country USA, 1999/2009 Skier Visit Numbers, http://media-colo radoski.com/CSCFacts/SkierVisits/.

28. United Nations Intergovernmental Panel on Climate Change, *Climate Change 2001: Synthesis Report*, http://www.grida.no/publications/other/ipcc_tar/?src=/climate/ IPCC_tar/vol4/english/008.htm.

29. Naomi Oreskes and Erik M. Conway, *Merchants of Doubt: How a Handful of Scientists Obscured the Truth on Issues from Tobacco to Global Warming* (New York: Bloomsbury Press, 2010), 169–215; Eric Pooley, *The Climate War: True Believers, Power Brokers, and the Fight to Save the Earth* (New York: Hyperion, 2010), 31–52.

30. NSAA Member Resorts to Senator John McCain and Senator Joe Lieberman, February 23, 2005, http://www.nsaa.org/nsaa/environment/climate_change/.

31. J. Francis Stafford, "The Heights of the Mountains Are His: The Development of God's Country," Pastoral Letter to the People of God on Northern Colorado Western Slope Growth (December 23, 1994).

BIBLIOGRAPHY

Archive Collections

Bill "Sarge" Brown. Papers. Denver Public Library Western History and Genealogy Department, Denver, Colorado.

Arthur H. Carhart. Papers. Denver Public Library Western History and Genealogy Department, Denver, Colorado.

Citizens for Colorado's Future, Records 1971–1972. Papers. Western History and Genealogy Department, Denver Public Library, Denver, Colorado.

Colorado Arlberg Club. Papers. Denver Public Library Western History and Genealogy Department, Denver, Colorado.

Colorado Environmental Coalition. Papers. Denver Public Library Western History and Genealogy Department, Denver, Colorado.

A Cooperative Highway Effort Thru the Rocky Mountains. Papers. Denver Public Library Western History and Genealogy Department, Denver, Colorado.

George E. Cranmer. Papers. Denver Public Library Western History and Genealogy Department, Denver, Colorado.

Denver Department of Parks and Recreation. Papers. Denver Public Library Western History and Genealogy Department, Denver, Colorado.

Denver Olympic Committee Records. Papers. Colorado Historical Society, Denver, Colorado.

Charles Minot Dole. Papers. Denver Public Library Western History and Genealogy Department, Denver, Colorado.

Forest History Society Archives. Durham, North Carolina.

Paul Hauk. Papers. Denver Public Library Western History and Genealogy Department, Denver, Colorado.

Edward Hilliard Jr. Papers. Western History and Genealogy Department, Denver Public Library, Denver, Colorado.

Jackson Family. Papers. Denver Public Library Western History and Genealogy Department, Denver, Colorado.

Lawrence Jump. Papers. Denver Public Library Western History and Genealogy Department, Denver, Colorado.

Richard Lamm Collection. Papers. Colorado Historical Society Archive, Denver, Colorado.

John E. Love. Papers. Colorado State Archives, Denver, Colorado.

William McNichols. Papers. Denver Public Library Western History and Genealogy Department, Denver, Colorado.

10th Mountain Division Collection. Denver Public Library Western History and Genealogy Department, Denver, Colorado.

Vail Associates. Papers. Denver Public Library Western History and Genealogy Department, Denver, Colorado.

Wilderness Society Records. Papers. Denver Public Library Western History and Genealogy Department, Denver, Colorado.

Winter Park Marketing Department Collection. Papers. Winter Park Ski Resort, Colorado.

Newspapers and Periodicals

Aspen: The Magazine

Cervi's Rocky Mountain Journal

Denver Municipal Facts

Denver Post

Denver Westword News

Eagle Valley Enterprise

Earth First!: The Radical Environmental Journal

Forest Service News Bulletin

Glenwood Post

Glenwood Sage

Grist.com

High Country News

Landscape Architecture

New York Times

NSAA Journal

The National Observer

Orion Magazine

Outside Magazine

Rocky Mountain News

Rolling Stone

Seattle Times

Ski Magazine

SKIING
Skiing Heritage
Sports Illustrated
Time Magazine
Vail Daily
Vail Trail
Wall Street Journal
Washington Post
Washington Times
Wilderness Magazine
Winter Park Manifest
Yosemite Nature Notes

Government Documents and Public Reports

Bramwell, Lincoln, et al. "The Yosemite Way: An Administrative History of Yosemite National Park." Lincoln Bramwell and Andrew Kirk, Principle Investigators, in Fulfillment of National Park Service Task and Great Basin CESU Cooperative Agreements, Preliminary Draft 2009.

Colorado Department of Highways. *Interstate Highway Location Study Dotsero to Empire Junction.* E. Lionel Pavlo Engineering Company, March 1960.

Foss, Phillip, ed. *Public Land Policy: Proceedings of the Western Resources Conference Fort Collins, 1968.* Boulder: Colorado Associated University Press, 1968.

Goeldner, Charles, et al. *Colorado Ski and Winter Recreation Statistics, 1972.* Boulder: University of Colorado Business Research Division, Graduate School of Business Administration, 1972.

———. *Colorado Ski and Winter Recreation Statistics, 1975.* Boulder: University of Colorado Graduate School of Business Administration, Business Research Division, 1976.

———. *The Colorado Ski Industry: Highlights of the 1997–1998 Season.* Boulder: University of Colorado Graduate School of Business Administration, Business Research Division, 1998.

———. *The Colorado Ski Industry: Highlights of the 1998–1999 Season.* Boulder: University of Colorado Graduate School of Business Administration, Business Research Division, 1999.

Goeldner, C. R., and Ted Farwell. *National Ski Areas Association: Economic Analysis of North American Ski Areas.* Boulder: University of Colorado Graduate School of Business Administration, Business Research Division, 1976.

Goeldner, Charles R., and Sally Courtney. *Colorado Ski and Recreation Statistics, 1977.* Boulder: University of Colorado Graduate School of Business Administration, Business Research Division, 1977.

Hartley, Ralph, and James Schneck. *Administering the National Forests of Colorado: An Assessment of the Architectural and Cultural Significance of Historical Administrative Properties.* Lincoln, NE: U.S. Department of the Interior, National Park Service, 1996, http://www.nps.gov/history/history/online_books/forest/colorado-nf/architecture.htm.

Laventhol and Horwath in Association with Ted Farwell and Associates, Inc. "Forest Service, U.S. Department of Agriculture Ski Area Price Evaluation Study," vol. 1 (April 1977), U.S. Forest History Collection, Durham, North Carolina.

Lloyd Levy Consulting. *Job Generation in the Colorado Mountain Resort Economy: Second Homes and Other Economic Drivers in Eagle, Grand, Pitkin and Summit Counties Executive Summary.* Denver: Levy, Hammer, Siler, George Associates, 2002.

National Ski Areas Association. *Sustainable Slopes: The Environmental Charter for Ski Areas.* Lakewood, CO: National Ski Areas Association, 2000.

National Ski Areas Association and RRC Associates, Inc. "Kottke National End of Season Survey 1994/1995." Lakewood, CO: National Ski Areas Association, 1995.

———. "Kottke National End of Season Survey 1998/1999." Lakewood, CO: National Ski Areas Association, 1999.

———. "Kottke National End of Season Survey 1999/00 Final Report." Lakewood, CO: National Ski Areas Association, August 2000.

———. "Kottke National End of the Season Survey 2005/06 Final Report." Lakewood, CO: National Ski Areas Association, August 2006.

National Ski Industry Demographics and Trends, 2008. Prepared by Colorado Wild and the Ski Area Citizen's Coalition, September 2008.

Outdoor Industry Foundation. *A Targeted Look at Participants with Potential,* July 2004.

Reese, Rick. "The Denver Winter Olympic Controversy," in Presentation by Rick Reese to Salt Lake Winter Olympics Feasibility Study Committee, November 16.

RRC Associates. *National Ski Areas Association: National Demographic Study.* Boulder, CO: RRC Associates, December 2000.

Stafford, J. Francis. "The Heights of the Mountains Are His: The Development of God's Country." Pastoral Letter to the People of God on Northern Colorado Western Slope Growth, December 23, 1994.

Talmey Research and Strategy, Inc. "1988 Winter Olympics Survey of Colorado Voters," October 1988.

United Nations Intergovernmental Panel on Climate Change. *Climate Change 2001:*

Synthesis Report. http://www.grida.no/publications/other/ipcc_tar/?src=/climate/IPCC
_tar/vol4/english/008.htm.

U.S. Department of Agriculture. *Land and Resource Management Plan—2002 Revision.*
U.S. Forest Service, Rocky Mountain Region, 2002.

U.S. Department of Agriculture. *Summary of the Final Environmental Impact Statement to
Accompany the Land and Resource Management Plan—2002 Revision.* U.S. Forest Service
Rocky Mountain Region, 2002.

U.S. Forest Service. *Final Environmental Impact Statement: Vail Category III Ski Area Development, White River National Forest, Holy Cross Ranger District, Rocky Mountain Region,*
vols. 1 and 2, U.S. Department of Agriculture, August 1996.

von Bickertt, Carl, Judith Oldham, and John Ryan. *A Profile of the Tourist Market in Colorado: 1968.* Denver: Denver Research Institute, University of Denver, 1969.

Books

Abbey, Edward. *The Monkey Wrench Gang.* New York: J. B. Lippincott, 1975.

———. *Hayduke Lives!* Boston: Little, Brown and Company, 1990.

Abbott, Carl. *The Metropolitan Frontier Cities in the Modern American West.* Tucson: University of Arizona Press, 1998.

———. *How Cities Won the West: Four Centuries of Urban Change in Western North America.*
Albuquerque: University of New Mexico Press, 2008.

Abbott, Carl, Stephen Leonard, and Thomas J. Noel. *Colorado: A History of the Centennial
State,* 4th ed. Boulder: University of Colorado Press, 2005.

Allen, E. John B. *From Skisport to Skiing: One Hundred Years of an American Sport, 1840–
1940.* Amherst: University of Massachusetts Press, 1993.

———. *The Culture and Sport of Skiing From Antiquity to World War II.* Amherst: University
of Massachusetts Press, 2007.

Amundson, Michael A. *Yellowcake Towns: Uranium Mining Communities in the American
West.* Boulder: University Press of Colorado, 2002.

Aron, Cindy. *Working at Play: A History of Vacations in the United States.* Oxford: Oxford
University Press, 1999.

Auran, John Henry, and the Editors of Ski Magazine. *America's Ski Book: A Comprehensive,
Illustrated Guide to Skiing.* New York: Charles Schreiber's Sons, 1966.

Bailey, Beth L., and Dave Farber, eds. *America in the Seventies.* Lawrence: University Press
of Kansas, 2004.

Baldwin, Donald. *The Quiet Revolution: The Grass Roots of Today's Wilderness Preservation
Movement.* Boulder, CO: Pruett Publishing, 1972.

Bari, Judi. *Timber Wars*. Monroe, ME: Common Courage Press, 1994.

Barney, Robert, Stephen Wenn, and Scott Martyn. *Selling the Five Rings: The International Olympic Committee and the Rise of Olympic Commercialism*. Salt Lake City: University of Utah Press, 2002.

Barringer, Mark Daniel. *Selling Yellowstone: Capitalism and the Construction of Nature*. Lawrence: University Press of Kansas, 2002.

Bass, Rick. *Winter: Notes from Montana*. Boston: Houghton Mifflin, 1991.

Bell, Daniel. *The Coming of the Post-Industrial Society: A Venture in Social Forecasting*. Special Anniversary Edition. New York: Basic Books, 1999.

Berkowitz, Edward. *Something Happened: A Political and Cultural Overview of the Seventies*. New York: Columbia University Press, 2007.

Birnham, Charles, and Robin Karson. *Pioneers of American Landscape Design*. National Park Service Historic Landscape Initiative, Inc. History. New York: McGraw Hill, 2000.

Biven, W. Carl. *Jimmy Carter's Economy: Policy in an Age of Limits*. Chapel Hill: University of North Carolina Press, 2002.

Black, Robert. *Island in the Rockies: The Pioneer Era of Grand County*. Granby, CO: County Printer, 1969.

Brechin, Gray. *Imperial San Francisco: Urban Power, Earthly Ruin*. Berkeley: University of California Press, 1999.

Brooks, Karl Boyd. *Before Earth Day: The Origins of American Environmental Law*. Lawrence: University Press of Kansas, 2009.

Brower, David. *For Earth's Sake: The Life and Times of David Brower*. Salt Lake City: Peregrine Smith Books, 1990.

Brown, Dona. *Inventing New England: Regional Tourism in the Nineteenth Century*. Washington, DC: Smithsonian Institution Press, 1995.

Brown, Robert L. *Ghost Towns of the Colorado Rockies*. Caldwell, ID: The Caxton Printers, 1968.

Buccholtz, C. W. *Rocky Mountain National Park: A History*. Boulder, CO: Colorado Associated University Press, 1983.

Burbank, Matthew, Gregory Andranovich, and Charles Heying. *Olympic Dreams: The Impact of Mega-Events on Local Politics*. Boulder: Lynne Rienner Publishers, 2001.

Burghardt Wright, John. *Rocky Mountain Divide: Selling and Saving the West*. University of Texas Press, 1993.

Burton, Hal. *The Ski Troops*. New York: Simon and Schuster, 1971.

Caldwell, Lynton Keith. *The National Environmental Policy Act: An Agenda for the Future*. Bloomington: Indiana University Press, 1998.

Campagna, Anthony. *Economic Policy in the Carter Administration.* Westport, CT: Greenwood Press, 1995.

Campbell, Colin. *The Romantic Ethic and the Spirit of Modern Consumerism.* Oxford: Blackwell Publishers, 1987.

Carr, Ethan. *Wilderness by Design: Landscape Architecture and the National Park Service.* Lincoln: University of Nebraska Press, 1998.

Catton, Theodore. *National Park, City Playground: Mount Rainier in the Twentieth Century.* Seattle: University of Washington Press, 2006.

Cawley, R. McGreggor. *Federal Land, Western Anger: The Sagebrush Rebellion and Environmental Politics.* Lawrence: University Press of Kansas, 1993.

Clawson, Marion. *The Bureau of Land Management.* New York: Praeger Publishers, 1971.

Clifford, Hal. *Downhill Slide: Why the Corporate Ski Industry Is Bad for Skiing, Ski Towns, and the Environment.* San Francisco: Sierra Club Books, 2002.

Clifford, Peggy, and John M. Smith. *Aspen/Dreams and Dilemmas: Love Letter to a Small Town.* Chicago: Swallow Press, 1970.

Clary, David A. *Timber and the Forest Service.* Lawrence: University Press of Kansas, 1986.

Cohen, Lizabeth. *A Consumers' Republic: The Politics of Mass Consumption in Postwar America.* New York: Vintage Books, 2003.

Cohen, Michael. *The History of the Sierra Club, 1892–1970.* San Francisco: Sierra Club Books, 1988.

Coleman, Annie Gilbert. *Ski Style: Sport and Culture in the Rockies.* Lawrence: University Press of Kansas, 2004.

Cronon, William, ed. *Uncommon Ground: Rethinking the Human Place in Nature.* New York: W. W. Norton, 1996.

Cronon, William. *Nature's Metropolis: Chicago and the Great West.* New York: W. W. Norton, 1991.

Dempsey, Paul Stephen, Andrew Goetz, and Joseph Szyliowicz. *Denver International Airport: Lessons Learned.* New York: McGraw Hill, 1997.

Devall, Bill, and George Sessions. *Deep Ecology: Living as If Nature Mattered.* Salt Lake City: Peregrine Smith Books, 1985.

Dilsaver, Lary, and William Tweed. *Challenge of the Big Trees: A Resource History of Sequoia and Kings Canyon National Parks.* Three Rivers, CA: Sequoia Natural History Association, 1990.

Domback, Michael, Christopher Wood, and Jack Williams. *From Conquest to Conservation: Our Public Lands Legacy.* Washington, DC: Island Press, 2003.

Dorsett, Lyle. *The Queen City: A History of Denver.* Boulder, CO: Pruett Publishing, 1977.

Fay, Abbott. *A History of Skiing in Colorado.* Montrose, CO: Western Reflections, 2003.

Findling, John E., and Kimberly D. Pelle, eds. *Encyclopedia of the Modern Olympic Movement.* Westport, CT: Greenwood Press, 2004.

Foreman, David. *Confessions of an Eco-Warrior.* New York: Harmony Books, 1991.

Foreman, David, and Bill Haywood, eds. *Ecodefence: A Field Guide to Monkeywrenching,* 3rd ed. Chico, CA: Abbzug Press, 2002.

Fox, Ray. *Raising Kane: The Fox Chronicles.* Montgomery, IL: Kindred Spirits Press, 1999.

Fox, Stephen. *The American Conservation Movement: John Muir and His Legacy.* Madison: University of Wisconsin Press, 1985.

Frum, David. *How We Got Here: The 70s: The Decade That Brought You Modern Life.* New York: Basic Books, 2000.

Fry, John. *The Story of Modern Skiing.* Hanover, NH: University Press of New England, 2006.

Gerlach, Larry R., ed. *The Winter Olympics: Chamonix to Salt Lake City.* Salt Lake City: University of Utah Press, 2004.

Glick, Daniel. *Powder Burn: Arson, Money, and Mystery on Vail Mountain.* New York: PublicAffairs, 2001.

Gold, John, and Margaret Gold, eds. *Olympic Cities: City Agendas, Planning, and the World's Games, 1896–2012.* New York: Routledge, 2007.

Goodstein, Phil. *Robert Speer's Denver: 1904–1920, The Mile High City in the Progressive Era.* Denver: Denver New Social Publications, 2004.

Gottlieb, Robert. *Forcing the Spring: The Transformation of the American Environmental Movement.* Washington, DC: Island Press, 1993.

Gutfreund, Owen. *Twentieth-Century Sprawl: Highways and the Reshaping of the American Landscape.* New York: Oxford University Press, 2004.

Guttmann, Allan. *The Games Must Go On: Avery Brundage and the Olympic Movement.* New York: Columbia University Press, 1984.

Gulliford, Andrew. *Boomtown Blues: Colorado Oil Shale, 1885–1985.* Boulder: University Press of Colorado, 1989.

———. *The Olympics: A History of the Modern Games.* Urbana: University of Chicago Press, 2nd ed. 2002.

Harvey, Mark. *Wilderness Forever: Howard Zahniser and the Path to the Wilderness Act.* Seattle: University of Washington Press, 2007.

Hauserman, Dick. *The Inventors of Vail.* Edwards, CO: Golden Peak Publishing, 2003.

Hays, Samuel P. *Beauty, Health, and Permanence: Environmental Politics in the United States, 1955–1985.* Cambridge: Cambridge University Press, 1987.

———. *Conservation and the Gospel of Efficiency: The Progressive Conservation Movement, 1890–1920.* 1959. Reprint, Pittsburgh: University of Pittsburgh Press, 1999.

————. *Wars in the Woods: The Rise of Ecological Forestry in America*. Pittsburgh: University of Pittsburgh Press, 2006.

————. *The American People and the National Forests*. Pittsburgh: University of Pittsburgh Press, 2008.

Helvarg, David. *The War against the Greens: The Wise Use Movement, the New Right, and Anti-Environmental Violence*. San Francisco: Sierra Club Books, 1994.

Hill, Christopher. *Olympic Politics: Athens to Atlanta, 1896–1996*. Manchester, UK: Manchester University Press, 1996.

Hirt, Paul. *Conspiracy of Optimism: Management of the National Forests since World War Two*. Lincoln: University of Nebraska Press, 1994.

Hise, Greg, and William Deverall. *Eden by Design: The 1930 Olmsted-Bartholomew Plan for the Los Angeles Region*. Berkeley: University of California Press, 2000.

Howe, Susanna. *Sick: A Cultural History of Snowboarding*. New York: St. Martin's Griffin, 1998.

Huntford, Roland. *Two Planks and a Passion: The Dramatic History of Skiing*. London: Continuum Books, 2008.

Hurt, R. Douglas, ed. *The Rural West Since World War II*. Lawrence: University Press of Kansas, 1998.

Hurup, Elsebeth, ed. *The Lost Decade: American in the Seventies*. Aarhus, Denmark: Aarhus University Press, 1996.

Jackson, Kenneth. *Crabgrass Frontier: The Suburbanization of the United States*. New York: Oxford University Press, 1985.

Jackson, Philip, and Robert Kuhlken. *A Rediscovered Frontier: Land Use and Resource Issues in the New West*. Boulder, CO: Rowman & Littlefield, 2006.

Jenkins, Mckay. *The Last Ridge: The Epic Story of America's First Mountain Soldiers and the Assault on Hitler's Europe*. New York: Random House, 2004.

Johnson, Charles A. *Denver's Mayor Speer: The Forgotten Story of Robert W. Speer, the Political Boss with a Rather Unsavory Machine Who Transformed Denver into One of the World's Most Beautiful Cities*. Denver: Green Mountain Press, 1969.

Johnson, Michael. *Hunger for the Wild: America's Obsession with the Untamed West*. Lawrence: University Press of Kansas, 2007.

Johnson, Norma Tadlock. *Soldiers of the Mountains: The Story of the 10th Mountain Division of World War II*. New York: PublishAmerica, 2005.

Kaff, Albert. *Crash: Ten Days in October*. Chicago: Longman Financial Services, 1989.

Kamphuis, Robert W., Jr., Roger C. Kormendi, and J. W. Henry Watson, eds. *Black Monday and the Future of Financial Markets*. Chicago: Mid-America Institute for Public Policy Research, Inc., 1989.

Kahn, Alfred Edward. *The Economics of Regulation: Principles and Institutions*. Boston: Massachusetts Institute of Technology, 1988.

Kendall, Wilson D. *A Brief Economic History of Colorado*. Denver: Center for Business and Economic Forecasting, 2002.

Kingery, Hugh. *The Colorado Mountain Club: The First Seventy-Five Years of a Highly Individual Corporation, 1912–1987*. Evergreen, CO: Cordillera Press, 1987.

Kirk, Andrew. *Collecting Nature: The American Environmental Movement and the Conservation Library*. Lawrence: University Press of Kansas, 2001.

———. *Counter Culture Green: The Whole Earth Catalog and American Environmentalism*. Lawrence: University Press of Kansas, 2007.

Lamm, Richard. *Pioneers and Politicians: 10 Colorado Governors in Profile*. Boulder, CO: Pruett Publishing, 1984.

Lamm, Richard, and Michael McCarthy. *The Angry West: A Vulnerable Land and Its Future*. Boston: Houghton Mifflin, 1982.

Lang, Otto. *A Bird of Passage: The Story of My Life*. Milltown, MT: Sky House Publishers, 1994.

Langston, Nancy. *Forest Dreams, Forest Nightmares: The Paradox of Old Growth in the Inland West*. Seattle: University of Washington Press, 1996.

Large, David Clay. *Nazi Games: The Olympics of 1936*. New York: W. W. Norton, 2007.

Lassiter, Matthew. *The Silent Majority: Suburban Politics in the Sunbelt South*. Princeton, NJ: Princeton University Press, 2006.

LeBaron, Rawlene. *The Lost Cities of Colorado*. Bowie, MD: Heritage Books, 2002.

Lee, Martha. *Earth First!: Environmental Apocalypse*. Syracuse, NY: Syracuse University Press, 1995.

Le Master, Dennis. *Decade of Change: The Remaking of Forest Service Statutory Authority during the 1970s*. Westport, CT: Greenwood Press, 1984.

Lewis, Tom. *Divided Highways: Building the Interstate Highways, Transforming American Life*. New York: Viking Books, 1997.

Liddick, Donald. *Eco-Terrorism: Radical and Animal Liberation Movements*. Westport, CT: Praeger, 2006.

Limerick, Patricia Nelson. *The Legacy of Conquest: The Unbroken Past of the American West*. New York: W. W. Norton, 1987.

Limerick, Patricia, William R. Travis, and Tamar Scoggin. *Boom and Bust in the American West*. Report from the Center of the American West, no. 4. Boulder: Center of the American West, University of Colorado at Boulder, 2002.

List, Peter. *Radical Environmentalism: Philosophy and Tactics*. Belmont, CA: Wadsworth Publishing Company, 1993.

Long, Douglas. *Ecoterrorism*. New York: Facts on File, 2004.

Louter, David. *Windshield Wilderness: Cars, Roads, and Nature in Washington's National Parks*. Seattle: University of Washington Press, 2006.

Lucas, John. *The Modern Olympic Games*. New York: A. S. Barnes, 1980.

Lunn, Arnold. *The History of Ski-ing*. London: Oxford University Press, 1927.

Lytle, Mark Hamilton. *America's Uncivil Wars: The Sixties from Elvis to the Fall of Richard Nixon*. New York: Oxford University Press, 2006.

MacCannell, Dean. *The Tourist: A New Theory of the Leisure Class*, 2nd ed. New York: Schocken Books, 1989.

Maher, Neil. *Nature's New Deal: The Civilian Conservation Corps and the Roots of the American Environmental Movement*. New York: Oxford University Press, 2008.

Malone, Michael, and Richard Etulain. *The American West: A Twentieth-Century History*. Lincoln: University of Nebraska Press, 1989.

Manes, Christopher. *Green Rage: Radical Environmentalism and the Unmaking of Civilization*. Boston: Little, Brown, 1990.

McGerr, Michael. *A Fierce Discontent: The Rise and Fall of the Progressive Movement in America, 1870–1920*. New York: The Free Press, 2003.

McGirr, Lisa. *Suburban Warriors: The Origins of the New American Right*. Princeton, NJ: Princeton University Press, 2001.

Miller, Char. *American Forests: Nature, Culture, and Politics*. Lawrence: University Press of Kansas, 1997.

———. *Gifford Pinchot and the Making of Modern Environmentalism*. Washington, DC: Island Press, 2001.

Nadeau, Robert. *The Wealth of Nature: How Mainstream Economics Has Failed the Environment*. New York: Columbia University Press, 2003.

Nash, Gerald. *The American West Transformed: The Impact of the Second World War*. Lincoln: University of Nebraska Press, 1985.

———. *The Federal Landscape: An Economic History of the 20th Century West*. Tucson: University of Arizona Press, 1999.

Nash, Roderick Frazier. *Wilderness and the American Mind*, 4th ed. New Haven, CT: Yale University Press, 2001.

Nicholas, Liza, Elaine M. Bapis, and Thomas J. Harvey, eds. *Imagining the Big Open: Nature, Identity, and Play in the New West*. Salt Lake City: University of Utah Press, 2003.

Nicolaides, Becky. *My Blue Heaven: Life and Politics in the Working-Class Suburbs of Los Angeles, 1920–1965*. Chicago: University of Chicago Press, 2002.

Nie, Martin. *The Governance of Western Public Lands: Mapping Its Present and Future*. Lawrence: University Press of Kansas, 2007.

Norris, Scott, ed. *Discovered Country: Tourism in the American West.* Albuquerque: Stone Ladder Press, 1994.

Nugent, Walter. *Into the West: The Story of Its People.* New York: Alfred A. Knopf, 1999.

Opie, John. *Nature's Nation: An Environmental History of the United States.* Fort Worth: Harcourt Brace College Publishers, 1998.

Oreskes, Naomi, and Erik M. Conway. *Merchants of Doubt: How a Handful of Scientists Obscured the Truth on Issues from Tobacco to Global Warming.* New York: Bloomsbury Press, 2010.

Pickering, Leslie James. *The Earth Liberation Front, 1997–2002.* Portland, OR: Arissa Press, 2007.

Perlstein, Rick. *Nixonland: The Rise of a President and the Fracturing of America.* New York: Scribner, 2008.

Pomeroy, Earl. *In Search of the Golden West: The Tourist in Western America.* New York: Knopf, 1957; reprint, Lincoln, Nebraska: University of Nebraska Press, Bison Book Edition, 1990.

Pooley, Eric. *The Climate War: True Believers, Power Brokers, and the Fight to Save the Earth.* New York: Hyperion, 2010.

Power, Thomas Michael. *Lost Landscapes and Failed Economies: The Search for a Value of Place.* Washington, DC: Island Press, 1996.

Power, Thomas Michael, and Richard Barrett. *Post-Cowboy Economics: Pay and Prosperity in the New American West.* Washington, DC: Island Press, 2001.

Quinn, Tom. *Public Lands and Private Recreation Enterprise: Policy Issues from a Historical Perspective.* Portland, OR: U.S. Department of Agriculture, Forest Service: Pacific Northwest Research Station, September 2002.

Riebsame, William E., et al., eds. *Atlas of the New American West: Portrait of a Changing Region.* New York: W. W. Norton, 1997.

Ringholz, Raye. *Uranium Frenzy: Boom and Bust on the Colorado Plateau.* New York: W. W. Norton, 1989.

Robbins, William. *Colony and Empire: The Capitalist Transformation of the American West.* Lawrence: University Press of Kansas, 1994.

Robinson, Glen. *The Forest Service: A Study in Public Land Management.* Baltimore: Johns Hopkins University Press, 1975.

Rome, Adam. *Bulldozer in the Countryside: Suburban Sprawl and the Rise of American Environmentalism.* New York: Cambridge University Press, 2001.

Rose, Mark. *Interstate: Express Highway Politics, 1939–1989,* rev. ed. Knoxville: University of Tennessee Press, 1990.

Rosebraugh, Craig. *Burning Rage of a Dying Planet: Speaking for the Earth Liberation Front*. New York: Lantern Books, 2004.

Rothman, Hal K. *The Greening of a Nation? Environmentalism in the United States since 1945*. Fort Worth, TX: Harcourt Brace, 1997.

——. *Devil's Bargains: Tourism in the Twentieth-Century American West*. Lawrence: University Press of Kansas, 1998.

——. *Saving the Planet: The American Response to the Environment in the Twentieth Century*. Chicago: Ivan R. Dee, 2000.

——. *The New Urban Park: Golden Gate National Recreation Area and Civic Environmentalism*. Lawrence: University Press of Kansas, 2004.

——, ed. *The Culture of Tourism, the Tourism of Culture: Selling the Past to the Present in the American Southwest*. Albuquerque: University of New Mexico Press, 2003.

Rowley, William. *U.S. Forest Service Grazing and Rangelands: A History*. College Station: Texas A&M University Press, 1985.

Runte, Alfred. *Yosemite: The Embattled Wilderness*. Lincoln: University of Nebraska Press, 1990.

Sanders, Charles J. *The Boys of Winter: Life and Death in the U.S. Ski Troops during the Second World War*. Boulder: University Press of Colorado, 2005.

Sax, Joseph L. *Mountains without Handrails: Reflections on the National Parks*. Ann Arbor: University of Michigan Press, 1980.

Scarce, Rik. *Eco-Warriors: Understanding the Radical Environmental Movement*. 2nd ed. Walnut Creek, CA: Left Coast Press, 2002.

Schulte, Steven. *Wayne Aspinall and the Shaping of the American West*. Boulder: University Press of Colorado, 2002.

Schwantes, Carlos, and James Ronda. *The West the Railroads Made*. Seattle: University of Washington Press, 2008.

Schulman, Bruce J. *The Seventies: The Great Shift in American Culture, Society, and Politics*. Cambridge, MA: Da Capo Press, 2001.

Sears, John. *Sacred Places: American Tourist Attractions in the Nineteenth Century*. New York: Oxford University Press, 1989.

Seibert, Peter W. *Vail: Triumph of a Dream*. Boulder, CO: Mountain Sports Press, 2000.

Sellars, Richard West. *Preserving Nature in the National Parks*. New Haven, CT: Yale University Press, 1997.

Shabecoff, Philip. *A Fierce Green Fire: The American Environmental Movement*. New York: Hill and Wang, 1993.

Shaffer, Marguerite. *See America First: Tourism and National Identity, 1880–1940*. Washington, DC: Smithsonian Institution Press, 2001.

Shelton, Peter. *Climb to Conquer: The Untold Story of World War II's 10th Mountain Division Ski Troops*. New York: Scribner, 2003.

Sibley, George. *Dragons in Paradise: On the Edge between Civilization and Sanity*. Frisco, CO: Mountain Gazette Publishing, 2004.

Simson, Vyv. *The Lords of the Rings: Power, Money, and Drugs in the Modern Olympics*. London: Stoddart, 1991.

Simonton, June. *Vail: Story of a Colorado Mountain Valley*. Denver: Vail Chronicles, 1987.

Smith, Duane. *Rocky Mountain Heartland: Colorado, Montana, and Wyoming in the Twentieth Century*. Tucson: University of Arizona Press, 2008.

Sobel, Robert. *Panic on Wall Street: History of America's Financial Disasters*, 2nd ed. Frederick, MD: Beard Books, 1999.

Spence, Mark. *Dispossessing the Wilderness: Indian Removal and the Making of the National Parks*. New York: Oxford University Press, 1999.

Steen, Harold. *The U.S. Forest Service: A History*. Seattle: University of Washington Press, 2005.

Steinberg, Ted. *Down to Earth: Nature's Role in American History*. New York: Oxford University Press, 2002.

Stewart, James. *Den of Thieves*. New York: Simon and Schuster, 1992.

Stiles, Jim. *Brave New West: Morphing at the Speed of Greed*. Tucson: University of Arizona Press, 2007.

Strom, Claire. *Profiting from the Plains: the Great Northern Railway and Corporate Development of the American West*. Seattle: University of Washington Press, 2003.

Sturgeon, Stephen. *The Politics of Western Water: The Congressional Career of Wayne Aspinall*. Tucson: University of Arizona Press, 2002.

Sutter, Paul S. *Driven Wild: How the Fight against Automobiles Launched the Modern Wilderness Movement*. Seattle: University of Washington Press, 2002.

Sze, Julie. *Noxious New York: The Racial Politics of Urban Health and Environmental Justice*. Boston: MIT Press, 2007.

Travis, William R. *New Geographies of the American West: Landscapes and the Changing Patterns of Place*. Washington, DC: Island Press, 2007.

Travis, William, David Theobald, Geneva Mixon, and Thomas Dickinson. *Western Futures: A Look into the Patterns of Land Use and Future Development in the American West*. Boulder, CO: Center of American West, 2005.

Udall, Stewart. *The Quiet Crisis*. New York: Holt, Rinehart and Winston, 1963.

Wall, Derek. *Earth First! and the Anti-Roads Movement: Radical Environmentalism and Comparative Social Movements*. New York: Routledge, 1999.

Waugh, Frank. *Recreation Use on the National Forests*. Washington, DC: 1918.

Weir, Tom, et al. *Winter Park: Colorado's Favorite for Fifty Years, 1940–1990*. Denver: Winter Park Recreation Association, 1989.

White, Richard. *"It's Your Misfortune and None of My Own": A New History of the American West*. Norman: University of Oklahoma Press, 1991.

Whiteside, James. *Colorado: A Sports History*. Boulder: University Press of Colorado, 1999.

Wicken, Ingrid P. *Pray for Snow: The History of Skiing in Southern California*. Norco, CA: Vasa Press, 2001.

Wickersheim, Laurel Michele, and Rawlene LeBaron. *The Lost Cities of Colorado*. Bowie, MD: Heritage Books, 2002.

Wiebe, Robert H. *The Search for Order, 1877–1920*. New York: Harper Collins, 1967.

Wilkinson, John. *Crossing the Next Meridian: Land, Water, and the Future of the West*. Washington, DC: Island Press, 1992.

Wilkinson, John, and H. Michael Anderson. *Land Resource Planning in the National Forests*. Washington, DC: Island Press, 1987.

Wilkinson, Todd. *Science under Siege: The Politicians' War on Science and the Truth*. Boulder, CO: Johnson Books, 1998.

Williams, Gerald. *The USDA Forest Service: The First Century*. Washington, DC: USDA Forest Service, 2000.

———. *The Forest Service: Fighting for Public Lands*. Westport, CT: Greenwood Press, 2007.

Williams, Raymond. *The Country and the City*. New York: Oxford University Press, 1973.

Wilmsen, Steven. *Silverado: Neil Bush and the Savings and Loan Scandal*. Washington, DC: National Press Books, 1991.

Wilson, William. *The City Beautiful Movement*. Baltimore: Johns Hopkins University Press, 1989.

Winter Park Recreational Association. *Winter Park: Colorado's Favorite for Fifty Years, 1940–1990*. Denver: Winter Park Recreation Association, 1989.

Wolf, Tom. *Arthur Carhart: Wilderness Prophet*. Boulder: University of Colorado Press, 2008.

Wrobel, David, and Patrick Long. *Seeing and Being Seen: Tourism in the American West*. Lawrence: University Press of Kansas, 2001.

Wrobel, David M. *Promised Lands: Promotion, Memory, and the Creation of the American West*. Lawrence: University Press of Kansas, 2002.

Wrobel, David, and Michael Steiner, eds., *Many Wests: Place, Culture, and Regional Identity*. Lawrence: University Press of Kansas, 1997.

Wyckoff, William. *Creating Colorado: the Making of a Western American Landscape 1860–1940*. New Haven, CT: Yale University Press, 1999.

Wyckoff, William, and Larry M. Dilsaver, eds. *The Mountainous West: Explorations in Historical Geography*. Lincoln: University of Nebraska Press, 1995.

Yochim, Michael. *Yellowstone and the Snowmobile: Locking Horns over National Park Use*. Lawrence: University Press of Kansas, 2009.

Yost, Nicholas. *NEPA Deskbook*, 3rd ed. Washington, DC: Island Press, 2003.

Zakin, Susan. *Coyotes and Town Dogs: Earth First! and the Environmental Movement*. New York: Penguin Books, 1993.

Authored Articles and Essays

Arave, Joseph. "The Forest Service Takes to the Slopes: The Birth of Utah's Ski Industry and the Role of the Forest Service." *Utah Historical Quarterly* (Fall 2002): 34–55.

Benson, Jack A. "Before Skiing Was Fun." *Western Historical Quarterly* (October 1977): 431–41.

Briggs, James. "Ski Resorts and National Forests: Rethinking Forest Service Management Practices for Recreational Use." *Boston College Environmental Affairs Law Review* 28 (2000): 78–118.

Bryne, Jason, and Jennifer Wolch. "Nature, Race, and Parks: Past Research and Future Directions for Geographic Research." *Progress in Human Geography* 33 (March 2009): 743–65.

Casewit, Curtis. "A City Owned Ski Area." *Journal of the American City* (April 1970): 120–22.

Carhart, Arthur. "Denver's Greatest Manufacturing Plant." *Municipal Facts Monthly* (September–October 1921): 3–7.

Carney, Elizabeth. "Suburbanizing Nature and Naturalizing Suburbanites: Outdoor-Living Culture and Landscapes of Growth." *Western Historical Quarterly* (Winter 2007): 477–500.

Coleman, Annie Gilbert. "The Unbearable Whiteness of Skiing." *Pacific Historical Review* 65, no. 4 (November 1996): 583–614.

Cronon, William. "A Place for Stories: Nature, History, and Narrative." *Journal of American History* 78 (March 1992): 1347–1376.

———. "The Trouble with Wilderness: or, Getting Back to the Wrong Nature," in William Cronon, ed., *Uncommon Ground: Rethinking the Human Place in Nature*. New York: W. W. Norton, 1996, 69–90.

Dant, Sara. "Making Wilderness Work: Frank Church and the American Wilderness." *Pacific Historical Review* 77 (May 2008): 237–72.

Downing, Warwick M. "How Denver Acquired Her Celebrated Mountain Parks: A Condensed History of the Building of America's Most Unique Park System." *Municipal Facts* (March–April 1931): 14.

Farwell, Ted. "The Olympic Bubble." *Colorful Colorado* (January/February 1973).

Foster, Mark. "Colorado's Defeat of the 1976 Winter Olympics." *Colorado Magazine* 53 (Spring 1976): 173–76.

———."Little Lies: The Colorado 1976 Winter Olympics." *Colorado Heritage* (Winter 1998): 22–33.

Funk, McKenzie. "Firestarter." *Outside Magazine*, August 2007.

Goeldner, Charles R. "Skiing Trends in North America," in *Mountain Resort Development: Proceedings of the Vail Conference*, April 18–21, 1991, Alison Gill and Rudi Hartman, eds. Burnaby, British Columbia: Simon Fraser University Centre for Tourism Policy and Research, 1991, 7–20.

Graves, Henry. "A Crisis in National Recreation." *American Forestry* (July 1920): 391–97.

Igler, David. "Diseased Goods: Global Exchanges in the Eastern Pacific Basin, 1770–1850." *American Historical Review* 109 (June 2004): 693–719.

Leopold, Aldo. "Wilderness and Its Place in Forest Recreational Policy." *Journal of Forest Policy* (November 1921): 718–21.

———. "Conservation Ethic," in *A Sand County Almanac with Essays on Conservation from Round River*. New York: Oxford University Press, 1968, 165–76.

McKinzie, C. Wayne. "Ski Area Development after the National Forest Ski Area Permit Act of 1986: Still and Uphill Battle." *Virginia Environmental Law Journal* 12 (1993): 308–12.

Merrill, Karen. "In Search of the 'Federal Presence' in the American West." *Western Historical Quarterly* 30 (Winter 1999): 449–473.

Morrison, James, et al. "The Effects of Ski Area Expansion on Elk." *Wildlife Society Bulletin* 23, no. 3 (Autumn 1995): 481–89.

Rivera, Jorge E., and Peter deLeon. "Is Greener Whiter? The Sustainable Slopes Program and the Voluntary Environmental Performance of Western Ski Areas." *Policy Studies Journal* 32, no. 3 (2004): 417–37.

Rivera, Jorge E., Peter deLeon, and Charles Koerber. "Is Greener Whiter Yet? The Sustainable Slopes Program after Five Years." *Policy Studies Journal* 34, no. 2 (2006): 95–221.

Robbins, William. "Creating a 'New' West: Big Money Returns to the Hinterland." *Montana: The Magazine of Western History* 46 (Summer 1996): 66–72.

Romin, Laura A., and John A. Bissonette. "Deer: Vehicle Collisions: Status of State Monitoring Activities and Mitigation Efforts." *Wildlife Society Bulletin* 24, no. 2 (Summer 1996): 276–83.

Rothman, Hal K. "Powder Aplenty for Native and Guest Alike." *Montana* (Winter 1998): 3–17.

———. "'A Regular Ding-Dong Fight': The Dynamics of Park Service–Forest Service Controversy during the 1920s and 1930s." *Western Historical Quarterly* 20 (May 1989): 143–45.

———. "Selling the Meaning of Place: Tourism, Entrepreneurship, and Community Transformation in the Twentieth-Century West." *Pacific Historical Review* 4 (November 1996): 525–557.

Schrepfer, Susan R. "Establishing Administrative 'Standing': The Sierra Club and the Forest Service, 1897–1956." *Pacific Historical Review* 58, no. 1 (1989): 55–81.

Scott, Amy. "Remaking Urban in the American West: Urban Environmentalism, Lifestyle Politics, and Hip Capitalism in Boulder, Colorado," in *The Political Culture of the New West*, Jeff Roche, ed. Lawrence: University Press of Kansas, 2008, 251–80.

Sherman, E. A. "The Forest Service and the Preservation of Natural Beauty." *Landscape Architecture* 6 (April 1916): 115–19.

———. "Use of the National Forests of the West for Public Recreation." *Proceedings of the Society of the American Foresters* 11 (July 1916): 293–26.

Siedensticker, John. "Aldo Leopold's Wilderness, Sand County and My Garden," in *Aldo Leopold and the Ecological Conscience*, Richard L. Knight and Susanne Riedel, eds. New York: Oxford University Press, 2002, 45–59.

Spencer, John W. "The Place of Recreation in the Multiple-Use Management of the National Forests." *Proceedings: Society of American Foresters Meeting, December 17–20, 1947* (Washington, DC: Society of American Foresters, 1948): 179–82.

Sticker, John. "Recreation on the National Forest." *Annals of the American Academy of Political and Social Science* (September, 1957): 129–31.

Stone, Christopher D. "Should Trees Have Standing? Toward Legal Rights for Natural Objects." 45 *Southern California Law Review* 450 (1972): 3–55.

Wilkinson, Charles. "Paradise Revised," in *Atlas of the New American West*. William Riebsame et al., eds. New York: W. W. Norton, 1997, 15–44.

Wolf, Robert. "National Forest Timber Sales and the Legacy of Gifford Pinchot: Managing a Forest and Making It Pay," in *American Forests: Nature, Culture, and Politics*, Char Miller, ed. Lawrence: University Press of Kansas, 1997, 87–108.

Wyckoff, William. "Postindustrial Butte." *Geographical Review* 85 (October, 1995): 478–96.

Dissertations

Ashenmiller, Joshua Ross. "The National Environmental Policy Act in the Green Decade, 1960–1981." PhD diss., University of California, Santa Barbara, 2004.

Olson, Laura Lee Katz. "Power, Public Policy, and the Environment: The Defeat of the 1976 Winter Olympics in Colorado." PhD diss., University of Colorado, 1974.

Philpott, William. "Consuming Colorado: Landscapes, Leisure, and the Tourist Way of Life." PhD diss., University of Wisconsin–Madison, 2002.

Richey, Edward Duke. "Living It Up in Aspen: Post-War America, Ski Town Culture, and the New Western Dream, 1945–1975." PhD diss., University of Colorado, Boulder, 2006.

Shellenbarger, Melanie. "High Country Summers: The Emergence and Development of the Second Home in Colorado, 1880–1940." PhD diss., University of Colorado, Boulder, 2008.

Thomas, Thomas A. "Roads to a Troubled Future: Transportation and Transformation in Colorado's Interstate Highway Corridors in the Nineteenth and Twentieth Century." PhD diss., University of Colorado, Boulder, 1996.

Music

Denver, John. "Rocky Mountain High," RCA, 1972.

Web Pages

Charter Institute, http://www.charture.org/a9.php

Colorado Department of Transportation, http://www.dot.state.co.us/

Earth Liberation Front, http://www.earthliberationfront.com/

Forest History Society, http://www.foresthistory.org

National Ski Areas Association, http://www.nsaa.org/nsaa/home/

Ski Area Citizens Coalition, http://www.skiareacitizens.com/

Ski Heritage, http://skiinghistory.org/

Films

Sykes, Hunter, Darren Campbell, Christi Bray, and Steve Siig. *Resorting to Madness: Taking Back Our Mountain Communities.* Olympic Valley, CA: Cold Stream Creative, 2006.

Interviews

Buchheister, Jack. Former vice president of public affairs, Winter Park Recreation Association.

Doon, Ben. Research director for Ski Area Citizens' Coalition.

Farwell, Ted. Former technical advisor to the Denver Olympic Committee and Owner of Winterstar Evaluations, Inc.

Foreman, David. Cofounder of Earth First!

Groswold, Jerry. Former president of Winter Park Recreational Association.

Lamm, Richard. Former governor of Colorado.

Martin, Erik. Former Winter Sports Resorts program manager, White River National Forest.

McGraw, Gary. Former vice president of marketing, Winter Park Recreation Association.

Smith, Rocky. Former staff forest ecologist for the Colorado Environmental Coalition.

Stricklin, Dan. Former chief lift mechanic for Mary Jane Ski Area.

INDEX